# DISCOVERING THE
# LEAD CODICES

## The Book of Seven Seals and the Secret Teachings of Jesus

### DAVID & JENNIFER ELKINGTON

WATKINS PUBLISHING
LONDON

**for Dorothy,**
**Alex and Eloise**


*If in that Syrian garden, ages slain,*

*You sleep, and know not you are dead in vain,*

*Nor even in dreams behold how dark and bright*

*Ascends in smoke and fire by day and night*

*The hate you died to quench and could but fan,*

*Sleep well and see no morning, son of man.*


*But if, the grave rent and the stone rolled by,*

*At the right hand of majesty on high*

*You sit, and sitting so remember yet*

*Your tears, your agony and bloody sweat,*

*Your cross and passion and the life you gave,*

*Bow hither out of heaven and see and save.*

'Easter Hymn', A E Housman


*Whoever loves instruction loves knowledge, but he who hates reproof is ignorant.*
*A good person draws out the will of the Lord in others, but a person of wicked*
*intention condemns.*

*Proverbs* 12:1 2

This edition first published in the UK and USA 2014 by
Watkins Publishing Limited
PO Box 883
Oxford, OX1 9PL
UK

A member of Osprey Group

For enquiries in the USA and Canada:
Osprey Publishing
PO Box 3985
New York, NY 10185-3985
Tel: (001) 212 753 4402
Email: info@ospreypublishing.com

1 3 5 7 9 10 8 6 4 2

Typeset by Manisha Patel

Printed and bound in the US

A CIP record for this book is available from the British Library

ISBN: 978-1-78028-766-9

Watkins Publishing is supporting the Woodland Trust, the UK's leading woodland
conservation charity, by funding tree-planting initiatives and woodland maintenance.

www.watkinspublishing.co.uk

# Contents

# Plates

# Authors' Note

The Biblical quotations in this book are from: the Orthodox Study Bible, the King James Version (*KJV*), the Jerusalem Bible and the Septuagint (*LXX*). I have retained the *KJV* on occasions for its poetry and rhythm of language.

The controversial nature of the discovery has made it necessary not to mention the names and institutions of a number of the eminent scholars involved. Certain character names have been changed.

Owing to the practical considerations of modern publishing, we have had to keep text and footnotes within a strict limit. The full text of endnotes, plus appendices and a glossary, are available online at www.sevensealedbook.com

Many of the telephone and voicemail messages quoted or referred to in this text have been recorded and transcribed by the British police.

The authors would like it to be known that although we have consulted a number of scholars throughout the writing of this book, and are thankful for their efforts on our behalf, our conclusions are very much our own.

Although this book results from a collaboration of two authors, David composed the historical text and Jennifer the contemporary narrative: this is presented as one voice.

Whilst every effort has been made to trace the copyright holders of certain texts in order to seek their permission, this has not always proved successful. Any omissions will be corrected in future editions.

# Overture

We have been privileged to be a part of a discovery that was made a few years ago, of a series of ancient books, or codices, each of which is made of lead. In these books we have a series of images and symbols, and enough information to determine that these documents are deeply challenging to existing ideas of Christianity and its origins. One particular image is profoundly moving: it shows Jesus as the King of Israel. The existence of such an image might well have been regarded as highly blasphemous in the religious climate of the 1st century, which prohibited figurative depictions of the divine. What emerges from a first glimpse of the codices is that, since they are sealed, they were meant to be seen by certain eyes only – the eyes of those who would understand them, who shared the knowledge of the ineffable: knowledge of the interior of the Temple of Jerusalem … of God. The existence of these images challenges assumptions about the age and theology of Christianity from its earliest period.

What these books reveal is the beating heart of early Christianity – for they are the very secrets that Jesus alludes to in the Gospels. Secrets that St John, friend and Apostle of Christ, writes of in *Revelation*, a text that speaks of sealed books and of the apocalypse that will occur upon their opening.

# Prologue

**April 2009, Northern Israel**

We rubbed our hands in front of the blazing fire to warm ourselves in the cold night desert air. Sparks flew up and the smell of olive wood was heady.

'You like, Mr David?' said Hassan with boyish glee, his long dark locks unfurled from their usual bunch and flowing, prophet-like, all around him. I smiled.

'Is very beautiful, yes?' He was relaxed, and this meant that we were about to hear something we had been dying to hear since we first laid eyes on a set of amateur, yet astonishing, photographs in Oxfordshire, England, the year before.

Tired from our journey, yet alive with the heady exoticism of our surroundings, we waited. In the distance tiny dots of light from Hassan's rural community could be seen beneath the dark blue sky; the pyramidal shadow of Mount Tabor lay before us.

Hassan sat back and drew on a cigarette he had just rolled, listening to the midnight baying of his camels, a last link to the past of the Bedu.

'God has blessed you, Hassan,' I said, breaking a brief silence. Zaid, the farmhand, stoked the fire. Hassan smiled quietly at us, nodding his head respectfully. The flames crackled and roared, stretching high into the air, lighting up Hassan's features, exposing the shadow of dark stubble on his angular face. He pulled up a chair next to us and sat down, and after a long rapturous drag on his joint he coughed slightly and began his story.

*It was September 2005. Torrential storms had swept the area for the past week. The two shepherds had been scouring the hillsides looking for stranded animals in the flash floods. They were about to call it a day when they noticed a vapour rising from the ground where the floods had begun to subside. As they went over to investigate, it appeared to be emerging from a crack in the ground that had been washed clean of topsoil.*

*Puzzled, the two men began to move aside some rocks that obscured the opening. On two of the rocks they could make out some markings. One of them had a cross – 'X' literally marked the spot. The other seemed to bear the image of a Jewish candlestick, a menorah. The shepherds worked away at the rocks, scrabbling furiously at the craggy earth, struggling against the humidity after the storm.*

*The mud was cloying and made hard work for them. It was possibly a false trail. On the verge of giving up, and when they least expected it, they suddenly saw that they had made an opening – a vast hole where the rocky plug had been: a cave.*

*Each of them held their breath, hardly daring look inside, for fear that in the darkness there might be more threatening things. Evoking the name of Allah, they cast their fears aside and peered into the darkness.*

*One of them dug out his cigarette lighter, and as their eyes adjusted slowly to the darkness they began to make out forms. They picked their way down a sloping tunnel that opened out into a large cave. The flickering flame cast ominous shadows that danced on the walls. Moving in closer, they became aware of rectangular niches carved into the rock face, and they saw that these niches contained objects. Carefully, they removed from one of the niches a little metal book, sealed on all sides by metal rings and stained by long years of lime-scale build-up and other detritus. Other niches were similarly furnished with little lead artefacts. They gathered a few of the objects to take with them, hoping that God would not curse them for disturbing what appeared to be a tomb.*

# Prelude

*My point once again, is not that those ancient people told literal stories and we are now smart enough to take them symbolically, but that they told them symbolically and we are dumb enough to take them literally.*

John Dominic Crossan, *Who Is Jesus?*[1]

The force with which St Paul of Tarsus (while he was still known as Saul) threw James, the brother of Jesus, down the steps of the Temple of Jerusalem was considerable. As a Nazorean his appearance was ascetic, a man who fasted regularly and did not wash, whose hair was long and whose every word his many followers clung to: he was a holy man. His shattered body was duly collected by his followers and carted off into exile – across the Jordan.

This is a true account, told in detail in a document little known outside Biblical scholarship. The *Clementine Recognitions* (long believed to have been composed by Clement, one of the early Popes) is a 1st-century text written by Hebrew-Christians (that is, members of the Jerusalem Church). They give a telling detail: that forever after, James limped when he walked. The text also tells us the number of the followers of James as he escaped the tense brutality of Jerusalem: 5,000. They were soon to be pursued by 5,000 followers of Saul (soon to become St Paul), a Temple agent who harried and persecuted the early Christians. The Book of Acts and Paul himself confirm this fact, but not the sheer number involved.

Somewhere, on the road to Damascus, 10,000 people met in combat in one of the most important, but little-known, episodes in Christian history. Important, because during this encounter, as we shall see, Paul was shown an object no bigger than the palm of his hand. It was so surprising: it shook him to the core of his soul. Paul's response was to fall from his horse, blinded. The object he had seen transformed him into the saint of legend – and changed the course of history.

This dramatic story challenges the idea of the early Christians as a small peace-loving group of Jewish idealists, largely unknown and not yet politically influential. What it tells us is the exact opposite: that the Temple authorities, who ruled in the name of Rome, were worried enough by the power of the early Church to send their chief and most resourceful agent with clear orders: seek and destroy.

The subsequent conversion of Saul was a landmark in the survival of the nascent Christianity, which was soon to be divorced from its Jewish background. However, the form of Christianity espoused by James, which adhered to the Law of Moses and rejected the idea of faith *without works,* was not so lucky. In the downfall of Judea at the hands of the vengeful Roman armies in the war of AD 66–70 much was destroyed, but by virtue of having reached Rome before this time, Paul's vision became the central motif of his new faith, the kind of Christianity that James and his followers had objected to – the Christianity that became the foundation-stone of the Church in the West.

There are other texts to which we can turn to when investigating the very early period of Christian origins, but there is not much that pre-dates the letters of Paul. The New Testament gives us surprisingly little detail about the period immediately after the Crucifixion. It is all very murky. With the discovery of the lead codices, however, some of our basic assumptions about these shadowy years in the formative era of Christianity are about to be challenged.

Amidst the shadows, all signs of James and the Jerusalem Church disappeared: what was not wilfully destroyed by the victors lay hidden for a very long time – in caves in northern Jordan. What is forgotten is that, in their rush to exile, the community of St James took their precious store of books with them, for James had been privy to the Secret Teachings of Jesus Christ.

# PART I
# SIGNS AND WONDERS

## Autumn 2007, Wallingford, Oxfordshire

'You've got to have a look at these things – I've no idea what they are, fakes probably, but I've never seen anything like them,' Ron said, perplexed. His researches had quickly come up against a brick wall.

Jennifer had met Ron Lyons, a journalist, when working on a big news story with him in London, and they had struck up a friendship. She had since met me and had closed down her business as a literary publicist to work full-time on a film project based on the research used in my previous book, some of which happened to cross over with the area of ancient history she represented. Fortunately it didn't take much to persuade her to leave London, as she had been longing to escape to the country. We reckoned we could work anywhere thanks to the Internet, and as she was eager to be close to her 13-year-old son Alex, who was starting his first year at boarding school in Oxford, this seemed the most logical place to go. So we decamped to Oxfordshire to get Alex settled in – only to find ourselves surprisingly close to Ron's house. An invitation to dinner immediately ensued.

Towards the end of the evening, the request that Ron had been building up to finally came. 'David,' Ron said, 'I want you to have a look at something – I think you might be able to help me.' It was the request that was to change the course of our lives. We had just finished dinner and noticed that Ron was getting agitated. He marched determinedly for the stairs and we followed.

'Take a seat,' Ron commanded. What I saw next hit me slowly. My initial reaction was bafflement: I had never seen anything like this. The objects in the photographs appeared to be antiquated books, or codices, made of metal, all of them ring-bound. The covers were replete with iconography and inscribed with what looked like an ancient script. Curiously, some of them were sealed on all four sides.

'Did you take these pictures?'

'No. A friend of mine, she knows the guy who has these books. She believes they were found somewhere in northern Israel. Anyway, he's got a few of them and thinks they might be important.'

'Probably fakes,' I said, taking a closer look. 'So, what's the story? How did he come across them?'

At this point Ron became rather evasive. He began to shuffle around nervously.

'So, hang on a minute. These are antiquities, right? Has your friend tried to have them authenticated? To have the metal tested and the language looked at?'

'All I know is that they contacted a couple of universities. The Hebrew University in Jerusalem, I think, and maybe the Sorbonne, but she reckons they're too hot to handle.'

'Well, all I can say is I've never seen anything like them before. So how are you involved?'

'There could be a great scoop here, and my friend reckons I could get access to these things. But we need to find out what they are. That's where I was hoping that you'd be able to help.'

I peered again at the photographs, making out the delicate symbols that adorned the covers of each book. Already there was enough here that fascinated me and made me want to know more.

'We're going to need some better photographs and some samples so that we can get them dated. May I have a couple of the images?'

'Sure,' he said, 'have these, but keep them to yourself.'

We left Ron's house in the early hours of the morning, having agreed to speak again in a couple of days' time. Ron was to gather more information, speak to his contact, and obtain more photographs of the books, whilst my job was to begin to determine what exactly they were.

\* \* \* \*

## Introduction to the Codices: The Enigma of Christian Origins

*Certainty is impossible, and so what follows is a hypothesis consistent with the evidence.*

Dr Margaret Barker, in a private conversation, June 2011

Modern Christianity is centered on three events that supposedly took place in the life of Jesus: the Incarnation, the Crucifixion and the Resurrection. The aim of this work in relation to the discovery of the codices is to demonstrate that these actions occurred as historical events – but not in the way that we have become accustomed to thinking. These are the central mysteries of the Christian religion and they encapsulate the founding movement of the whole.

However, there is a lack of detail in the Gospels that only an investigation into other, non-canonical texts begins to fill, particularly when it comes to the events surrounding the Passion. The details represented on the codices go some way to suggest that what may actually have occurred, within the context of the Temple of Jerusalem, was as prominent as the figure of Jesus in the later sections of the Gospel stories – *stories* because they would appear to be a coagulation of real events involving messianic ritual.

But what exactly is a *messiah*?

The Christian idea of the Messiah is the singular concept of someone who is the *only* begotten Son of God, whereas in the ancient Hebrew religion, all the Kings of Israel were sons of God. This stems from other, wider, more archaic traditions that come not from paganism or from the influence of Hellenism as many have asserted, but from within the liturgical and theological history of Israel. The main problem with looking at this history and deriving a proper context from it is sorting out fact from fiction, interpretation from misinterpretation. Further complicating matters is the fact that the inconvenient parts of both Hebrew and Christian histories have been written out at various dates in the past, both before and after the lifetime of Jesus.

5

Also, in the 1st century there were many sects holding all sorts of differing beliefs within Judaism and emergent Christianity, particularly in some of the more remote areas of Judea – Galilee especially. Some of these beliefs would later contribute to the ideas that have been handed down in the guise of 'Gnosticism' – seen by later Christian orthodoxies as heretical. Others were merely offshoots of mainstream Judaism. All were affected in one degree or another by the increasingly apocalyptic climate of the times – a direct consequence of centralized Temple worship, Roman oppression and a corrupt regime that ran Judea with an often cruel hand.

A view of this 'central ideal' comes from the way in which religious texts were 'edited' in order to justify and illustrate the way the situation was many years on. As Robin Lane Fox has observed:

> … the scriptures have grown with a splendid incoherence. There was not a single block of early 'scripture' which was then padded by later users … Padding has certainly been added to older writings: it is obvious in the books of particular prophets and has had important effects in the older narratives. A covenant, for instance, with God has been added into the earlier stories of God and Moses on Sinai … Some of the texts were compiled from older, separate texts and, unlike bricks and plaster, these earlier building blocks had led a separate meaningful life.[2]

It may come as a surprise to learn that most of what we know as the Old Testament, upon which the New Testament was founded, is in fact propaganda, not history. As Richard Heller said in a review of Robin Lane Fox's book (from which the above quotation is taken), 'the Ten Commandments, as set out in *Exodus*, would have been unknown to David and Solomon because they were written at least 300 years later.'[3] Christianity tells us that Jesus was the Messiah, that he was a King and that he was crucified and resurrected from death three days later. However, it makes by implication an even greater claim, that, by virtue of his status as the Messiah, he is in some way semi-, or even fully, divine: that he is in fact *the* Son of God.

The Gospels are cited as first-hand testimony to this fact; and the New Testament as a whole provides the single uniting factor of Christianity, which in reality is an agglomeration of disparate trends, sects and sub-sects – namely, the idea of the Crucifixion and the Resurrection that gives Christianity its unique identity.

Christianity was to become a curiously divided religion in a remarkably short time after the passing of Christ, even though we are still inclined to think of it as a singular entity, an entity brought together by the (misleading) view that the Gospels are historical documents.

The last of the canonical Gospels, written by St John, is deemed to be the most reliable in terms of historical detail and first-hand knowledge: it reveals a surprising level of topographical information about Jerusalem in the 1st century. It contains incidents and names that do not occur in the other Gospels. St John's is the only Gospel most likely to have been written by an actual disciple of Jesus. The other, Synoptic Gospels (from the Greek *syn* meaning 'with', 'together' and *opsis* meaning 'view' or 'similar') were written by outsiders, not likely to have known Jesus personally – people unfamiliar with Palestine and therefore not conditioned to its way of thinking.

It is important here to bring to mind an important distinction: that the history of the human Jesus is remarkably different from the divine story of Christ. In Catholicism the difference is spelled out in stark fashion: the theological Christ and the historical Jesus. It is my conviction that the two coalesced in the Temple – and that reference is made to such an episode on the codices.

The key point to remember here is that the Gospels to be found in the New Testament were composed in an alien language and in an alien environment for an alien people: by Greeks for Greeks. Greek was not widely spoken in Palestine. It was inevitable that the intrinsic message would have changed emphasis, from one landscape to another, from one politics to another, and thus from one meaning to another.

7

Furthermore, until now, no Hebrew texts from the first Christians have survived or have been located, although there were plenty around in the first few generations of Christianity. Given that the Gospels were compiled many years after the events they describe, as eyewitness accounts they are unreliable: in fact they should be seen more as articles of faith than as documents of history (and yet, paradoxically, as articles of faith they make interesting historical reading).

For a start, there are few independent eyewitness accounts of the most important parts of Jesus's life, so the Gospels are the only guide to what might or might not have happened. The very few references in the classical sources, particularly in Josephus' *Antiquities of the Jews*, are regarded as suspect owing to the editorial influence of pious Christian editors during the early centuries of the rise of the faith. It is even likely that these editors destroyed much that they did not agree with or did not want to be seen by others, viewing the material as heretical or, possibly, too revealing.

In the *Antiquities of the Jews*, compiled towards the end of the 1st century, Josephus reports as follows:

> Now, there was about this time Jesus, a wise man, if it be lawful to call him a man, for he was a doer of wonderful works – a teacher of such men as receive the truth with pleasure. He drew over to him both many of the Jews, and many of the Gentiles. He was [the] Christ; and when Pilate, at the suggestion of the principal men amongst us, had condemned him to the cross, those that loved him at the first did not forsake him, for he appeared to them alive again the third day, as the divine prophets had foretold these and ten thousand other wonderful things concerning him: and the tribe of Christians, so named from him, are not extinct at this day.[4]

The *Testimonium Flavianum* is much disputed. It bears all the hallmarks of having been tampered with. Josephus, the turncoat Jewish general, to those unfamiliar with him comes across as a closet Christian; and

8

as others have pointed out, the *Testimonium* almost conforms to the Apostolic Creed. However, much of the text does indeed have the flavour of Josephus' style, his vocabulary and his way of thinking. The jury is still out on whether the passage is original or not – particularly as Josephus in his narrative, *The Jewish War*, blames the Messianists and the Zealots for the destruction of his people in the war of AD 66–70.

The four canonical Gospels, with perhaps the exception of John, in being written after Paul's letters, reflect to a large extent Paul's influence: his theological musings were not unknown to the authors, yet at the same time the Gospels reflect traditions and writings prior to Paul's theological input. Every deed and word of Christ seems overlaid with a divine context, and this is a testament to the sheer weight of influence that the character of Paul brought to bear on the early Church and its writings – those that he managed to inspire.

The immediate period after the disappearance and death of St Paul in AD c60 seems to draw a demarcation line in the early story of the Gospels and thus the story of early Christianity. What non-canonical Gospels such as the Gospels of Peter or of Philip demonstrate is that there were many Christianities co-existing in the era of the early 1st millennium AD, versions of the faith that until relatively recently were still condemned as *heretical* or 'off message'. It was not really until the discovery of the Nag Hammadi texts in the desert of Egypt in 1945 that a whole cache of Gnostic and alternative manuscripts came to light and our ideas about the origins of Christianity began to change. For much of this material had been hidden away by those condemned in the various Church Councils following the acknowledgement of Christianity as the official religion of the Roman Empire by Constantine the Great in AD 313.

By this stage Pauline thought had taken over the Church of Rome and was never in any danger of being toppled; except at the Council of Nicaea, when Arianism and its view of the human Jesus almost became the sole religion of the empire. However, the crisis was averted and Arianism went the way of all the other differences of opinion – heresy

9

(from the Greek, *haireseis*, to make a choice). These were the events that saw the rise of Christianity in the Western world. Within Christianity itself much also had changed. St Paul's original inspiration had begun to metamorphose into what we would now recognize as orthodox Christianity centred on the concept of the Saviour Messiah.

The idea of the Messiah is a far more complex and ultimately revealing concept than is generally considered by mainstream Christianity. In the millennium prior to Jesus, Israel had undergone significant changes; and perhaps when considering the subject of the Messiah, it is necessary to understand that everything changed in 722 BC, when the northern kingdom of Israel (as opposed to the southern kingdom of Judah), comprising ten of the tribes of Israel, was destroyed; and again in c586 BC when Judah was in large part sent into the Babylonian exile. It was during this time of exile that the term 'Jew' was coined – it was Babylonian slang for a member of the tribe of Judah.

In the New Testament Epistle of James the very first words are: 'To the twelve tribes scattered among the nations ...' Consistent reference is made by the Apostles and by the early Church Fathers to Israel – explicitly Israel in the sense of the twelve tribes of which Judea was merely one part. Jesus has to be seen as the King of all Israel, not just of Judea; or else his mission, his story and the liturgy that has built up around Christianity would make no sense. Jesus must therefore have had a good claim on such a title. In this sense, the term *Messiah* means truly the acknowledged King of the 12 tribes of Israel. How doubly cruel it was to Christ, as he hung in his death agony from the cross, to display the *titulus* above him that read with bitter irony: *King of the Jews.*

The first real acknowledged Messiah, King of Israel, is David, whose intermarriage with the 12 tribal heiresses sustained and confirmed his title. Kings of later Judea and the northern Kings of Israel would have had to claim descent from David in order to assert their entitlement to the throne. The role of the Messiah was to act as a kind of semi-divine interlocutor between the populace and God. When the candidate became King, the spirit of God would descend into him, and thus in an almost shamanic way he was half in this world and half in the next.

However, it is from the northern kingdom of Israel, which had seceded from Judah at the death of Solomon, c900 BC, that we derive the most interesting concept and the one that Jesus fits most accurately: the Suffering Servant, the Son of Joseph – the one exception to the idea of the Messiah always being a warrior king. Joseph is the famous patriarch with the coat of many colours, whose father was Jacob, also known as Israel (*Ish-Ra-El*, a probable translation being 'The Man Who Saw God').

The Suffering Servant is mentioned most famously by the prophet Isaiah, who lived around 740–680 BC. What Isaiah has to say is probably one of the most significant passages in the whole of the Old Testament, as we know it.

> He was despised and rejected by others, a man of suffering, and familiar with pain, like one from whom people hide their faces. He was despised and we held him in low esteem. Surely he took up our pain and bore our suffering, yet we considered him punished by God, stricken by him and afflicted. But he was pierced for our transgressions, he was crushed for our iniquities: the punishment that brought us peace was on him, and by his wounds we are healed.
>
> *Isaiah* 53.3–6

The passage goes on, a few lines later, as follows:

> ... and though the Lord makes his life an offering for sin ... after he has suffered, he will see the light of life and be satisfied; by his knowledge. My righteous servant will justify many and he will bear their iniquities ... because he poured his life unto death, and he was numbered with the transgressors.
>
> *Isaiah* 53.10–12

But it is this next (and last) line in the passage that justifies my earlier comparison of Isaiah in the midst of his prophetic ecstasy with the tribal shaman:

> For he bore the sin of many, and made intercession for the transgressors.
>
> *Isaiah* 53.12

Perhaps it is my Western Christian conditioning, but this idea, this specific concept of the Messiah, has about it such an extraordinary touch of humanity and an implicit awareness of the human condition that one can fully understand, not only its popularity, but also its meaning. That is to say, when we read about the Messiah, son of David, we get the impression of a ruthless slashing and hacking warrior king out for glory, in the usual testosterone-filled sense of the word; but with the idea of the Suffering Servant we have almost the exact opposite.

But surely, what is most striking of all is that this should have emerged from northern Israel – the place where Jesus made his home and pursued his mission before going on to Jerusalem and higher things.

In the Old Testament book of *Numbers* (24.17) there is an even older prophecy about the Suffering Servant: 'I see him ... but not in the present, I behold him – but not close at hand, a star from Jacob takes the leadership, a sceptre arises from Israel' (*Jerusalem Bible*).

To truly understand these texts we have to appreciate that most of them were rewritten or 'adjusted' in order to underline the importance of certain specific issues – and to cover up others. This was undertaken in response to the early Christian movement – the people who were largely held responsible for the fall of Jerusalem in the war of AD 66–70.

The early Christian writer Justin Martyr, who was born AD c100 in the former Roman city of Flavia Neapolis (modern-day Nablus), near the old territory of Samaria, took issue with the Jews over their rewriting of texts. In conversation with Trypho he declares:

I certainly do not trust your teachers who refuse to admit that the translation made by the seventy elders who were with Ptolemy [king] of the Egyptians is a correct one and attempt to make their own translation. And I wish you to observe that they have altogether taken away many Scriptures composed by those elders.'[5]

Justin then reveals precisely which Scriptures he knows to have been altered. This is entirely relevant to our understanding of the Lead Codices, for what Justin is saying is that the parts recognized by Christians as messianic texts were being removed. Trypho denies this but Justin quotes deleted words from *1 Esdras*, which cannot be found today – but they were certainly known to Lactantius (AD 240–320), a later Christian author, and adviser to the first Christian Roman emperor, Constantine.

And Esdras said to the people, this Passover is our Saviour and our refuge. And if you have understood, and your heart has taken it in, that we shall humble Him on a standard, and thereafter hope in Him, then this place shall not be forsaken for ever, says the God of hosts. But if you will not believe Him, and will not listen to His declaration, you shall be a laughing-stock to the nations.[6]

Justin also refers to words deleted from the *Book of Jeremiah*, now lost to us, but quoted by another Church Father, Irenaeus.

From the *Book of Jeremiah* Justin informs us that the following words, though 'still found in some copies of the Scripture in Jewish synagogues', were deleted:

I was like a lamb that is brought to the slaughter: they devised a device against me, saying, Come, let us lay on wood on His bread, and let us blot Him out from the land of the living; and His name shall no more be remembered.

*Book of Jeremiah* 11.19

In addition Justin points out that the text of *Psalm* 96.10 has also been tampered with, since it no longer reads, 'The Lord reigns from the tree,' the last three words having been deleted.

It is interesting that a Christian scholar of the mid-2nd century should claim that the older Greek version of the Scriptures was being replaced by new translations, and that parts being used by the Christians as messianic texts were being removed, for there is more than an intimation here of what we recognize today as Christian writings – even though they pre-date the era of Jesus.

Warning about the accuracy of his translation from Hebrew into Greek, Ben Sira (2nd century BC) wrote: 'You are urged therefore to read with goodwill and attention, and to be indulgent in cases where, despite our diligent labour in translating, we may seem to have rendered some phrases imperfectly. For what was originally expressed in Hebrew does not have exactly the same sense when translated into another language.'[7]

The Hebrew Scriptures had been translated into Greek under the aegis of Ptolemy of Egypt around 285–247 BC. When the work, called the Septuagint (*LXX*), was finished, it was read to the Jewish community of the city, who agreed it was an accurate translation, going so far as to lay a curse on anyone who should attempt to alter it (*Letter of Aristeas* 311). The Septuagint was regarded with honour in the lifetime of Jesus, yet by the end of the 2nd century AD it was being condemned (*m. Soferim* 1.7).

At a much later date St Jerome (AD c400) made a new translation of the Bible into Latin, but where possible used Hebrew translations as a source, abandoning the Greek Old Testament, which until this point had been the Scripture of the Church. The early Church Father Origen (AD 184/5–253/5) had known passages important to the Christians that were not in the Jewish Scriptures, but also he was well aware that Jewish Scripture had passages not in the Christian texts. Scripture had become a war zone.

The unacknowledged consequence of the Western Church accepting the Jewish canon and the text of the Old Testament as its Scripture, to the exclusion of other books, has been profound. Evidence shows clearly that the earliest Church used a very different set of Scriptures. After the destruction of the Temple (the blame for which was laid firmly at the door of the Christians), some of the Hebrew books came to be accepted as Scripture by the Jewish community, whilst others were excluded. That Rabbi Akiva could say that anyone 'who read a book excluded from the Scripture would have no part in the world to come' (*m. Sanhedrin* 10.1) shows the starkness of the distinction. The decision to adopt the newly altered canon is thought to have taken place at Jamnia in the years after the fall of the Temple in AD 135. There is a disguised account of this process in *2 Esdras*, describing how Ezra heard the Most High speaking to him from a bush (*2 Esdras* 14.1).

Ezra was the new Moses. He was told to write the new canon in the form of a series of books, only some of which were to be made public. The remainder, containing the source of understanding, wisdom and knowledge, were therefore of utmost importance. It is possible that they were the pre-Christian books that came to be preserved only by the Christians: *The Ascension of Isaiah, 1* and *2 Enoch* and so on. The discovery of the Dead Sea Scrolls in the 1940s has brought this issue into sharp relief, since texts long cited as major, yet written out of the Scriptures, were found in the hoard, and were obviously important to the Dead Sea community (see Margaret Barker, *The Great High Priest*, p298ff).

The alteration of scripture was remembered ever after. Later, Muslim scholars too would also cite their accusations that the texts had been altered. What was being hidden away or completely rewritten was nothing less than the secret history of Hebraism, the long-lost original theology – and the fact that it was based upon ritual performed at the Temple of Jerusalem.

The 1st century was the era of the Second Temple, built by Herod the Great – he who tried to massacre the innocents according to Scripture. It bore little resemblance to the original Temple of Solomon. In antiquity the Temple had played a crucial role as a mouthpiece of the divine through the person of the King-Messiah; and as these traditions were altered, redacted and edited down the centuries, there came into being movements that sought to preserve them, and came to see the later, reconstructed Temple as somehow polluted.

By the time of Jesus the image of the Temple was tarnished; for the truth of the matter is that God's name resided in the middle of what was effectively Judea's central bank. In this capacity the Temple attracted the rather unwelcome attentions of Judea's ruling élite on a regular basis. The very thing that had caused the secession with the ten northern tribes of Israel at the end of the reign of Solomon had made the Temple an extraordinarily wealthy place: taxes. Payment of Temple tax was compulsory for every devout pilgrim, and such a captive following – thousands went up to Jerusalem every year for the Passover – brought phenomenal power to the heart of the city. But it was also a hotbed of intrigue, strife and political assassination, as various parties struggled for prestige and influence.

The latent power of Jerusalem's ancient traditions and practices was to resurface in the 1st century – in the teachings of the early Jerusalem Church.

The Christians adopted Temple ways of thinking in their liturgies and continued to worship in the Temple. Jesus went to the Temple often and even after it was destroyed in AD 70 'the Christians,' as Dr Margaret Barker put it to me in private conversation, 'continued to use the Temple ways of thinking, Temple styles of decoration, Temple styles of worship; and a lot of the Temple, in every sense of the word, passed into Christianity.'

When we first looked upon the codices and their iconography, an image of the Temple, with its accoutrements, was precisely what stood out for us. One of these accoutrements strongly affirmed that this was indeed the holy place in which Jesus had preached and worked: the seven-branched menorah. This singular item was to be found in only one place: deep inside the hall of the Holy of Holies, the most sacred place in 1st-century Palestine. In Christian memory it was held to reside *inside* the Holy of Holies. It was a piece of God's furniture – forbidden from representation at the time on the grounds of blasphemy. Seeing the Menorah on the codices was the moment of confirmation – that the codices abounded in hidden knowledge, sealed in books and then hidden away for many, many centuries.

At this time no Christian iconography existed. All that there was were the vivid descriptions in *Revelation*, the last book in the Bible. One missing letter in the Book of Haggai was said to indicate that five items were now absent from the Second Temple. Later Jewish texts remember what these were: the Menorah, the Ark, the Spirit, the Fire and the Cherubim. We were soon to realize that at least two of these, the Menorah and the Spirit, are to be found in or around the discovery of the codices; furthermore, if the discovery comprises a 'New Covenant' with God as seems to be suggested, then the fact that they were contained in a series of lead boxes would also imply the Ark. However, it was only when we first saw, on one codex, the face of Jesus, the Man of Woes, with all of its power and the sadness in its eyes that we began fully to appreciate the codices as repositories of early Christianity.

According to one of the eminent scholars who has examined the codices, the Key of Heaven, often to be seen in the hands of St Peter and other saints, is actually a reference to a seal, as in the seal of a book. In stained-glass windows in churches St Peter is often to be seen holding both a key and a sealed book: according to Clement of Alexandria (in *Hypotyposes*) he was a recipient of the secret teachings of Jesus and was also a Nasorean – a guardian of these mysteries and guardians always have a key.

In the light of this, it is significant that the very texts Justin Martyr mentions as being altered are also writings that mention secret books and other items hidden away in caves. In *2 Maccabees*, written c140 BC, which placed the prophet Jeremiah at the end of the First Temple period, we read specifically of Jeremiah sealing and hiding away the Ark of the Covenant in a cave in Jordan near Mount Nebo (2.1–8). Specifically the passage tells of 'images of silver and gold'.

And how that the prophet, having given them the law, charged
them not to forget the commandments of the Lord, and that
they should not err in their minds, when they see images of
silver and gold, with their ornaments.

*2 Maccabees* 2.2

Jeremiah is said to have been the last person to see the Ark of the
Covenant before its disappearance from the Temple, and it was he
who secreted it away, never to be seen again. However, the account in
*2 Maccabees* was written by Hebrew-Christians in the 1st century. Were
they hinting at something? Not necessarily the Ark of the Covenant but
perhaps a new Ark, a New Covenant, a treasure held to be of equal
importance: a treasure hidden in a cave.

More than this, *2 Esdras* 14 describes in explicit terms the making
of many books and an instruction from God to keep 70 of them and give
them only to the wise. It is the last few lines that are revealing:

… but keep the seventy last, that thou mayest deliver them only
to such as be wise among the people: For in them is the spring
of understanding, the fountain of wisdom, and the stream of
knowledge.

*2 Esdras* 14.46–7

The final reference is telling, for the female figure of Wisdom resided
deep inside the original temple and her story was to play a major part in
the upheavals of the 1st century – for there were those who sought her
return to the centre of Temple worship and rite, preservers of the old
ways. These people were Nazoreans and at their heart were the secret
teachings of Jesus, their rightful King, whose prophecies told of the
destruction of Jerusalem if the polluted temple was not cleansed and
whose words were sealed and hidden away in caves across the Jordan –
until the end of time.

\* \* \* \*

## 15 September – 18 October 2007: The Codices

Over the next few days I poured over the four images that Ron had given me. They were crude photographs, printed on photocopy paper, but at least there was enough to begin a rudimentary analysis. The first thing that struck me about the images was the variation in size and thickness of the codices, which could be easily ascertained as they had been helpfully placed next to a bright green plastic ruler. Two were reasonably large, the size of a standard hardback book, whilst the other two were so small they could fit into the palm of a hand. One of the photographs showed a book resting face up, and through the outward-facing binding I was able to count four or five metal leaves (the thick detritus covering them made it difficult to ascertain precisely how many). On the smaller books there was one motif I struggled to work out at first, eventually identifying it as the flower of a pomegranate tree.

The covers of the larger books were of a different order: they were festooned with palm trees and palm branches, and I could just make out a wall that seemed to be either crumbling or under construction. In the centre of the entire tableau was a column of what I thought to be Palaeo-Hebraic text. The best overall explanation of the codices, however, seemed to be offered by the menorah, or Jewish candlestick. At first sight it had taken my breath away: it was the very same candlestick that was to be found in the inner sanctuary of the Temple of Solomon. What was odd about this candlestick was that it did not have the usual seven branches; rather, it appeared to have nine. However, the eighth and ninth branches were literally that – tree branches formed of leaves, or fronds, though elsewhere in the photos there were also menorahs bearing the standard seven branches. I repeatedly counted the branches to make sure that there were indeed nine and not seven: there were menorahs all over the covers of the books, always within a boundary of palm trees.

The extraordinary nine-branched candlestick is called the *chanukiyah* and, in a later pious Jewish myth, symbolizes a miracle wherein one day's worth of oil burned for eight days, after the rededication of the Temple in the time of the Maccabean Kings (immediately before the time of Jesus). The nine-branched menorah was a symbol of the Jewish Exile to Babylon, which had occurred at the end of the kingdom of Judah way back in c586 BC.

It was to Babylon that Nebuchadnezzar had exiled the Jews, in c586 BC; and it was from here that some elements of Judaism familiar to us today had begun to emerge. An earlier King of Babylon, Hammurabi, had been presented with a gift of two tablets by the god Shamash – tablets that contained the Law, echoing most obviously the story of Moses on Mount Sinai. To represent the seven-branched menorah was utterly forbidden by edict of the Elders of the Hebrew community, since the original was uniquely sacred: it was the golden candlestick placed at the heart of Solomon's Temple, housed in the Holy of Holies – the place wherein God Himself was said to reside. After the last great rebellion of the Jews in AD 132–5, this edict was destroyed, along with the Temple that housed it. From then on the image was freely portrayed.

Another thing I noted was that almost all of the books were covered in eight-pointed stars (see plate 2) – so many of them that it was impossible to ignore their implied importance. To the people of ancient Judah and those who followed after, these motifs were not simple ornamentation: every depiction had meaning and was placed upon the page with purpose and intent, mere decoration being potentially blasphemous.

It was the stars that prompted my first insight: they were symbolic of kingship. The six-pointed star is familiar to us today as a symbol of black magic and of Israel: it is derived from the famous King, Solomon. The seven-pointed star denoted Solomon's father, King David. However, of particular interest to me at the time was the fact that the eight-pointed star was indicative of the enigmatic figure of Melchizedek, the figure to whom Abraham showed obeisance. Melchizedek appears in

*Genesis* 14 as the King of Salem. Moreover, his role is that of High Priest, and a cursory inspection of the codices showed definite High Priestly and regal references. Could the codices possibly be early Christian documents? It was an intriguing thought.

The symbols gathered around the square in the middle of some of the books were largely of menorah and palm trees and, everywhere, eight-pointed stars. All of this was turning over in my mind: the books were trying to tell me something, but I was struggling to understand what it was. I looked again at the palm trees. They looked remarkably similar to the symbols often seen on coins from the era of Simon bar Kokhba, the last of the Jewish 'rebel' leaders and a messianic candidate whose symbol was a star – his name translates as 'son of the Star'. Bar Kokhba's revolt took place in AD 132–5 and was, at first, successful. But it was only a matter of time before the Romans struck back. The Temple of Jerusalem had been utterly destroyed at the end of the first Great Revolt in AD 70. Roman rule had been brutal, but it was matched by the fanaticism that the occupying force had witnessed first-hand in this most reluctant of provinces. The rebellion had started as most rebellions do. Jerusalem had become a tinder-box of ill-feeling towards its rulers, both foreign and domestic, over a long period. There was a rumour that the rebellion had been stirred in the aftermath of the death of St James, brother of Jesus. When Roman retaliation eventually came, it was swift, brutal and horrific. This was the final punishment for a province long seen as a thorn in the imperial flesh. With the final Roman victory and the death of bar Kokhba and his cohorts, Jerusalem was destroyed and a new, Roman city was built upon its ruins: Aelia Capitolina. Another messianic hope of the people had been annihilated.

Bar Kokhba had issued his own coinage, and on some of the examples I had seen online I was able to make out the very same palm trees that appeared on the codices. This is where I began to make a bit of headway in my interpretation. The palm tree was symbolic of the House of David, King of Israel. Furthermore, on the codices they are in fruit, which implies that an offshoot of David will arise to claim the throne. Palm fronds, as is well known, were used to usher Jesus into the Holy City of Jerusalem on what is now called Palm Sunday (*John* 12.12– 19; *Mark* 11.1–11). There are separate representations of palm branches (that is, as single details rather than on the whole tree) throughout the codices, and they immediately struck me as indicative that what was being celebrated here was something to do with kingship.

Moreover, the eight-pointed stars, my researches had told me, represented stars of the House of Jesse, the father of David. Epiphanius (AD c315–403), the early Church Father, claims that the Essenes took their name from him. The star of Jesse, most famous as the Star of Bethlehem, is an unmistakable messianic symbol. Strangely, it was only when I took note of these particular stars (see plate 2) that I was struck by how often they appear in churches all over Europe – particularly medieval churches. If these were kingly documents, then the presence of *lulavim* and *etrogim* would go some way to confirming it.

*Lulavim* are bundles of branches that included palm branches. They were laid in the path of Jesus on his entry into Jerusalem. They are a sign of kingship. *Etrogim* are a kind of Rubenesque lemon – citrus with cellulite. They were one of the four species brought by the Israelites out of Egypt during the Exodus. (See plate 14 for a row of *etrogim*.) They are still used in the festival of Sukkot, otherwise known as Tabernacles. Two thousand years ago this annual event in the calendar was called the Feast of the Messiah. I had a strong intuition regarding the orthodox Jewish connection, and felt compelled to pursue this. The books, to my mind, were likely to be Hebrew-Christian.

We all too often forget that the first Christians were Jewish, but it is even more difficult to appreciate the idea of a 'Hebrew-Christian'. We shall use this term for the first followers of the early Church surrounding Jesus, the last King of Israel, to avoid confusion with later converts. Jesus was Jewish, as they all were. To them he was the *fulfilment* of the Law of the prophets. However, he was one King among the many that Israel had had in her long history. All the Kings of Israel were Messiahs: all the word *Messiah* means is the 'anointed one'.

To these people Greek was a foreign language – and, of course, the New Testament was written in Greek. Thus, the New Testament was foreign in their eyes and bore little resemblance to what these early believers had witnessed. The Hebrew-Christians were the actual family, as well as the followers, of Christ. Until now, no existing texts from these groups have survived, with the possible exception of the newly restored Gospel of Judas. They were either hidden away or ordered destroyed by the winners in the game of competing Christianities.

\* \* \* \*

### 18 October 2007: A Secret Meeting

Jennifer and I were excited. It was the day of our first official meeting about forming a team of professionals to authenticate and investigate the codices. I had in the meantime been in touch with Allen Ferkel, a well-respected metallurgist whom I had met at the London Book Fair. I also suggested to Ron that we include Shane Kimberley. Shane was a businessman from Melbourne whom I'd met in Bath some time back when he was project-managing for the Wisdom of the Ancients trust. We picked up Shane from Didcot Parkway station and drove over to Ron's, only 15 minutes away. He greeted us enthusiastically.

There was a woman already in the room, in a stylish tunic and beaded necklace. Her demeanour was stern. Ron introduced her as Maryam.

'Maryam is here from Israel representing the owner of the artefacts. She is a museum curator and archaeologist in Palestine.'

Allen had arrived by this time, and we were all shown through into the dining room. Ron gave a brief assessment of the discovery and informed us that as an indication of the owner's serious intentions he was prepared to provide research funds for testing and analysis. Midway through the discussion that ensued, Maryam reached into her handbag and pulled out a small velvet pouch. Carefully removing the object, she unfurled it from its wrapping. It was a tiny lead book. Everyone leaned forward, straining to get a closer look. It was without a doubt one of the most beautiful and surprising things I had ever seen.

My hands quivered with anticipation as Ron passed the little book to me. I weighed it in my hand; it was surprisingly heavy, much heavier than I had expected considering its small size. Its weight determined that the metal had to be lead. The book emanated power that both intrigued and fascinated me. It had quite obviously been cleaned, but with great care. Turning it over, I could see that it comprised a collection of five lead plates bound together by thick lead wire. It was inscribed both inside and out. My immediate reaction was that it seemed to impart a religious or magical intent. The book appeared to represent a scheme or pattern: both front and back displayed a stylized palm tree in fruit with two eight-pointed stars below. At the top there was a nine-branched menorah, just as I had seen in the earlier photographs, only this one had an inscription above it.

As I held the little book in the palm of my hand, taking in its delicate beauty, everything around me seemed to fade. My mind was racing. Who made this? Who would have carried it? Why lead? Why make a collection of books out of this metal?

Allen had brought a camera and had just taken it out of his tote bag and rested it on the table when Ron barked out, 'No pictures!'

'Why not'? Allen enquired dejectedly. 'I have a very good camera with a 50mm macro lens that can take a much better photo than the images you have on your computer. It will be helpful to use for research.'

'No pictures,' Maryam echoed firmly. 'Not yet.'

Allen reluctantly backed down, instead producing a jeweller's loupe with which he studied the book closely. By this stage Maryam was getting agitated: she clearly could not wait to put the little book back in its pouch and out of the thrall of everyone in the room. I wondered how on earth she had sneaked it past airport customs.

Having asked various questions of the team, she packed up the booty and left, looking at all of us suspiciously as she said her hasty goodbyes.

It was Allen who broke the silence. He told us he had done some online research and found that someone had already posted a few images on a website. Clearly we were not the only ones to know about the discovery. Ron explained that Maryam had shown a few of the codices to a couple of universities, but he did not know who else had seen them.

Less than half an hour after Maryam had left, Ron received a call. His expression was grim as he hung up. Maryam had been in a car accident: the brakes had failed. She was fine but the car had been written off. She was lucky to be alive. Jennifer and I did not say this out loud, but somehow it felt like a warning. Apprehension clouded our initial excitement.

Allen set out his plan for an initial investigation of the codices.

The lead is likely to be Roman in provenance,' he said. 'There's a lot of information on Roman lead – I'll gather what I can. I think that my first guess would take us to Anatolia, modern-day Turkey. The Romans used lead the way we do today – for pipes and roofing ... although we've stopped using it for piping – for obvious reasons, of course. But a book? I've certainly never come across anything like that, but I have plenty of notes and sources at home. I'm sure I'll come up with something. I remember an article on some lead artefacts that were discovered a couple of centuries ago, which have since disappeared into the Vatican archives. I'll dig that up and email it to you.'

A strategy was devised, with a role for everyone. When we got up to leave, Allen extended his hand, giving me what seemed like an unmistakably Masonic handshake – pressing his thumb to the knuckle of the forefinger.

'How well do you know him, David?' Shane asked.

'Not very well,' I admitted, 'but he does have a good reputation as a metallurgist.'

Jennifer and I had talked a lot about the discovery over the past month, and had decided to throw everything at it once the metal analysis had confirmed the age and authenticity of the hoard. It was agreed that

Allen would get together with Ron and arrange for samples to be taken and sent to the two laboratories he recommended: the Oxford Materials Characterisation Service (OMCS) at Oxford University Begbroke Science Park; and the Swiss Federal Laboratories for Materials Science and Technology (EMPA) in Dübendorf, Switzerland. Scrapings would be taken from the edges, leaving no traces; and if possible perhaps a small cutting would be taken from one side. These would be obtained from the book that Maryam had brought with her, as it would save time. Ron would gather more background information on the discovery and I would continue my search to establish the identity of the codices.

We needed more information about the cave where the books had been discovered. Ron had a photograph that he thought would be helpful, so we drove over to visit him. The image he handed to me depicted what appeared to be a wall of niches carved into a dusty limestone wall. Thick roots were growing out of the sides where the undergrowth had matured over the years, pushing its way through the rocky soil.

'Some of the books were found *in situ* in those series of individually carved niches,' Ron said, pointing to the shallow recesses.

'Did the owner tell you where this cave site is?' I asked.

'Israel. Somewhere in the north, but I'm not saying any more.'

I had gathered that much. Apart from the obvious fact that Maryam was Palestinian and Ron had mentioned that she had taken the books to the Hebrew University in Jerusalem to be analysed, for me the script on the codices had narrowed down the possibilities for the location.

\* \* \* \*

**The Early Christians**

> ... *behold, how great a matter a little flame kindleth.*
>
> *James* 3.5

From my initial study of the images it was easy to conclude that they may well be Hebrew-Christian, the work of people who saw themselves as preservers or restorers of writings and rituals that had long ago been taken away from them. They were not therefore abandoning their identities, just reasserting them. The shock of this realization is that Christianity was not a new religion. Furthermore, in the early 1st century there was no such thing as 'Christianity', just a miscellany of sects representing variations upon a theme. Therefore, if Christianity, as the codices seem to suggest, harks back to the days of Solomon's Temple, then it also harks back to the days of the original twelve tribes of Israel – the Hebrews. What we are looking at is Hebrew-Christianity or, in a 1st-century context, Christian Hebrews.[8]

The 'earliest Christians' were known as the Jerusalem Church – a far better term for this breakaway movement, composed not only of Jews but of Samaritans and others too. They believed that Jesus was the rightful King, the expected Messiah – the King/God of Israel. This was the movement that in due course would become defined as Christianity. They were also called Nazarenes or Nazoreans. The term comes from the Hebrew *notsrim*, meaning 'keepers' or 'preservers' or even 'guardians'; this is turn comes from the root *nezer*, meaning 'branch'.

From the time of Solomon until the Seleucid period (c176 BC), Temple ritual, it is believed, had been overseen by priests of the House of Zadok (meaning 'Righteous'). This practice had come to an end after Antiochus Epiphanes, the Seleucid King, had deposed the last of the Zadokite High Priests in 175 BC.[9] However, with the restoration of independence, the Maccabean rulers chose priests from within their own family. They became Kings *and* High Priests. The House of Zadok was to remain in exile. Scholars believe that a group from within this house had separated themselves from the Temple and settled by the shores of the Dead Sea: they became known as the Essenes.

The Essenes had ever since then been a thorn in the side of the Temple authorities, for it was widely believed that only a High Priest from the House of Zadok, the *Righteous*, could give legitimacy to the Temple ritual. Only they could speak on behalf of the people before God – and therefore make the offering of Atonement once a year at the Temple. Their emphasis was purity: ritual and liturgical. They believed that the Temple of Herod was polluted, that the rituals there were improper, involving practices that they saw as abominable. They insisted upon the proper practice by the proper people; and they yearned for the coming of the Messiah King of Israel to cleanse the sins of the nation.

When Herod the Great had ascended the throne he had restored the High Priesthood to the House of Zadok, giving himself the right to depose High Priests when he saw fit: traditionally it had been a hereditary office and a lifelong one. Politics ruled the day and demands for purity by the traditionalists became ever more urgent. These factors play a part in the significance of the codices, most obviously in their representation of the Temple. They have the shape and the feel of sectarian documents produced by a community in exile.

The Temple authorities were confronted by a double-edged sword: on the one hand, they had the Romans, wanting to impose peace under their own terms; on the other, they had the many factions of Judea wanting to be forever rid of the Romans. Ever practical, the Temple, its High Priesthood and the Sanhedrin walked the tightrope between the Romans and the destruction of all they held dear. This was the extremely tense situation shortly before and after the Crucifixion of Jesus.

By the time that the Church came to take on a recognizable form, Jerusalem had fallen and Christianity was beginning to develop in two distinct regions: the Greek-speaking area of Asia Minor, the playground of St Paul; and the Aramaic, Syriac area north of Palestine, including the region of Antioch. It is in this latter area that very early Christian writings were formulated from what were older Christian traditions.

Before the author of *Matthew* composed his Gospel in Greek, the saint to whom authorship is ascribed is credited with a now lost collection of the sayings of Jesus in Aramaic. A small but important selection of these sayings, or *logia* (from *logos*, the Word) as they are sometimes called, has been partially incorporated into the Gospel. An earlier work that incorporated more of the sayings was described by St Jerome as the Gospel According to the Hebrews. 'I had an opportunity of copying it,' he writes, 'afforded me by the Nazarenes who use the book, at Beroea, a city of Syria.'

It is significant that St Jerome (AD c330–420) should have had in his hands a copy of the original Nazarene gospel. He was private secretary to Pope Damasus and after the latter's death demonstrated his scholarly talent by translating the Bible from its original Hebrew into Latin.

Of all the Gospels, Matthew's is the most symbolic in its use of mythic imagery: there is a tension here, an urgency, suggesting a writer eager to impart something important, something encoded. Many scholars in recent years have asserted that the Gospels are more myth than history, and in Matthew we get a taste of why this argument has emerged. The idea of Jesus that we get from Matthew and the other Gospels is like a reflection in a plate-glass window. This is the Jesus of faith, the Son of God, tangible but ghostly: Jesus appears every inch the hero, performing miracles and doing good – only for it all to end when he is brought before the Roman procurator Pontius Pilate on an unspecified charge and condemned to death by the most gruesome means possible: crucifixion.

The Gospels were not only written long after the events they describe but with an eye to their readership – a largely Roman audience. Suddenly we can see why Matthew appears to be holding back. It is all a matter of subtlety. The Gospels show a keenness to appear free of anti-Roman sentiment: this at least is the view of modern Biblical scholarship.

Around AD 110, Papias, Bishop of Hierapolis, wrote a work in five books entitled *Exposition of the Oracles of the Lord*, in which he reports that Matthew, the disciple, compiled the sayings of the Lord in Hebrew. This has been taken to mean the first Gospel, whereas it is known that St Matthew's Gospel used the Greek Gospel of Mark as a source; the many scriptural quotations within Matthew's Gospel are from a Greek translation rather than from a direct Hebrew source.

... all the Gospels, except the patently fictitious ones, were based on notes taken by Greek-speaking converts from the Aramaic Gospel orally current among the Nazarenes; and ... each evangelist, as Papias reports; 'interpreted them as best he could' – that is to say, uncritically and, in general, with studied ignorance of their historical background.[10]

St Matthew's Gospel[11] and the *Exposition of the Oracles of the Lord* are two entirely different works, and one might have come from out of the other – the Oracles first, the Gospel second. Furthermore, the shape of Matthew's Gospel was very likely to have been inspired by the Oracles, even though its narrative form relied on notes taken in Greek.[12] (Oracular retelling of various traditions was common throughout Asia Minor and Palestine at the time of Jesus.)

Unfortunately, Matthew's use of Greek is confusing. He uses the Greek 'Nazoraios' – a 'preserver of the old ways'. It later became associated with the place called Nazareth; but there is no archaeological evidence to show that Nazareth existed at this time. Matthew states: 'He [Jesus] will be called a Nazarean' (*Matthew* 2.22–23). This does not correspond at all closely to anything in either the Old or New Testaments. As Professor J R Porter points out:

> ... many scholars think that it is based on *Isaiah* 11.1, a well-known messianic passage where the Messiah is described as a 'branch' (Hebrew '*nezer*') of the tree of Jesse (the father of King David). But Matthew normally cites the Septuagint, the Greek version of the Hebrew Bible, which has nothing like Nazaraios at this point. However, he may be translating directly from the original Hebrew ...[13]

In one of the fragments mentioned by Eusebius, Papias describes his viewpoint:

I will not hesitate to add also for you to my interpretations which I formerly learned with care from the Presbyters [elders or priests in local Christian congregations] and have carefully stored in memory, giving assurance of its truth. For I did not take pleasure as the many do in those who speak much, but in those who teach what is true, nor in those who relate foreign precepts, but in those who relate the precepts which were given by the Lord to the faith and came down from the Truth itself. And also if any follower of the Presbyters happened to come, I would inquire for the sayings of the Presbyters, what Andrew said, or what Peter said, or what Philip or what Thomas or James or what John or Matthew or any other of the Lord's disciples, and for the things which other of the Lord's disciples, and for the things which Aristion and the Presbyter John, the disciples of the Lord, were saying. For I considered that I should not get so much advantage from matter in books as from the voice which yet lives and remains.[14]

Papias is telling us that he had these things from an unwritten oral tradition passed directly from Jesus's immediate Nazarene followers and that they were written in the native language:

Matthew put together the Oracles [of the Lord] in the Hebrew language, and each one interpreted them as best he could.[15]

In the years after the Council of Nicaea in AD 325, when Church teaching had been formalized under the aegis of Constantine the Great, much was subsequently destroyed as heretical or inconvenient. The consequence of these actions has led to many misunderstandings about the Jerusalem Church. This was the Mother Church. However, in the West it was the Christianity of St Paul that had won out – and it bore little resemblance to the early Church of the 1st century. It has even sought to play down the image of the early Church, as Hyam Maccoby points out:

It is, after all, implausible, to say the least, that the close followers of Jesus, his companions during his lifetime, led by his brother, should have so misunderstood him that they reversed his views immediately after his death. The 'stupidity' motif characterizing the disciples in the Gospels is best understood as a Pauline attempt to explain away the attachment of the 'Jerusalem Church' to Judaism, rather than as historical obtuseness.[16]

In the *Clementine Literature* (the *Homilies* and the *Recognitions* attributed to St Clement of Rome, who died in AD 99, but more likely authored by early Hebrew-Christian Church communities) there is a scene in which James, brother of Jesus, is preaching in the Temple and on the verge of converting a substantial group within his audience. It is at this point that an 'enemy' appears and starts to incite a crowd against James. In the ensuing mêlée James is thrown down the Temple steps, suffering great injury, whereupon he is quickly taken away to safety by his followers. The enemy was Saul of Tarsus, soon to change his name to Paul.

In AD 42 James was forced to leave Jerusalem on pain of death; and so it was that his burgeoning community vacated the divided powder-keg of a city, taking their archive with them and carrying the shattered remains of his lame body.

Many scholars believe that this single act of persecution against James was a contributory factor in the eventual rebellion of the Jews against the might of Rome. Paul, being a representative of the ruling élite of the city, the Sanhedrin, was probably all too aware of the need for the authorities to keep a lid on any perceived threats to the might of Rome. Jerusalem was faced with its gravest crisis in years.[17]

In everything I have read about James he is described as a good man, always placed in high regard. His supremacy was recognized throughout

Christendom. 'Good' in this sense would mean to a person of 1st-century Palestine, a man of God.

Hegesippus, a 2nd-century saint, in a remaining fragment from his lost *Commentaries* writes the following about James:

> After the apostles, James the brother of the Lord surnamed the Just was made head of the Church at Jerusalem. Many indeed are called James. This one was holy from his mother's womb. He drank neither wine nor strong drink, ate no flesh, never shaved or anointed himself with ointment or bathed. He alone had the privilege of entering the Holy of Holies since indeed he did not use woollen vestments but linen and went alone into the Temple and prayed on behalf of the people, insomuch that his knees were reputed to have acquired the hardness of camels' knees.[18]

From an early age James had been an avowed Nazirite, an ascetic in the service of God. The fact that he was allowed to enter the Holy of Holies also suggests that he was not only a High Priest but also a member of the exiled community by the shores of the Dead Sea, the community that the Greeks called Essenes.[19]

In the early texts there is an intriguing dearth of references to the figure of St James: the Epistle of James in the New Testament says little about him, and so too does the Book of Acts, where we see him as the leader of the Jerusalem Church in the wake of the Crucifixion.[20] Clement of Alexandria (AD c150–c215) wrote:

> For they say that Peter and James and John after the ascension of our Saviour, as if also preferred by our Lord, strove not after honour, but chose James the Just bishop of Jerusalem.[21]

He also relates:

> The Lord after his resurrection imparted knowledge to James the Just and to John and Peter, and they imparted it to the rest of the apostles, and the rest of the apostles to the seventy, of whom Barnabas was one.[22]

The 'knowledge' spoken of by Clement is what, in likelihood, gave James the level of power and influence that he so clearly enjoyed. However, it also made him a lot of enemies, particularly within the organization of the Temple. But if such knowledge was dangerous to James, then it was dangerous also to his entire family, for it seems that the Jerusalem Church was run on the principle of dynastic succession. There is enough strong historical evidence to demonstrate that James was in turn succeeded by another relative of Jesus: James' cousin, Simeon.

Moreover, for a few hundred years after Jesus's death, a remnant of this sect of Jewish Messianists, known as *Ebionim* or *Ebionites* ('poor men'), still survived. They revered Jesus as one of the last prophets without attributing to him anything of the divinity that Paul accorded him. Within this sect were a select group called the *Desposyni*, descendants of Jesus. There is a reference to these descendants by Eusebius (AD c260–340), Bishop of Caesarea and the Father of Church History. Commenting on the earlier words of Hegesippus (2nd century), Eusebius writes:

> But there still survived of the family of the Lord the grandsons of Jude, his brother after the flesh, as he was called. These they informed against, as being of the family of David; and the *evocatus* [a soldier in the Roman army who had gained his discharge but chosen to stay in service] brought them before Domitian Caesar. For he feared the coming of the Christ, as did also Herod. And he asked them if they were of David's line and they acknowledged it. Then he asked them what possessions they had or what fortune they owned. And they said that between the two of them they had only nine hundred *denari*, half belonging to each of them ... after this Domitian in no way condemned them, but despised them as men of no account.[23]

Domitian Caesar, the younger son of the Emperor Vespasian and brother of Titus (victor of the battle to re-take Jerusalem from the Jewish rebels after a fanatical four-year struggle) had good reason to be afraid of the remnant of the family of Jesus; but how low they had fallen, truly they were now *poor men*. Some writers and scholars have interpreted this as evidence of an attempt to depict the Jerusalem Church and the followers of James as a part of the general fanaticism of the time, to theorize that they were Zealots, or *Sicarii* ('knife wielders'). This is pure speculation, and to my mind misguided, since according to the precepts of practising Essenes and their various off-shoot movements, violence was something to be abhorred.[24] The fact that such texts as the Dead Sea Scrolls sometimes speak in violent terms does not mean to say that this was reflected in reality. (Ironically, modern scholarly debate on the subject can be just as contentious, without necessarily resorting to physical violence in the aftermath of heated argument.)

Paul also mentions James the Just, writing in *Galatians* 1.19: 'Other of the apostles saw I none, save James, the Lord's brother.' Paul was a divisive figure in the early Church after his famous conversion. Two warring factions developed: the Jerusalem Church, which did not see itself as separate from the general Hebrew-Jewish community; and the Gentile Church of Paul – *gentile* because by this time Paul had begun to travel across the breadth of the Roman Empire, beyond the remit of Judaism, with his message of salvation.

Meanwhile, the situation in Jerusalem continued to be fraught. James was leading the Jerusalem Church, a Nazarene party riven by factional fighting.[25] It was only after the return of Paul from various of his post-conversion foreign travels, around AD c43–4, that the Jerusalem Church began to look anything like a focused entity – focused on mutual enmity towards Paul and his 'deviant' message.[26]

* * * *

**November 2007: Reading Between the Lines**

Ron called in a panic. He was having misgivings about the project and asked if we could come over as soon as possible. He had decided to take the little book to nearby Reading University to perform a test on the lead with a spectrographic gun. I was surprised to discover that he had the codex in his possession. And to take the whole book and not just a few scrapings to Reading was, in my opinion, unwise. He had potentially sent out a huge advert to the academic community as a whole, and we hadn't even begun to determine whom we could trust yet. We were still in the very first stages of analysis and it was crucial that, until we had more of an idea of what we were working with, we treated our discovery as highly confidential.

Ron told us that the metallurgist had said, 'Artefacts like this shouldn't be in the hands of someone like you.'

'Did they give you any results from the spectrographic test on the metal?' I asked.

'Yes,' Ron replied. 'The good news is that he confirmed that the provenance of the lead is indeed ancient, although the professor recommended we get more testing done to arrive at a more comprehensive and detailed analysis.'

'I haven't yet told you the bad part,' Ron continued. 'I got an email from Scotland Yard yesterday. Apparently Reading University contacted them.'

The metallurgist clearly wondered what on earth a British journalist was doing toting around an observably unique and potentially important artefact. Ron would have been obliged to tell him that the codex had come from Israel, as provenance is a key aspect in obtaining accurate and relevant test results. How did it come to be in the UK? Was there no archaeological or academic team behind this discovery? Admittedly, the scenario was highly suspicious.

Upstairs in his office, Ron showed us the email, which said that the police had been contacted by the university about a 'matter of possible illegal stolen antiquities'. Ron was simply asked to get in touch with the police to cooperate with them on this.

I asked him what proof he had that the artefacts were legitimately owned, and he informed me that the owner had provided him with a document showing legal ownership. I wondered why he hadn't shown it to anyone, and suggested that this might be a good idea. I also recommended that he give Allen a call, as the two of them were supposed to be sending samples to laboratories in Oxford and Switzerland. Ron had trust issues with this, but I told him I thought he was making a mistake. So Ron agreed to give Allen a call and tell him about Reading and hopefully speed up the process with the other laboratories, as the Israelis were already starting to pressure him for results.

\* \* \* \*

## December 2007 – March 2008, Castle Combe, Wiltshire

It was late November when Jennifer and I relocated to my old neck of the woods, near Bath, in Wiltshire. I was looking forward to getting on with my research unencumbered and furthering the historical analysis, as well as discussing key points with the others. For the moment, pieces of the puzzle were still floating loosely around my mind. I wanted to put everything in some kind of order, to step back and try to piece the fragments together as a whole. In the meantime I also had to wait for the scientific tests on the metal. Although the Reading University test for antiquity was positive, Ron seemed to be withholding essential elements from me, and this made me uncomfortable, creating doubt in my mind over the authenticity of the codices.

'I thought I'd let you know what happened with Scotland Yard,' Ron told me next day in a phone call. 'I went in last week and showed them the letter I told you about. They seemed to accept it.'

'That's good news indeed. And have you had any luck tracking down the person behind the website?'

'Oh yes, I meant to tell you. She's actually known to the owner. Her name's Yvette something or other. He knows her from when he lived in Sweden, although she's a British journalist. I spoke to her and she's agreed to take the photographs off the Internet and to keep quiet about them.'

Weeks passed by without any news from anyone. I called Shane, who said he had organized a conference call with his lawyer friend in Melbourne to discuss Heads of Agreement, but Ron had backed out at the last moment.

'We don't seem to be getting anywhere,' I said despairingly.

'Well, at least Hassan has agreed to pay for the research and analysis. In fact Ron's going to visit him sometime in March.'

I rang off, more than a little perturbed. Why had Ron not mentioned his trip to Israel last night when we had spoken? However, at least I now knew the name of one of the protagonists – it was some sort of breakthrough.

Knowing that Ron was going to be on a plane to Israel sometime within the next two months, my next task was going to be to draw up a set of guidelines for his visit: upon this we had agreed. We would need forensic protocols for handling the books and on-the-spot research would be essential – without it there was not much further I could go beyond mere speculation.

As I continued my research, I was beginning to realize that the codices were even more important than I had appreciated. It was now time to call in help from more specialized scholars, but for the moment I had to be more certain of the codices' authenticity, so as not to waste anyone's valuable time, let alone make a fool of myself.

One of the things that preoccupied me about the codices was the language – and the fact that it did not seem to be Aramaic, the language of 1st-century Palestine. My guess was that it could possibly be a Phoenician-Canaanite script. The problem was that nothing we had researched had matched it. I knew, moreover, that the search for a match would be futile, as I already felt in my bones that the writing was Palaeo-Hebrew, an obscure form of the ancient Phoenician-Canaanite.

Aramaic was the language of the Palestinian region in the first few centuries of the rise of Christianity. It had its origins in Syria. The Judeans and other peoples of Palestine would have been Aramaic speakers. By the time of Jesus, Hebrew had become a script reserved largely for sacred texts, and rarely, if ever, used for everyday purposes. There are examples of it on the Dead Sea Scrolls written in an elegant hand and with great care. However, Aramaic was the everyday language used for note-taking and doing business.

Looking at the lettering on the codices, I observed the way the characters seemed to rise up from the base metal, as if they were embossed, the equally strange way in which detached single letters were scattered here and there, and the archaic character of the language. All this sent my mind into a spin. For a 1st–century text to be written in such an archaic script could mean only one thing: that the texts were very holy indeed. Why else would the writers hark back to such a long-forgotten language?

I remembered what my researches had told me: that Hebrew had first been formulated on Mount Sinai, probably by Hebrew slaves. Apparently the latest thinking is that the language we today know as Hebrew was originally a series of *graffito* which were interpretations of Egyptian hieratic – a style of communication in large part incomprehensible to these people, who sought an easier way to understand it. In this early language, called Western Sinaitic by philologists, the letters Y, J and G were from the start *one* letter as represented by one specific glyph. The letter Shin, the S in today's Western alphabet, was represented by one specific glyph also.

The original glyphs for these letters were a hand pierced by a nail and a spear entering between the fourth and fifth ribs – for anyone who knows the story of Christ's Passion, obvious bells will be starting to ring. *Jesus* has these letters in its spelling. It would appear that his name was actually a prediction of what the Gospels would later describe as his sacrifice.

Looking at icons of the Orthodox Church repeatedly, one thing struck me like a bolt from the blue – an idea that was to have vital repercussions for the project. In my earlier years I had studied painting at the Bath Academy of Art. Colour and form have always held a fascination for me, but it was the wonderful aroma of artists' pigments and the lingering odour of linseed that especially moved me. As a former student of fine art, I knew the painter's palette like an extension of myself.

Once, I had been given a lesson on all the different versions of white available. There was painter's white, titanium white, zinc white, and so on. And then there was *lead* white, which was always used as a base on which to put other colours.

I already knew about the use of lead by medieval icon painters as the background on which they made their images. As a trained painter myself, I knew that Renaissance artists often used a substance called *litharge*. This was a mixture of lead monoxide and lead. Then one day, in the catalogue of an academic publisher specializing in Orthodox Christian art, I came across a reference to the symbolic importance of lead. Apparently, this metal represented the veil of the Temple and its promise of the world beyond. Lead was the base physical nature of the earth devoid of all spirit. It was a ground through which the idea of the divine might shine – to someone in the right frame of mind to perceive it. The idea was that meditating upon a holy icon might bring about the revelation of a secret inherent in the image.

White was light. The light itself was within the painting, within the image of the divine or of the saint depicted there. Was this an ancient tradition that had been passed down through the centuries, originating long before it was expressed in practice by the icon painters. Was it a time-honoured way of thinking about, and celebrating, the divine? My instinct was telling me that I was on the right path. What we were now looking at was nothing less than a series of icons: possibly the very first icons.

What initially seemed strange to me, that metal should have played such an important but understated role in the history of the icon, was starting to make sense. At the base of the icon was lead; and on the very top, as a symbol of immortality, the eternal quality of the divine, was gold. This brought me full circle to the view held by the alchemists, of lead as representing the base nature of our existence and of gold as somehow stating the obverse of that: our understanding of perfection.

This idea of the *baseness* of lead intrigued me. Such was its popularity that in the age of Queen Elizabeth I of England, lead was used as a make-up to whiten the complexion of the skin. It was a sign of breeding and of wealth – of someone wealthy enough not to have to work outside in the sun. (It is extraordinary to think that, 400 years later, exactly the opposite is true: the mark of affluence is a suntan, denoting leisure in the sun, with pallor perhaps denoting poverty.) However, in the centuries before Elizabeth, lead was seen differently: as the veil between worlds, which kept us at a safe distance from the divine. It seemed to me, by extension, that we too were being characterized as base, that our natural element was the lead in the alchemist's alembic.

To gaze upon an icon, and to meditate in its presence, was gradually to strip away the layers, pierce the veil and look, however briefly, upon the divine mystery – and in the process transform the viewer into spiritual gold. Many saints and holy people within the Orthodox Church and beyond claim to have experienced precisely this. The idea is that God's eternal light, the very essence of divinity, is so ultra-intense that we can see, feel or witness it only rarely, under special and testing conditions. To experience the divine, we need to be correctly attuned.

This makes perfect sense, given our limitations as a species. Our experience as human beings is of a small planet located somewhere within a vast cosmos. Our consciousness is highly localized, and incapable of cosmic understanding. To the ancient mind, ironically, the concept of God or divinity as a whole was imagined on a grand scale, although the ancients also had the humility to realize their own inadequacy in meaningfully grasping such a scale. A transcendent understanding was attainable, but the problem was how to explain it when it happened. Thus they resorted to symbols. A deeply felt symbolism is at the heart of all iconography, conveying the personal sense of revelation that words can never capture. A person who could penetrate the leaden veil of the mysteries was someone to be reckoned with, someone with priceless insight. How appropriate that our codices were composed of this very same substance: lead.

I had by this time deduced that the codices seemed to encapsulate a representation of Solomon's Temple. The larger of the books portrayed in the photographs that I had been given had a rectangular column of text hemmed in by half-menorahs and messianic stars, palm trees, and lemon-like *etrogim*. What seemed significant to me is that the text within the rectangle was untouched by any of these symbols. The text stood alone, as if uniquely special: holy, even.

* * * *

I rang Shane again the following week. I was more than a little surprised to find out that he and Ron had been to various meetings with the Israelis.

'Yes, we all met up in London a few times.'

'You met the *Israelis?*' I asked unable to disguise the surprise in my voice.

'Yup. And you'll be surprised to hear that, Hassan, who owns the artefacts, is not the poor farmer that we were led to believe he is. Hassan is actually quite well off, though I don't know exactly what his business is.'

'I guess that's why he was able to underwrite the initial research costs,' I answered.

'Ron took them to a dealer in London to get an appraisal of the books.'

'Well, what happened with the dealer?' I asked, astonished that he would do such a thing.

'Apparently he offered them all of fifty pounds for the book that Hassan had with him.'

I shared the news with Jennifer: 'I don't buy it. Either Ron's being economical with the truth or the dealer believed them to be fakes.'

It seemed to me that any dealer who had the good fortune to be shown the books, upon seeing them simply would not have believed his luck – so did not. This scenario was reminiscent of the initial reaction to the discovery of the Dead Sea Scrolls. The priceless artefacts had at first been dismissed in exactly the same manner: at first they were thought to be medieval forgeries, then they were advertised 'for sale' in the *Jerusalem Post*.

Ron seemed to have been following his own agenda. Selling the artefacts had not been discussed with the group – or at least not with Jennifer and me. Why had he not extended us the courtesy of a call or an email? The best that I could do was to give him the set of protocols that I had prepared to act as a guide in the event that he laid his hands upon the codices. What was required was dust and pollen samples; and, if possible, good clean images shot on a white background in order to adduce the darkness and coloration of the images. We needed a true sense of what they really looked like and an accurate assessment of their size. In my memorandum I asked Ron not to handle the artefacts with his bare hands and to provide me with a set of photographs that were taken from all angles – so that we could deduce the thickness of the books and what kind of condition they were in. I called a few days later and wished him *bon voyage*.

∗ ∗ ∗ ∗

### March 2008: An Astonishing Evaluation

Jennifer and I set out for Ron's house in Oxfordshire. Ron had returned from Israel and we were eager to see his photographs and to hear all about the trip. Confronted with the pictures, I stared open-mouthed at what I could only describe as 'archaeological porn'. The lead books had been propped up against a series of plush velvet backdrops as if stylized for a glossy adult publication. For academic use and study they were quite useless.

Moving in to get a closer look at the screen, I had to admit the codices were indeed more beautiful and astonishing than I had ever expected. They varied in size, and there were a *lot* of them. They were very similar to the one Maryam had brought – no more than the size of the palm of a hand.

Ron seemed uncomfortable about showing us *all* the pictures. What he had not told us was that he took a photojournalist with him. I could tell because when he scanned his mouse over the images the text box came up showing that they had been taken by a Nikon D2X – a top-of-the-range professional digital camera. Ron was unlikely to have had one in his kit: they cost a small fortune. My hunch was confirmed by the next set of photos, which were quite obviously taken by a different camera. The images were indistinct; many of them were out of focus. On a cheap veneered table that took up 90 percent of the photograph was a book. It was hardly recognizable, since it was so out of focus and was held in Ron's ungloved white hand. In other photos were more books, and an assortment of bizarre 'artefacts' leaning against empty Marlboro packets.

I stopped looking – I could not bear to see any more. 'Did you take any pollen or dust samples?' I dared to ask. He replied that there not been time to do this. 'So what about the inside of the books – from the looks of things, some of them have been opened?'

'Yes, not much in them though, just a lot of writing,' he said casually, handing me a CD he had burned for me of his photography.

'Oh, did I tell you? Allen came over a while back and took some metal samples, which have now been sent to two laboratories, one in Oxford and one in Switzerland? Only, the results are not expected to come in any time soon.' I was pleased to hear that Ron had been working with Allen, and told him so.

'Yes, Allen's been great. He told me he knows some collectors in New York and Israel who'd be interested in buying some of the books.' This last piece of information really knocked me sideways. Allen was purportedly an academic: we could not imagine that he might have considered selling the codices.

'Two of the books have been evaluated by Christie's New York in excess of 50 million dollars!' he exclaimed excitedly.

A few weeks later I decided to give Shane a call to hear his take on things. He told me that he and Ron had attended more meetings in London with the Israelis, who had agreed to fund further research. This baffled me, as the initial funding was more than enough to carry out preliminary testing. We still had no results back from the labs to show for this money, which concerned me, especially as the testing at the Oxford lab had cost £10,000, according to Shane. This seemed a huge amount to pay to wait months to test a tiny scrap of metal. Shane agreed that it all seemed a bit fishy. He admitted that he and Ron were not quite seeing eye to eye, as the trip to Israel had been a waste of time and expenses, with little to show for it apart from the useless photographs. I gleaned as much as I could from the conversation, particularly the intriguing fact that during their meetings Hassan had brought an adviser.

* * * *

**Unfamiliar Christianity**

> *He who controls the past controls the future.*
>
> George Orwell, *Nineteen Eighty-Four*, chapter 3

We rarely hear about the unfamiliar aspects of Christianity, the events that unfolded in the immediate aftermath of the death of Jesus. The Gospels end with the Resurrection; and the Book of Acts speaks mainly of the arrival and the career of Paul – from a Pauline perspective. There are few non-Pauline Letters. And then we are confronted with the Book of Revelation. However, when we take a look at some of the supposedly apocryphal texts of the New Testament, judged by certain Churches to be either anathema or of doubtful provenance, we can see that they actually contain some intriguing information, making us question their exclusion in the first place. One such text is the *2 Esdras*.

In *2 Esdras* Ezra has a vision whereby he is commanded to restore the Law. He does this by producing a series of books, 94 in number. The first 24 of these books are assumed to be the Tanakh, the canon of the Hebrew Bible – these were published openly. However, the last 70 are the secret books, containing the real wisdom that was to be made available only to a select few. God gave a specific command that the secret books were to be given to the wise among the people. Significantly, these texts were written by the early Hebrew-Christians: when James and his followers had fled Jerusalem, they had taken their secret books with them. In my discussions about the hoard with Hassan, it became clear to me that 70 books was about the sum of it. They were more important than the Tanakh: *they were the source of understanding, knowledge and wisdom.* It is likely that they were off-limits to anyone outside the early Church, which would have included anyone identified as Jewish who was a supporter of the new Hebrew translations. As Dr Margaret Barker puts it, in her book *The Great High Priest*, 'If, as seems likely, they were the pre-Christian texts that were only preserved by the Christians, eg the earlier strata of the Ascension of Isaiah, the texts known as *1* (and *2*) *Enoch* ... there must have been something of great importance in these texts.'[27]

The *Clementine Recognitions* tell us that James and his community fled Jerusalem north-east to Pella and beyond – to the area where the codices were discovered. Eusebius, probably using Hegesippus as a source, writes:

> But the people of the Church in Jerusalem had been commanded by a revelation, vouchsafed to approved men there before the war, to leave the city and to dwell in a certain town of Perea called Pella.[28]

This episode has presented quandaries for scholars, many of whom may have been unable to understand or accept it: the lack of evidence from Jordan until now has justified their doubts. There seems to have been more than one exodus of the early Jerusalem Church to Pella – and beyond. Epiphanius, the Church Father, writing in AD c374, gives a little more detail:

> The Nazoraean sect exists in Beroea near Coele, Syria, in the Decapolis near the region of Pella, and in Bashan in the place called Cocaba, which in Hebrew is called Chochabe. That is where the sect began, when all the disciples were living in Pella after they moved from Jerusalem, since Christ told them to leave Jerusalem and withdraw because it was about to be besieged. For this reason they settled in Peraea and there, as I said, they lived. This is where the Nazoraean sect began.[29]

I soon realized that at least one part of the story had to be more or less true. Saul of Tarsus had shortly afterwards been given a remit by the Jerusalem Temple authorities to go in pursuit of James and his community. It was while he was engaged in this pursuit that Saul, or Paul as he was soon to become known, witnessed something secret, something that today would be classified as 'for your eyes only', hidden away from us all. And the only secret thing or things that he could have seen were in the hands of James and his community. This was the event that was to change Western civilization.

The problem is that at a very early stage much was either rewritten or destroyed by both Christians and Jews. The Tanakh or Hebrew Canon – the Old Testament, as we think of it (though there are differences) – is riddled with inconsistencies as a result of being rewritten and edited to exclude anything that might be perceived as Christian. For example, *Genesis* 22 tells of the sacrifice of Isaac: this was omitted as a result of antipathy to the Christians. There is evidence of redacting in the apocryphal Gospel of Barnabas as well as in the Quran, which mentions the Jews altering their books.

Although most Christians are hardly aware of the fact, the Quran is a reliable source of the history, and the only reason it is not often quoted in this context is that it does not agree with mainstream Christian doctrine. It is quite specific in mentioning that the Temple authorities removed the line from *Isaiah* 7, 'He shall be named a Nazarene.' This is reflected by Gregory of Nyssa (AD 335–95) who wrote that the Old Testament prophet Isaiah 'knew more perfectly than all others the mystery of the religion of the Gospel'.[30] In praising Isaiah St Jerome states tellingly:

> ... he was more of an evangelist than a prophet, because he described all of the mysteries of the Church of Christ so vividly that you would assume he was not prophesying about the future, but rather was composing a history of past events.[31]

If we look at the New Testament from an Old Testament perspective we can see many inconsistencies in how Jesus lives up to the promise of the prophets, yet this is not reflected in the surviving Old Testament Scriptures that have come down to us. St Jerome (AD c347–420), when compiling his translation of the Bible, one of the most influential events of Western history, took the view that the Hebrew text used by the Jews and not the Greek Septuagint was the most reliable text of the Old Testament. He used this translation for his Latin Vulgate Bible and it was this that was gradually accepted into the Catholic Church. Jewish authorities, in altering their texts, were understandably antipathetic to Christians, holding them responsible for the destruction of the Temple of Jerusalem in AD 70. It was other groups who preserved the hidden and altered traditions, much to the ire of the Temple authorities and the later editors and redactors.

In Jesus's own lifetime the Septuagint had been held in the highest esteem and was greatly honoured. According to Philo, the translators were 'prophets and priests of the mysteries whose sincerity and singleness of thought has enabled them to go hand in hand with the purest of spirits ...'[32] Indeed, such was the regard in which the translators were held that there was an annual celebration at Pharos, where they had worked on the text.

By St Jerome's day this situation had altered radically. The Diaspora Jews had accepted a new translation by Aquila[33] in the 2nd century AD and had condemned the Septuagint translation in the strongest possible terms. This condemnation was itself condemned in a 5th-century text, the *Dialogue of Timothy and Aquila*, thought to be a reworking of much earlier material. Timothy, a Christian, writes of the corruption not only of the Greek text of Scripture but also of the Hebrew: 'If you find that a testimony to Christ has disappeared from the Hebrew or has been concealed in the Greek, it is Aquila's plot.'[34] The problem of Old Testament Scriptures was one that beset the early Church for many years.[35] In *The Clementine Homilies* (18.20) Jesus says:

> On this account do you go astray, not knowing the true things of the Scriptures [cf *Mark* 12.24] and for this reason you are also ignorant of the Power of God. Therefore every man who wishes to be saved must become, as the Teacher said, a judge of the books written to try us. For he said: 'Become experienced bankers.' Now the need for bankers arises when forgeries are mixed up with the genuine.[36]

This points to the central enigma of Jesus and the early Church and the struggle by scholars to understand what actually happened. The problem for scholarship has been the recognition of what was lost or rewritten. The Christian view was often dismissed on the grounds that the lost passages must be interpolations, as they cannot be found in the original Hebrew. The discovery of the Dead Sea Scrolls began to change this view, prompting a re-evaluation of old assumptions. Basically, the heart of the problem is that the Western Church has as a major part of its Scriptures the Jewish canon: the early Church used very different Scriptures. This explains why certain texts are listed as non-canonical and are little known. The general reader, coming across them for the first time, is likely to find their content surprising:[37]

> The Jews ... had it written in their sacred oracles, 'That then should their city be taken, as well as their holy house ...' [There was] an ambiguous oracle that was also found in their sacred writings how, 'about that time, one from their country should become governor of the habitable earth.'[38]

In *Revelation*, the last book of the Bible, the seventh angel sounds his trumpet and voices are heard in heaven: 'The kingdom of the world has become the kingdom of our Lord and of his Christ' (*Revelation* 11.15). In his Gospel and in *Revelation*, John, who had a close relationship with James, the leader of the early Church, criticizes 'the Jews', but what he is criticizing more specifically is the abolition of the older traditions, the failure to preserve the older writings.

Josephus, who seems antagonistic towards the Messianic movement in his writings, fled to the Roman side during the Jewish Revolt. He managed to gain the ear of the future Emperor, Vespasian, by declaring that it was the Roman General himself who was destined to fulfil the prophecy (*The Jewish War*, 3.400–02).

From this brief assessment it will be appreciated that the later 'heretics' of the Western Church after the great Council of Nicaea in AD 325 were highly misunderstood figures who were, in some cases, aware of the rewriting of scripture and were familiar with some of the texts in their original form. The idea of John's Gospel being seen at the time of Nicaea as verging on the Gnostic seems understandable. The Western Church was using an inaccurate canon on which to base its decisions in council. The ship of the Church had only to be one degree off course and the destination would change profoundly. If this seems shocking, that is down purely to our conditioning – *it is what we have been taught.*

There is another statement that is equally strange, or so it seems, in the *The Jewish War* by Josephus. It was brought to my attention in conversation with Dr Margaret Barker and Professor Philip Davies. When they first made the remark, I was caught slightly unawares and thought, somewhat bizarrely, that they were referring to a song by the late George Harrison. For apparently, the Great Revolt of the Jews was led in part by nationalist Hebrew-Christians, who when they saw the approach of the armies of the Romans, come to destroy them, shouted 'Here comes the Son.'[39] What is remarkable is that this too would appear to be a reference to *Revelation*, whose prophecies were to be a significant factor in the war against Rome. Josephus seems to be referring either to *Revelation* or to a common source. Yet until this moment scholars have had a difficult time determining if Josephus had anything to say about the Christians that had not since been tampered with by Christians.

The effect on those of us who are not familiar with the early years of Christianity is to tell us that the movement was not as meek, mild and loving as we have been led to believe. This view also goes some way to explaining why Rome remained ever-suspicious of Christians and threw them to the lions.

It also explains why Sulpicius Severus, writing in the 5th century, contradicted Josephus (Sulpicius is quoting from a lost book of Tacitus) by stating that Titus, son of the Emperor Vespasian, wanted to pull down the Temple because it was important to both Jews and Christians. Josephus suggests that Titus had no clear wish to demolish the building: he was in two minds about whether it was necessary. It is discomfiting to think that we have been fed the illusion that events were other than they really were.

\* \* \* \*

## October 2008 – January 2009, Wiltshire

Although hard to pin down, Shane had become our only source of news regarding the project. Our own role was proving troublesome to the group. Jennifer and I had made clear our feelings against selling the codices. However, the others could not afford to lose my wide knowledge and my grip on the essential facts and interpretation. It was impossible to sell the books without knowing what they were. Hence, begrudgingly, they kept in touch with me through Shane, although even he was keeping me at arm's length. We felt that they perceived our intentions to see the artefacts in a museum as naïve.

When I had last spoken to Shane, he told me of the Israelis' frustration that it was taking so long to get the report that they had been patiently waiting for. They had paid what was asked of them and now they wanted results – not an unfair demand. We too were mystified as to quite why it was all taking so long.

I contacted Allen to see if he had heard back from the laboratories. He would only tell me what we already knew, that scrapings from two of the books had gone off to the OSMC lab in Oxford and to the EMPA lab in Dübendorf, Switzerland. He said he had spoken to his contact at OSMC, who told him that they had a backlog of work to get through before they could do our testing for us, and that it could take up to another two months. Jennifer and I could not help thinking that this was an inordinate amount of time.

I called Shane out of courtesy to report back on my conversation with Allen. He said they had lined up a few more meetings in London and were seeing a few potential buyers over the coming weeks. Then he dropped the bombshell:

'Yes, there's a good 10 percent commission in it for us – of course, it will have to be split four ways, but it will still be substantial.' I remained silent, knowing that until I had a copy of the metal analysis no definite move could be made. As far as I knew, we were still waiting to hear back from the laboratory.

'By the way, I'm heading off to Ukraine for a couple of weeks to renew my visa.' Jennifer and I wondered why Ukraine and where was Shane getting the money to travel there? We had been funding him out of our own pockets, something we could scant afford, but he had assured us he would be able to repay us. We were starting to get increasingly uncomfortable about the direction in which things were heading. It would help if we could speak to the Israelis ourselves.

Then I put in a call to Ron, who had been quiet for far too long. The research funds had come in at last and he wanted the analysis to be written up as soon as possible. I reminded him that he would need to send me a full set of photographs before this could happen. A few days later I received the CD and swiftly looked through the images stored there. To my surprise, they included scrolls, tablets, incense dishes and other artefacts. My eyes went over these in hurried anticipation, eager to see what else there was. I halted in astonishment at the next image. The photograph was lacking definition, but there was enough of a contrast on the codex to make out what was unmistakably portrayed on the cover: the face of Jesus Christ.

\* \* \* \*

## Romans and Christians

> *'What is truth?'*
>
> Pontius Pilate in *John* 18.38

Fact: Jesus was declared King in an occupied country. Fact: Christianity as a word did not exist until it was coined in Antioch at the end of the 1st century.

The early written history of Christianity is not nearly as antagonistic towards the Romans as might have been the case, particularly in the aftermath of the Great Revolt against Rome and the subsequent destruction of the Temple. The roots of the Jewish revolt of AD 66–70 and the rise of Western Christianity lie within the Temple itself. For, once a year at the feast of Yom Kippur, great swathes of the population of Judea would descend upon Jerusalem to pay court to God. The people hated the compulsory Temple tax, which led to further dissent and occasional revolt, all of which were ruthlessly suppressed by the Temple authorities, working in tandem with their Roman overlords.

Herod the Great had ascended the throne of Judea around 40 BC, and immediately set about the refurbishment of the Temple. It was a vast structure. As the building rose at the heart of Jerusalem, its ever more splendid presence must have been a source of great wonder and pride to the people of Judea, who had finally wrought a palace worthy enough for their God. Herod had spared no expense. A period of significant prosperity ensued: a great army of craftsmen, architects, priests, sub-priests and suppliers needed to be fed and housed as the Temple grew and grew over the next 80 or so years.

By the time of Jesus, the Temple was nearing completion, and this had led to a reduction of work for the skilled labourers who now called Jerusalem home. This in turn led to significant problems with the economy. When Jesus foresaw the downfall of the Temple, it was in fact a justifiable prediction. The stage was set for an explosive confrontation, one that would see the ruin of Jewish hope to be free of Roman dominion and the end of the Temple.

Judea was a hornet's nest of dangers for any Roman governor, made worse by the fact that it was not considered important enough to send from Rome an official of senatorial status. As a result of Roman greed, Temple mismanagement and general dissatisfaction, revolt broke out in AD 66. It proved easy to overwhelm the Romans stationed in the city and to gain the upper hand. This in turn led to false hopes on the part of the rebels, and more than a little fanaticism in their approach to outsiders who dared cross them with anything approaching a rational assessment. The Jewish historian Josephus was caught up in the revolt and witnessed the utter destruction of his beloved country from behind Roman lines. Josephus came from a High Priestly Jewish family and practised the Pharisaic mode of Judaism that was less reactive and reactionary than the path trodden by the Sadducees. From the very beginning of the revolt, Josephus was a reluctant participant, becoming a general and, from his own account, a good one. However, he soon tired of war, disgusted by the fanaticism displayed by some of his fellow countrymen. As far as Josephus was concerned, it was the intolerance of these fanatics that had led to the revolt: how could they possibly hope to win against the might of the Roman Empire?

Having jumped ship to the Romans, Josephus was brought before the Roman general Vespasian, whereupon he effected a shrewd bargain in an opening gambit that he guessed might save his life: he predicted that within a very short space of time Vespasian would be Emperor. When the prophecy came true, Josephus was adopted into the imperial family as Flavius Josephus, and thereafter he whiled away his days by writing his histories of the Jews.

Josephus is a rich source for the story of the revolt, although despised by scholars and contemporaries alike for no other reason than that he was a turncoat. Personally, I think this is unfair, as he is nowhere near comparable to, say, Benedict Arnold, the infamous traitor who switched sides to the British during the American War of Independence. He was merely a shrewd observer, and preserver of the once-doomed culture of his people.

Not surprisingly, Judea was retaken by the Romans three and a half years later; and after Vespasian's son Titus had walked, with impunity, right to the heart of the Temple and into the Holy of Holies, into the presence of God Himself, he was astonished to discover that after all of that the room was empty.

Judea was re-conquered. The Temple was razed to the ground.

When, 60 years later, the Jews rose up again in revolt against the Romans, the Temple yet again lay at the heart of the problem. The Emperor Hadrian had offered to rebuild it in an attempt to mend fences with the Jews, but when his request to have his statue placed within its environs was made, the response was as volatile as it was disastrous: a re-run of the First Great Revolt was set in train.

Led by the last of the messianic claimants, Simon bar Kokhba (the 'son of the star'), the ferocity of the initial assault by the rebels was such that for three years Jerusalem and large parts of Judea remained independent – but all to no avail. When the Romans returned, this time they meant business. Jerusalem was put to the sword and Judea destroyed once and for all, in name and in deed: the death toll was terrible. The Jews were forbidden entry into Jerusalem and the city's name was changed to Aelia Capitolina. The surviving remnants of the Jerusalem Church, unable to withstand such a fury, were largely eliminated. All that appeared to be left of Christianity, ironically, now resided in Rome.

Some early Christians, in their enthusiasm for all things Roman, did their best to obscure or even remove the traces of their origins in the feverish race to orthodoxy. Accusations of *heresy* abounded, and those who disagreed, however minute their differences, were hounded into oblivion, on occasion facing death for their pains. The genius of Constantine the Great was in moulding the new orthodoxy to the needs of his empire. Gone was the story of a remarkable man; in came the supergod, with the power of the Roman spin machine behind him. It was a brilliant, but ultimately tragic, PR job. I say 'tragic' because what remained of the original story may well have been far more accessible if its sheer humanity had been allowed to shine through; and also because, in its context, the narrative is strikingly more spiritual, precisely because of its humanity. The Gospels too were depoliticized; and, in order to achieve this, the true history also had to be altered.

In the aftermath of Christianity becoming the official religion of the Roman Empire in the days of Constantine the Great, it was necessary for the message of Christ to become more uniform, particularly from a theological point of view. This may, in part, account for some of the apparent inconsistencies in the message that the Gospels give out. When reading them we are dazzled by what they have to say, and yet struck by the occasional lumpiness of the text. It is easy to see that there are things that they are trying to say, even while they seem to be missing their aim. It is almost as if they have been redacted as stories, rewritten to be more 'on message'. The sense of history in these Scriptures has been replaced more by a sense of story as ritual. For example, St John's is the only Gospel that tells of the raising of Lazarus; and yet Professor Morton Smith describes how, one day in 1958 deep inside a monastery not far from Jerusalem, he stumbled across a missing chapter from the Gospel of St Mark. The missing fragment had never been detected as such by Biblical scholars, and if Professor Smith had never encountered it, there it would have remained. The subsequent controversy that raged was prompted by the fact that the fragment had been suppressed in antiquity – by none other than the Church Father, Clement of Alexandria. Clement had received a letter from someone calling himself 'Theodore'. In it Theodore complains about the practices of a Gnostic – and thereby heretical – sect called the Carpocratians. Members of this sect were apparently interpreting specific passages in the Gospel of Mark according to their own ritual practices, practices of which Clement and Theodore disapproved. Their interpretations are revealing. In the letter discovered by Professor Smith, Clement, responding to the 'unspeakable teachings of the Carpocratians', speaks of secret things.

> [As for] Mark, then, during Peter's stay in Rome he wrote [an account of] the Lord's doings; not, however, declaring all [of them], nor yet hinting at the secret [ones], but selecting those he thought most useful for increasing the faith of those who were being instructed. But when Peter died as a martyr, Mark came over to Alexandria, bringing both his own notes and those of Peter, from which he transferred to his former book the things suitable to whatever makes for progress towards knowledge [*gnosis*, hence Gnosticism]. [Thus] he composed a more spiritual gospel for the use of those who were being perfected. Nevertheless, he yet did not divulge the things not to be uttered, nor did he write down the hierophantic teaching of the Lord, but to the stories already written he added yet others and, moreover, brought in certain sayings of which he knew the interpretation would, as a mystagogue, lead the hearers into the innermost sanctuary of that truth hidden by seven [veils]. Thus, in sum, he prearranged matters, neither grudgingly nor incautiously, in my opinion, and, dying, he left his composition to the Church in Alexandria, where it even

yet is most carefully guarded, being read only to those who are being initiated into the great mysteries.[40]

It is then that Clement, in Donald Rumsfeld mode, makes an astonishing, though at the time secret, admission:

> For, even if they should say something true, one who loves the truth should not, even so, agree with them. For not all true [things] are the truth, nor should that truth which [merely] seems true according to human opinions be preferred to the true truth, that according to the faith.[41]

So at an early stage, Clement, who lived in the 2nd century (AD c150–c215), was admitting that all was not as it seemed. In his response he admits that there is indeed an authentic Gospel of Mark, but he instructs Theodore to deny it. What they are corresponding about is the real nature of Jesus's raising of Lazarus from a state of apparent death … *apparent* because in his response Clement reveals the truth by giving a verbatim description of what is in the original text:

> And they came into Bethany, and a certain woman, whose brother had died, was there. And coming, she prostrated herself before Jesus and said to him, 'Son of David, have mercy on me.' But the disciples rebuked her. And Jesus, being angered, went off with her into the garden where the tomb was, and straightway a great cry was heard from the tomb. And going near, Jesus rolled away the stone from the door of the tomb. And straightway, going in where the youth was, he stretched forth his hand and raised him, seizing his hand. But the youth, looking upon him, loved him and began to beseech him that he might be with him. And going out of the tomb they came into the house of the youth, for he was rich. And after six days, Jesus told him what to do and in the evening the youth came to him, wearing a linen cloth over his naked [body]. And he

> remained with him that night, for Jesus taught him the mystery
> of the kingdom of God. And thence arising he returned to the
> other side of the Jordan.[42]

Now, it is only proper to mention that many scholars question the antiquity and genuineness of this document; however, *pace* such objections, it does have the Marcan style of composition and writing. The implication of the text is that the raising of Lazarus, mentioned as one of the most remarkable miracles in St John's testimony, was a ritualistic affair. The connection of both men seems particularly strong, as if the youth were expecting Jesus to arrive and to be initiated into the central mystery. What this instance demonstrates is that this Gospel was changed, and it is likely that others too suffered the same fate. Gospels were expurgated, revised and edited into a form that suited the needs of the soon to be organized religion of Christianity. Matthew, Mark and Luke tell the story of the betrayal of Jesus by Judas, as does John (who omits the Last Supper). However, when we come to the events of Jesus's execution, each is seemingly at odds with the other, particularly regarding the actual day of the Crucifixion: in the Synoptic Gospels it occurs the day after the Passover, whereas in John it is the day before.

The fact that the Gospels agree on the circumstance of Jesus's death is intriguing: all concur that he was crucified between two criminals, as well as conveying the prophetic nature of his agony. However, when we arrive at the moment of his death, the discrepancies really do stand out. Matthew has him cry out one final futile question: '*Eloi, Eloi, lama sabachthani?*': 'My God, my God, why hast thou forsaken me?' Mark agrees with this version of events. Luke does not quite contradict them, but in *Luke* after his final agonized question Jesus makes one last cry, not detailed by Matthew or Mark: 'Father, into Your hands I commend my spirit.' The sheer despairing power of Jesus's last prophetic cry from the cross in his death agony is lost. When we come to John's Gospel, he states simply: 'It is finished.' Then comes the Resurrection.

Given the noticeably different details (within an overview of events that is broadly consistent), we can only conclude that much has been tampered with. This is certainly borne out by the discovery by scholars that when Mark's Gospel was composed, it ended at the site of the empty tomb. The Resurrection text was written into it subsequently, possibly as much as 150 years later.

This is merely a taste of what had happened to the Gospels in the early years after they were written. However, this is also a good description of what happened to those other Gospels called 'non-canonical' written around the same time and shortly after the four Gospels familiar to most Christians from the New Testament. Some of these appear as very obvious forgeries, even dating into the Middle Ages – reflecting a practice that has 'a long and distinguished history'.[43]

After the Crucifixion, the main centre of the new religion was, initially, Jerusalem. However, from AD 40 the focus of ideas shifted to Antioch in Syria; and from thence, around AD 60 to Ephesus; and eventually to Rome around AD 180. Constantine convened the Council of Nicaea in AD 325. It was at this council that Jesus was finally voted as having divine status, the creed was agreed upon and the dating of Easter was confirmed. Jesus was God, and now equal, if not superior, to all of the other gods – no longer was he a dangerous mortal. It was also at Nicaea that the orthodoxies of the faith were established: for the first time the word 'heresy' began its intimate association with the Church. Our view of early Christianity is derived mainly from the work of Eusebius, an early Church Father and adviser to the Emperor Constantine. Unsurprisingly, Eusebius' work appears biased towards what had come out of Nicaea as accepted Christianity. By this time, anything that went against such views was condemned and ultimately destroyed. Image, to the new Church, was everything. Eusebius was a godsend to the new 'literalist' Christianity: he lent it a power and authority previously lacking, and very soon it would go on the rampage. It was Eusebius who drew up the Nicaean creed, the article of faith that is still used in modern times. People who objected were themselves objected to, and eventually banished. It was the Christianity of Eusebius that set the course for the future of the faith. Under the auspices of Constantine the united front of Christianity papered over a lot of cracks. Christianity even rewrote and, in one sense, reconstructed its own history. When the tomb of Christ at Jerusalem was discovered, a pagan temple stood upon the site. Special permission was sought from Constantine to demolish this, and a new construction was begun. Uniformity was paramount and Christianity was the new politics.

The early Church Father Tertullian (AD c160–225) had stated only a hundred years before the accession of Constantine: 'The world may need its Caesars, but the Emperor can never be a Christian, nor a Christian ever be the Emperor.'[44] In Tertullian's day, Christians considered themselves as Jesus had: as bringers of peace. Suddenly, and by association with Constantine's victory against his brother-in-law Maxentius at the Battle of Milvian Bridge (AD 312), all of that had changed. Christianity had now become corporate.

\* \* \* \*

### January – March 2008: The Showdown

Ron called to say that the metal analysis had come back from the Oxford laboratory, but he had no idea how to read it. He urged me to call Allen for his opinion of the report. Allen was non-committal about when he would be able to send me a copy, but offered to go over the findings on the phone with me.

'It states here in the report, that *lead sheets bound together as a codex are not previously known from Roman times, and the present samples may well be unique,*' he said, reading a key passage verbatim.

'According to the report, how likely is it that the samples are fakes?' I asked.

'Well, basically they're saying that the lead samples have significant levels of impurities and can be paralleled with ancient lead ingots from Western Europe. Furthermore,' he read aloud, perusing the conclusion, '*the analysis of the two samples taken showed compositions consistent with a range of ancient lead, one recycled, the other probably from ingot lead. The corrosion on the surface has built up over a period of time making it clear that the book is not a recent production.'*

Although elated that the codices were starting to look as if they were indeed genuine, suspecting that important information was being withheld from me made me uneasy. My request for a copy of the report, which I was sure held vital clues that would back up my own historical notes, went ignored. Much to my relief, the report was conclusive: if the books had been forged, then that could not have been done in the past 100 years – and 100 years ago the process of genuine enquiry into the origins of Christianity was only just beginning.

Before I received the full OMCS laboratory report many months later, all I had to go on was what seemed to me to be an abridged version that had been sent to me following my phone conversation with Allen. Not only did it appear to be lacking in detail, but I sensed that something had been withheld from me, for in his summary Allen wrote: 'The conclusion from the analysis of the two samples is that both are compatible with an ancient date, and fall within the range of compositions known from the Roman-period lead relics. *Also the conclusion is consistent with the location site of the original discovery* [my italics].

So, there it was. The location must have been given to Ron whilst he was in Israel, despite his reluctance to tell me where it was. Although I could not be sure, I felt that he and Allen had to be working closely together, and likely had been for some time. At Jennifer's suggestion, I called Allen: I was determined to get to the bottom of the matter. I relayed my discomfort about the air of mistrust between us as a team, as well as my conviction that if we were all going to work together there had to be a certain level of disclosure between us.

'I'm not interested in getting involved in the politics of it,' was all Allen would say.

Despite my reservations about the group, I decided that I would honour my side of the bargain and write my report, but after that I was going to throw in the towel. It had been a privilege to come across the codices, but against a wall of silence there was no point in continuing to be involved.

\* \* \* \*

The question of what caused the divide between the Orthodox Church and the Catholic Church began to nag at me: what is the main difference between the two? The Churches went their separate ways in AD 1054 – and have wrangled over their differences ever since. Basically the distinction is that the Orthodox Church has retained, to a large extent, the ancient rites centred upon the Temple in Jerusalem, whereas the Catholic Church follows Pauline doctrine.

When we look at the New Testament, we see that it is brimful of Temple references. Perhaps the most famous example is that of Jesus cleansing the Augean Stable (to use an ancient Greek analogy) that the Temple had become in his day. His spat with the money-changers makes compelling reading even now. What we see in modern-day Orthodoxy, in terms of rite, architecture and foundation, is reminiscent of the Temple and its practice. Perhaps the other major difference is that in the West St Paul plays a bigger role than he does elsewhere. In the East it is St Andrew or St John the Evangelist, also known as the Beloved Disciple, who assumes the prominent role. Both Paul and John had visions of how the Church should be, and what moral precepts it should follow.

St John is perhaps best known as the author of the Book of Revelation – the last book of the Bible. Look around you next time you go into an Orthodox Church and you will see icons everywhere, and in many of these you will also see St John and scenes from *Revelation*. These are found in many Western churches but not to the same degree as in the East.

\* \* \* \*

Christmas 2009 came and went. I called Shane early in the New Year to get an update on the latest meeting with the Israelis. We had hardly heard from him since he had returned from Kiev, but he was still our link with Ron and with what was going on. Somehow we had to keep open the lines of communication.

I remonstrated with Shane that I had remained patient for long enough, but he did not offer me much encouragement. There was no mistaking that we were being left in the dark. I decided on one last throw of the dice and decided to have it out with Ron. Over the next two days I received a flurry of emails from him trying to justify his position, the last one challenging me to call Hassan myself ... and passing on Hassan's phone number.

# PART II
# FROM AFAR

## January 2009: A Call to the Wilderness

'Am I speaking to Hassan?' I enquired, both nervous and curious. There was a moment's pause filled with a torrent of raucous laughter from what sounded like a sizeable gathering.

'Who is this?' I had heard so much about this man – his fiery temper and his unpredictable mood swings. I was not expecting the conversation to be easy.

'I have never heard of you, Mr David.' It was an inauspicious start, since as far as I was concerned this man had commissioned me to write his report.

'Hassan, I am the David Elkington who has written the report about your wonderful books.'

'What books?'

'The lead books – I have something to tell you about them. Look, Hassan, I'll be straight with you – I don't trust Ron or the others involved in this project.'

'You tell Ron, and he will tell me everything,' he commanded.

'Then I'm sorry, we cannot do business,' I said. Hassan was clearly distracted by something that was going on in the room. It seemed that I had called at a bad time.

'Call me tomorrow, we will speak and then you will tell me everything.' The phone went dead.

'Forgive me, Mr David', said the voice. 'Last night was good, I was drunk – and you know we had some good hashish.' He was laughing. He had an almost child-like way of stating the obvious; and when calm, and not under the influence of smoke or drink, he could be quite disarming. But when in one of his riotous moods, he would listen to no one.

In truth, we did not know exactly what Ron had been up to. He had asked me for the report, for which he had apportioned a nominal sum from the funds made available by Hassan – it was a rudimentary analysis after all. That was back in September 2007. I had assured Ron at the time that I could give him my initial thoughts in a matter of weeks.

'Look, Hassan, you've paid a lot of money for this research. You deserve to hear it straight. You've got some very valuable artefacts on your hands.'

'Tell me now what you think is important – for me they are interesting, but they are fakes.' Hassan had changed tack, but I was not convinced. He was testing me.

'I cannot tell you, unless it is to your face,' I said firmly but politely. 'It's too important for me to tell you over the phone.'

'OK, my friend, we will meet, I will see you in one month, we will talk, and then you will tell me what they are.'

### An Unexpected Party

'Hello, Mr David, how are you?' It was Hassan, and from the clear reception on the line he sounded a lot nearer than Israel. It had only been three days since our last conversation.

'I'm fine, my friend. Where are you?'

'Well, I must tell you that I do not like this British weather.' It was early February and it was snowing heavily. Hassan was calling from London. I was stunned.

Knowing that Hassan had only ever rendezvoused with the others in cafés and shady nightclubs in London, Jennifer and I thought that, since he had flown over just to meet us, it would be proper to offer Hassan our hospitality; and to show him that we had nothing to hide by giving him an insight into our lives and our home. Much to our surprise he accepted. He told us that he would be travelling with his adviser, and then he passed the phone to Boaz, leaving him to introduce himself and take down my instructions to get a train from Paddington station to the West Country.

They arrived at Chippenham station the following morning. It was freezing cold and the ground was blanketed with snow. All three stood there shivering. Boaz and his assistant, Noam, were wearing heavy, dark grey overcoats, appearing every inch the Middle Eastern bureaucrats that they were. Hassan looked like a cross between a Hell's Angel and

Jesus Christ, if such a thing can be imagined. His appearance would have been intimidating if he had not had a big smile on his face as he returned our wave.

Jennifer found herself making endless cups of black coffee, whilst the three visitors filled several makeshift ashtrays with mounds of cigarette ash and stubs. Hassan paced about the room nervously.

'Well, my friends, this discovery of yours is really rather interesting,' I initiated.

'Tell me what it is I want to know?' Hassan responded, eager to get to the point.

I started off by giving them a run-down of what had happened up until now, making clear my disapproval of the length of time that it had all taken, and of the intention of selling the codices.

As Jennifer began to lay the table for lunch, Hassan made it clear that he was not happy about my assessment of the way things had been handled thus far. We could not blame him for his annoyance at having to wait so long for the analysis. I fetched some of the photographs Ron had given me. One by one I went through them, highlighting what I saw of significance, pointing out certain marks or symbols that were of interest, concluding with my overall assessment. I wanted to show him that I knew what I was talking about.

I laid a photocopy of the well-known icon of Christ Pantocrator (the all-Encompassing) on the table in front of them. Hassan seemed unimpressed.

'Go on, look *carefully* at the image,' I encouraged. 'Look particularly at the head and what he's holding ... a sealed book.' Next to the image of the icon I placed an enlarged photograph of the lead book with the face on it. All of a sudden Hassan got it. He stood up and punched the air laughing. He looked across to Boaz, exclaiming animatedly.

'I knew it! I knew it! What did I tell you? It's Jesus, isn't it? I *knew* it was Jesus!'

The two of them spoke hurriedly in their native tongue, gesturing in the direction of the photographs. I had no idea what they were saying, but I could see from Boaz's face that he was trying to quieten down Hassan's excitement, but Hassan was not having it. Suddenly he reached his hand into the neckline of his jumper and pulled out a miniature book that had been looped through one of its binding rings by a leather strip. He unlooped it over his head and moved in closer to us, opening the tiny codex.

'This is one of my favourites. I make a promise to myself that if you are true, I will show you this thing.' Jennifer and I were stunned. Boaz and Noam looked at each other, clearly not happy about Hassan's gesture.

'I knew that the face on the book was Jesus,' he repeated with satisfaction. 'You make me really happy, Mr David. Now what we do?'

'I think that in the future we should be very careful not to sell them to a dealer for 50 pounds!' I replied with stern amusement. Hassan slapped me on the back and laughed out loud.

Later the same evening I rang Shane. I had already informed him after my showdown with Ron that I had every intention of getting in touch with the Israelis sooner rather than later. Shane replied that he had arranged a meeting with them and would tell me how it went.

'No need,' I said, ignoring his smug manner. 'They were here today and we got quite a lot sorted. Hassan and Boaz came over for lunch. It was a good meeting,' I assured him.

'I wish you hadn't done that, it confuses the issue of who they're dealing with.'

'There is actually nothing confusing about it – they're dealing with me.' Shane reproached me, reminding me that Ron was still in charge. 'But the codices belong in a museum,' I argued for the umpteenth time. 'They're far too important to be sold off into a private collection.'

\* \* \* \*

## The Assumptions of Conditioning

*A great and wondrous mystery is made known to us this day: a new thing is done in both natures: God is made man. That which was, remained. That which was not, he assumed; suffering neither confusion nor division.*

'Antiphon' in *Vespers and Lauds*

In 1990 the late Professor John Strugnell, former head of the international team on the Dead Sea Scrolls, gave an interview to the Israeli newspaper *Ha'Aretz* in which he denounced Judaic belief with surprising ferocity: 'Judaism is a horrible religion, based on folklore. It is a Christian heresy.'[1] Professor Strugnell went on to say that it was a phenomenon 'that we haven't managed to convert ... and we should have managed'. His remarks were immediately condemned, and soon afterwards he was admitted to hospital showing all of the signs of the stress of overwork. A long-term sufferer of manic depression, the professor later withdrew his remarks and received the support of a number of Jewish scholars, with whom he had retained a long-term friendly relationship. Professor Frank Cross said that Strugnell's comments were based on a theological argument of the early Church Fathers. What intrigued me about them, however, was that they raised an interesting anomaly.

According to accepted history, Judaism has existed since the time of Moses, c1400 BC, whereas Christianity has only been around since AD c33: so how could a scholar at professorial level with over 40 years' experience say, even in a moment of off-guardedness, that Judaism was a heresy of Christianity? It is akin to saying that George Washington stole all his ideas from Franklin D Roosevelt. Was there something that we were not being told? Was this a case of something emerging in the 1st century that had only the outward appearance of being original? Something that in fact had been around for a very long time, but had been re-packaged and re-branded?

There is a clear sense in many respects that the early Christians were actually trying to preserve something that had come out of First Temple Hebraism. I write 'Hebraism' because it has only become clear in the past few decades or so that what we thought of as a well-defined belief system based around the Temple of Jerusalem was in fact part of a larger story.

It was the rise of Christianity as a focused organization that served to force definition, in turn, upon the equally nascent Rabbinic Judaism that had itself emerged from the destruction of Jewish hopes after the two great revolts ending in AD 70 and AD 135. The echoes of the past that existed in the many forms of these sects, scattered all over the Holy Land, hark back to the period of Solomon. But what was the original united religion like? The answer to this questions lay in the environs of the Great Temple of Jerusalem.

I was going over the extraordinary interview with the late John Strugnell when I was struck by a dramatic thought, one suggested by Strugnell himself – and by the early Church Fathers. Everything within the New Testament would seem to be a description of the Temple and what happened within it: including the story of Jesus, which appears to be its culmination. The Old Testament description of creation is a description of the Temple – its areas, boundaries, and holy places. The New Testament to a certain degree intimates this; and its last book, *Revelation*, seems to confirm it in the form of a series of visions. Everything that we see in the Old and New Testaments of the Bible is actually a metaphor for the greater mysteries – which would explain certain motifs found upon the codices. What I mean by *metaphor* is that for years many sceptics have been saying that the whole Christian story, as told in the Gospels, is pure myth. In thinking about this I have come to the conclusion that they are right – but not in the way we might guess.

For *myth* read *ritual*: ritual told in the form of myth. This was a way of preserving that which was most secret. It was this aspect of secret wisdom that must have most horrified the Temple authorities about early Christianity. The story of Jesus as it has come down to us is true, it is real, in so far as its subject involves the rituals deep inside the Temple of Jerusalem, his rebirth as a son of God, his ascension into heaven (also known as the inner sanctum of the Temple). The story is about not only his facing the Presence of God, but his whole relationship with God: his mythic quality as the Son of God. It is rather like the difference between Clark Kent and Superman. In the movie when Clark enters the Fortress of Solitude to meet his destiny, he emerges as Superman; but, once he re-enters Metropolis, he can only relate to other humans as Clark Kent, as they are too much in awe of Superman. Jesus was a real man, a mortal human; but when he entered the Temple, he became more than human, the reality became the myth because deep inside the two merged into one. The Gospels only tell us one side of the story.

It is habitual for many of us, in our advanced technological age, to consider that people 2,000 years ago were intellectually inferior to ourselves. In fact, they were actually very complex thinkers, in some ways more so than today. It is almost as if their idea of religion was actually a lost language of science. The Temple functioned much like a modem for spiritual receptiveness: a focusing point for the people.

Looking at the layout of the Temple, it is easy for us to see that it is divided into seven sections, corresponding to the seven levels of Heaven. The Temple was Heaven on earth, and in this regard represented the outpouring of physical creation, the outward flow of the Word: the perfection of heaven was reflected in the perfection of creation. The Temple was seen as a Garden of Eden, as Paradise; and Adam, who is often confused with the literal idea of the first man, was very probably a historical High Priest within its environs – for the Temple was the meeting point of humanity and the cosmos. It was always called the centre of the earth, the navel point, as all ancient temples were, but in reality there is no centre – except in the figurative sense.

In the Gospels Jesus is actually called the 'cornerstone': he is the link – the physical link, in his role of King and High Priest – between humanity and God. When he entered the Temple it was to arbitrate on behalf of man, to renew the Covenant between humanity and God, and to renew, then and for all time, creation, of which humanity was the culmination. The Temple was right at the heart of nascent Christianity – because that is where the deal was struck with God Himself. Jesus was the man who became God.

The *angels* mentioned throughout the Old Testament were actually *priests*: the term *angel* means 'messenger'. In the context of heaven on earth, their true role becomes obvious: they were the messengers or bearers of the secrets of God. Jesus, when he went into the holiest place in Israel, himself became an angel. *Israel* was the name given to the Patriarch Jacob when, falling asleep at Bethel, he dreamt of angels ascending and descending a ladder to Heaven (*Genesis* 28.10–22). Jacob became Israel, 'the man who saw God', as did Jesus after him. Jesus was trying not only to renew the ancient Covenant but also to purify the Temple, or Eden, through an act of self-sacrifice. It was Jesus who founded what became known as Christianity. Furthermore, the idea of Christianity may well have been far, far older, predating even the time of Kings Solomon and David when the 12 tribes were united in the idea of Israel.

The First Temple of Israel, though we know very little about it, was not actually in Jerusalem: it was in Bethel, 17 miles (27 km) north of Jerusalem. It was sited at the place where Jacob had had his famous dream about the angels on the ladder, and where he actually wrestled with an angel. Jesus came as the restorer of the true Temple and would have known that this was where it all began, before Judah and Israel split and went their separate ways, by which time the Temple had been removed to Jerusalem by Solomon. There is further evidence for this point in the Gospels themselves. In the oldest version of the Gospel of Luke, the *Codex Bezae*, we have the familiar scene of the disciples encountering Jesus after the Crucifixion, except that here there is a remarkable difference. Jesus, the manuscript tells us, was on the road not to Emmaus, as in the canonical version, but to Oulammaus (*Luke* 24.3): this is the old name for Bethel, and the point is underlined in the Septuagint, since in *Genesis* 28.19 the identification is confirmed. Jesus is making his point overwhelmingly. He is making reference to the most archaic form of Israelite belief. He is sending out a message that the original Temple worship should be restored and that the abuses carried out in the name of God at Jerusalem should be brought to an end. He is pointing out the illegitimacy of the priesthood at Jerusalem – and as King he has the right to effect the necessary reform.

The idea of God residing in the Temple brings to mind the Indiana Jones movies, which in the context of ancient cultures portray the idea of God as an awesome force – a thing of exceeding power. Such was this power that it could be barely be contained even within the Ark of the Covenant, above which God was held to reside. Woe to he who treated the Presence with anything but awestruck and devout humility. The power would strike a man down and turn him to ashes in a matter of seconds – or at least that was the gist of the matter in the Bible stories.

Before the destruction of Solomon's famous Temple by the Babylonians in the 580s BC, its Sancta Sanctorum, or Holy of Holies, was the most hallowed place in Israel. However, it was the reforming king, Josiah, who first destroyed it in 600 BC. The essential items kept in the Temple in the period immediately before Josiah's reforms were hidden away and remembered. These were the objects in the Holy of Holies that enjoyed the holiest status: the Ark of the Covenant, containing the two tablets of the Law and Aaron's rod; the seven-branched candlestick; the cherubim; and the image of Wisdom – the Queen of Heaven. These are the same relics that can be seen represented in paintings and stone carvings in any church or cathedral today – which demonstrates Christianity keeping at its core the memory of things more ancient than the story of Jesus.

These relics in ancient times were icons of absolute divinity and could only be approached by the purest of the pure. The Temple of Jerusalem was the power-house of the people, and right in the heart of the edifice the presence of God resided between the two cherubim of the Ark seated upon the *Kapporet* – the Mercy Seat.

The most extraordinary evidence comes from *Genesis* in the episode of Abraham and his meeting with a very powerful semi-divine king of

Salem called Melchizedek (*Genesis* 14.18–20) – the name Melchizedek is actually two words: *milku* meaning 'king' and *zedek* meaning 'righteous'. Melchizedek was the King of Righteousness – exactly how Jesus is described in churches the world over. The Melchizedek text found at Qumran is one of the more obscure of the Dead Sea Scrolls. It speaks of the restoration of the Temple away from 'accursed' practices. It expresses the importance of returning to the older belief system. In this text Melchizedek is an anointed prince who is also the High Priest. He has come to Jerusalem to perform the Great Atonement and to establish the Kingdom of God. He even does this using bread and wine.

The story of Jesus was a restoration of the ancient practice. Everything in the Gospels points to Jesus actually achieving his aim: this is the sole reason why the Church has survived all these years. Crucially, if he had failed, there would be no Church. Jesus's victory rewrote history. His actions in the Temple, specifically reflected in the codices, made *him* the Church, and it made Christianity what it was and still is today. Suddenly the Temple was in man. God was a concept no longer rooted to a particular, centralized spot: he was everywhere, but particularly within us. And from here onwards, the orthodox and the unorthodox Church movements went their separate ways. Churches became mini-Temples of Jerusalem, all over Europe; and eventually the world, as the Word and the Way, flowed outward. However, Gnosticism (from the Greek, *gnosis*, 'to know'), which was the remnant of the older Temple worship that flowed into and out of Christianity, and was at the very heart of the faith, was never allowed to take root in such glories and was doomed to become the underground stream – a secret that the populace was never quite allowed to know. As Dr Margaret Barker puts it,

> There was far more to the teaching of Jesus than is recorded in the canonical gospels. For several centuries a belief persisted among Christian writers that there had been a secret tradition entrusted to only a few of his followers. Eusebius quotes from a now lost work of Clement of Alexandria, *Hypotyposes:* 'James

the Righteous, John and Peter were entrusted by the Lord after his resurrection with the higher knowledge. They imparted it to the other apostles, and the other apostles to the seventy, one of whom was Barnabas.' (*History* 2.1) This brief statement offers three important pieces of evidence: the tradition was given to an inner circle of disciples; the tradition was given after the resurrection; and the tradition was a form of higher knowledge, ie gnosis.[2]

Once Jesus had been recognized as the returning King, he would have been acclaimed, and though his reign was brief (Josephus mentions 'a king who did not reign'), it would have given the spark to incipient change that only a Messiah could bring about – hence the rise of the new Messianism: Christianity, seen by the people who acclaimed him for what it truly was – a restoration movement for the original Temple practice.

What this also demonstrates is another critical and fascinating historical as well as theological point: that the period of the First Temple, the era of David and Solomon, was not one of monotheism. A monotheistic form of faith, based on the worship of one god, came much later, introduced under the reforms of the Deuteronomists. As Dr Barker informs us, in *The Risen Lord*,

> Yahweh, the Lord, had been the second God, the guardian angel and patron deity of Israel, the Son of El Elyon. Once the Deuteronomists had introduced monotheism into the life and, more importantly, into the records of the people of Judah, Yahweh and El Elyon were no longer distinct. The older beliefs, however, did not disappear and the evidence of Philo confirms that this second deity was still known in the period of Christian origins.[3]

When I first began to read of this period, and the nature of worship in Davidic times, my Christian cultural conditioning was such that I was unable to take in the ramifications of it all. Jesus, as Messiah both historical and theological, was the Son of God: but in this case the Son of God Most High, rather than the Son of Yahweh.

There is a passage in *Luke* where Jesus is called the 'Son of the Most High' by the Angel Gabriel (*Luke* 1.2). This has always intrigued me, for in the earlier texts Yahweh is hardly ever referred to as 'the Most High'; in fact he is the 'Son of the Most High' himself – 'Most High' in Hebrew is El Elyon.

El Elyon is first mentioned in *Genesis* 14.18–22:

> Melchizedek king of Salem brought forth bread and wine: and he was priest of God Most High [El Elyon]. He blessed him, and said, 'Blessed be Abram of God Most High [El Elyon], possessor of heaven and earth, and blessed be God Most High [El Elyon], who has delivered your enemies into your hand.

Although distinct at first, all of these gods, or concepts of God, became one and the same thing with the passage of time, under pressure of editorial processes that brought in the concept of monotheism. This concept was challenged when Christianity came along with its idea of the Trinity and alluded to its preservation of the long-lost or altered faith: the Dead Sea *Melchizedek* text is about the return of the Messiah and the restoration of the teachings that had been hidden. So, in a sense, with Christianity we have three variations upon a single theme of God: God has always been a difficult concept contained in a very short word. It is all beautifully summed up by Dr Barker in another of her books, *The Great Angel*:

> There were many in first-century Palestine who still retained a world-view derived from the more ancient religion of Israel in which there was a High God and several Sons of God, one of whom was Yahweh, the Holy One of Israel. Yahweh, the Lord, could be manifested on earth, in human form, as an angel or, in the Davidic king. It was as a manifestation of Yahweh, Son

of God, that Jesus was acknowledged as Son of God, Messiah and Lord.[4]

Now we come to the crux of the matter: suddenly, long-held secrets emerge into the light of day. At the beginning of the Gospels of Matthew and Luke we have an angel of the Lord, come to annunciate the coming birth of the Messiah. *Angel*, in this sense, means 'messenger'. It may still come as something of a shock to us to see the term *angel* used to mean not a supernatural being in the ordinary sense of the word, but a priest – in this context, most probably an Essene priest. There are references in various of the Dead Sea Scrolls to such a human interpretation, but let us cast aside all supernatural considerations, which even in our secular age are still the first things that come to mind. Two thousand years ago these things were seen entirely as human concerns. Therefore, when we look at the Temple, and read of it in the Gospels, we must see it in this vein.

\* \* \* \*

## The Round Table

As we had promised Hassan, Jennifer organized a meeting in London with the purpose of launching into the public domain a responsible news agenda for the discovery. The meeting was to take place in the boardroom of a leading London PR agency in Kensington. In attendance were the Chairman and the MD; two media executives; Helena, a friend and patron of the project; and Charles Merchant, a prominent businessman and mentor. We had invited Allen to join us, but he was out of the country. We wanted to show the Israelis that we meant business.

Hassan and Boaz were running late, but finally showed up breathless and excited, having rushed to the meeting directly from Heathrow. It was the first time I had spoken publicly about my research on the discovery, so I had no idea how it would be received. I knew that my presentation had been a success when everybody got up to offer their congratulations on what had for them been a profound and compelling experience. After the meeting broke up an hour or so later, Jennifer and I felt elation as well as a huge sense of relief: our mission seemed to be going somewhere at last and we had a team of professionals supporting our efforts.

It was late afternoon when the group retired to a dark basement wine bar nearby. We needed a quiet, unobtrusive place for Charles and Boaz to work out a media strategy, one that would protect both parties. As a highly experienced negotiator with a legal background, Charles insisted that we hammer out an agreement before proceeding further. He stressed that it was of utmost importance to determine the rightful ownership of the artefacts. During their tête-a-tête, Boaz was adamant that Hassan had proper and rightful ownership. Charles challenged him, requesting written confirmation from the proper authorities, and this Boaz promised to deliver. It was finally agreed that a contract would be drafted based on the verity of Hassan having legal ownership; if this premise proved to be false, the contract was to be declared null and void. Charles had grave doubts but kept them to himself as he proceeded with the negotiations.

Hassan, who had been drinking copious amounts of wine, wandered around the dusky room in his element, a chaotic spirit, all of us orbiting around him. No one could deny his exotic charisma. His euphoric high, however, suddenly and without warning turned aggressive. Just as Charles and Boaz had reached an accord, Hassan stepped in and made an unexpected new demand. We feared we were back to square one. However, Charles must have worked some sort of magic, as they eventually backed down from what we felt to be an unreasonable position.

I joined Hassan outside on the street, watching as he smoked one hash-laced cigarette after another, whilst trying to remonstrate with him. He merely laughed off my attempts to get him to see sense. I felt terrible at the thought of what Charles was going through. He was much too dignified a man to be a target of such grubby tactics. What had I got us all into?

Inside, Jennifer gathered information. Boaz's assistant, Noam, was boasting to her that they were going to approach Schlomo Moussaieff, the well-known Israeli antiquities collector and jewellery dealer, with a view to selling some of the codices. Was today's show of altruistic cooperation just pretence? It seemed that all of our efforts would be thrown away in favour of the highest bidder.

More than four hours later, the meeting finally adjourned. The parting was tense. However, Boaz and Hassan seemed pleased, confirming their desire to work with us, though quite what that meant we could not determine. Boaz confirmed that they would await his initial Heads of Agreement and we would take it from there.

## Help in High Places

Jennifer and I had started to go to church in the nearby village of Castle Combe where we had met and befriended the local vicar, the Reverend Valerie Plumb, who turned out to be someone quite special. We found ourselves confiding in her – we needed to talk to someone we could trust. We showed her some of the photographs of the codices. Being an Oxford scholar, she studied the images carefully and sat there in silence as I delivered my appraisal of them.

'Do you want me to put you in touch with my friend Bishop Rowan?'

Noting our quizzical expressions, Val clarified: 'The Archbishop of Canterbury. I think he should know about this, he's a good man and you're going to need his guidance.'

She insisted on writing to the Archbishop then and there. A week or two later she received his reply. He was delighted that she had been in touch with him and said that he would write to us in turn, but had we heard of the work of Dr Margaret Barker? He passed on her email address in the letter. I duly emailed Dr Barker later that day, expecting a long wait before I heard from her. She responded 20 minutes later: 'Wow!' She asked that I call her at once.

## Mounting Temple Issues

Because of the intense political issues surrounding the Temple Mount in Jerusalem, archaeologists have had little access to the area recognized as the site of Solomon's Temple. This has led to speculation that it may never actually have existed, but such a view speaks only of the frustration of researchers forbidden to work in a site of extreme religious tension prone to outbreaks of violence from time to time. Solomon's Temple, if it did exist, was swallowed up by the sheer magnificence of Herod's refurbished Second Temple. However, the important question is, why should such an extraordinarily sensitive site still be important to Christians? The answer to this was to be found in the work of one of our most admired Biblical historians. Dr Margaret Barker stresses that, from the very outset, Christianity was based in and around the Temple. This is something of a puzzle, until we understand that beyond the familiar episode with the money-changers in the Gospels, the role of Jesus *inside* the Temple was far more important than has previously been understood. The intimation is that something happened there, something that most Christians little appreciate or understand: something upon which our codices might cast new light.

In the battle of Christianities the victors had written the history – only they had forgotten to throw away the notes. Wherever I had looked there was very little information available about the earliest Christians, virtually nothing about the Ebionites/Nazarenes, or the Poor, as they were commonly known, and only a few references from the early Church Fathers, who had a tendency to disagree with each other on more or less every point. It was too early yet to come up with a proper analysis. However, I had a strong feeling about what the codices were. I lacked evidence, but for the moment it was enough to know that the iconography and the circumstance came together precisely. I had a firm conviction that they had to be Hebrew-Christian.

Following my fascinating conversation with Margaret, I returned to studying the codices with renewed vigour. The fuzzy colour photocopies that I had initially been given had by now been supplemented by slightly upgraded images on a CD from Ron. As awful as they were from an analytical standpoint, they were nevertheless good enough to make an initial assessment. I sat at the kitchen table that was doubling as my study and got out a large magnifying glass. I began to study the language on the images, which appeared to me, as I have already mentioned, to be a form of Palaeo-Hebrew.

One of the photographs got my mind racing even more. The codex it showed had a chalice on it; and coming from out of the chalice was a strange-looking 'W' hieroglyph, very much like the Greek letter *omega*. It was Christ who said 'I am the *Alpha* and the *Omega*' – the First and the Last, the Beginning and the End. The *Omega* is the equivalent, in this sense, to the Hebrew *Shin* – in terms of rendering, the two are very similar, and I wondered if this was what the Greeks derived this letter from when they founded their version of the Christian Church. This brought to mind the reference in *Revelation* to the end-times and its allusion to the Temple of Solomon, where the Messiah would potentially reappear to judge 'the quick and the dead'. I had the feeling, as I was pondering such matters, that I had seen or read something like this before, but I was unable to place it.

The 'W'-shaped letter was the Hebrew letter *Shin,* or S or SH as it would appear in English. In ancient Hebrew, as in many Middle Eastern languages, each letter of the alphabet had esoteric significance – a symbolic ritual purpose. The use of *Shin* in the codices was intriguing, for it offered a clue to the very early dating of these artefacts. It seemed to me that an enthusiastic Greek copyist had seen or heard of the codices and had translated the *Shin* literally, in other words visually, as the Greek letter *omega* – which looks almost exactly the same, whereas the last letter of the Hebrew alphabet is *T* or *Tav*, which in Palaeo-Hebrew script is *x*. However, the Greek letter translates differently and has now come down to us as the famous saying of Christ, 'I am the beginning and the end.' This was very intriguing, as the idea of the Divine Feminine in ancient Israel was called the *Shekinah,* and the letter *Shin* was always used to illustrate this fact. This was a reference to the feminine figure of Wisdom, which can most famously be seen in the poetic 'Song of Songs', thought by some to have been composed by Solomon himself. The figure of Wisdom was cast out under the reforms of King Josiah in the 600s BC.

The cup or chalice that appears on many of the codices could be easily mistaken, by those not versed in the origins of Christian theology, for the chalice from the Last Supper. Given the ritual context of the artefacts, this is a direct reference to the Cup of Wisdom, which was also a part of the Temple rite. These thoughts, and others of a similar kind, crossed my mind as I studied the codices.

One line of thought took me to the northern hinterlands of 1st-century Palestine, to Samaria, the remnant land of ancient Israel. The Samaritans may well have preserved much more than has previously been understood. If an ancient sacred script was deployed by any group in the region, this group was most likely to have been responsible. Although there was still much to learn about the Samaritans, and I would dig deeper in the months to come, the one thing I did know was that part of their grievance against the priests and ruling powers of Judah in the ancient period was the reformation of their history and religion – in other words, the complete rewriting of their identity. It was for a good reason that the Jewish authorities despised the Samaritans: they were a permanent reminder of an uncomfortable past.

It had been suggested that the Palaeo-Hebrew might in fact be Samaritan: I therefore made a cursory investigation into the script. That it had survived as the alphabet of this remarkable group was an extraordinary story in itself. However, looking at it made me sharply aware of my own limitations: this was definitely going to be a matter for the experts.

Once I had come to this conclusion, my attention was drawn back to other aspects of the books. I could barely refrain from poring over them obsessively: they were exquisite and mysterious. It was clear that a great deal of craftsmanship and attention to detail had gone into them. But it was something else that drew me in. I had an ever-growing suspicion that these codices were part of an early Christian library – a library far, far older than any texts we know.

I kept going back to the eight-pointed stars in particular. Contrary to what I told Ron, I had already ascertained that they did not belong to the period of Simon bar Kokhba but expressed a much older symbolism. I had seen them somewhere else. But where?

A few days later it hit me. In a travel bookstore I had been looking at some photographs of churches from the Near East and there, festooned upon their ceilings, were representations of the same star. In fact, now that I was attuned to them, strangely I was starting to notice them closer to home in British and European churches.

\* \* \* \*

**A Shadow of the Past**

The phone rang, and it was Boaz. After the nonsense they had put us through the other evening, he was the last person I wanted to speak to.

'Mr David, we want to apologize to you, we were wrong about you. We need your help.'

'Well, for starters you can stop changing the goalposts on our agreement,' I said, not particularly softened by his attempt at an apology.

'OK, no problem.' Then following a pause he announced: 'We're in Paris, we've been to see Professor Lemaire. He could not tell us much, but he said that we should trust you.'

While their visit was still fresh in his mind, I called Professor Lemaire at the Sorbonne. André Lemaire was a contact of Allen's and personally unknown to me, although I was aware of his reputation as a scholar. He had come to public prominence in 2002 through the case of the James Ossuary, a small limestone box for the containment of bones with an inscription that read: *Yaakov bar Yoseph Achui de Yeshua* ('James son of Joseph, Brother of Jesus'). If authentic, it would have been the first archaeological proof for the historical existence of Jesus. Professor

Lemaire had dated the object to the 1st century AD, stating that 'it was very possible that the ossuary had belonged to the biblical James'. However, others contested this, among them Professor Robert Eisenman, who considered the artefact just a little 'too perfect', and Jeffrey Chadwick of Brigham Young University, Utah, who stated that the 'brother of Jesus' part of the inscription was not genuine. The disagreement took the form of an explosive controversy, which continued until June 2003 when the Israel Antiquities Authority published a report concluding that the inscription was a modern-day forgery. Lemaire stuck by his words, even in the face of increasing evidence that the ossuary inscription was faked. In fact, it would seem he had good reason to do so. Herschel Shanks, the founder and editor of *Biblical Archaeology Review* (*BAR*), wrote in an article in the September – October 2003 issue describing a conversation he had with Lemaire:

> I had originally received a call from the owner of the ossuary (Oded Golan) and that he had offered me a thousand dollars a month for ten years if I would publish the article about the ossuary and its inscription. I replied that that was not enough money. I then received a call from André Lemaire urging me to accept the offer because he, too, had been offered a thousand dollars a month for ten years and he would not get his money if I refused to take Golan's money and publish the article. I told Lemaire that I would publish the article only if, in addition to the money I was to receive from Golan, Lemaire would give me half of the money he was to receive. Lemaire agreed and that was how the article was published in *BAR*. It was clear, even to Ganor,[5] that I was joking.

Nevertheless, the academic establishment was split over whether the ossuary was a forgery, and remains so to this day. Lemaire was also involved in the identification of an ivory pomegranate, which dated to the era of the First Temple. It was later purchased for a significant sum, but was ultimately proven to be a forgery. The professor's record, I was surprised to discover, was mixed, but I wanted to give him the benefit of the doubt: he was and remains a reputable authority with a professorship at a prestigious institution. However, I was still a little wary.

He was out when I rang but soon returned my call. I outlined my involvement with the codices and related a few of my estimations. The discussion was curiously ambiguous. When I spoke about the symbolism on the covers of the codices, he dismissed it straight away as 'unimportant'; then he went on to dismiss the texts that Allen had shown him as 'gobbledygook'.

'These things, they are full of nonsense, I cannot make anything of them. It is all so haphazard. The texts do not read very clearly if at all. I think that they are magical, probably curse tablets or something.'

I called Margaret later that day to tell her about my bewildering conversation with Professor Lemaire. 'Poppycock!' she exclaimed. 'To ignore the symbolism is to miss the whole point of the thing.' I also reported on Lemaire's view that the codices were from the era of Simon bar Kokhba (d. AD 135), who was very likely to have mass-produced them to use as propaganda against the Romans to keep morale high during his revolt – a theory I found inconsistent with what the symbolism represented and with the circumstances of the find. Why would bar Kokhba have expended so much time, effort and money on smelting lead tablets as a means of promoting his movement, when parchment would have been so much more cost-effective, as well as being easier to produce, conceal and – in the event of being tracked down by the Romans – destroy? On these grounds alone, the argument made no sense. However, in stark contradiction, the professor curiously let slip the thought that the portrait on the cover of one of the codices bore remarkable Hebraic qualities and that the facial features seemed indicative of some kind of Herodian connection prior to the period of bar Kokhba. (See plate 1, The Face of Christ.)

Allen had been away on holiday in Israel at the time of our eventful meeting in London, but was now back in the UK. Still wanting to believe that we could work together on the analysis, I invited him to lunch, so that we could catch up. As I was the one who had introduced him to the discovery, I was frustrated that he refused to discuss my concerns over what was happening amongst the group and I hoped we could discuss a way forward. I wanted to bring everything into the open for the sake of the project, hoping to defuse any politicking.

I showed Allen into our living room and briefed him on the events of the past two weeks. To my surprise he handed me a copy of the OMSC analysis on the lead – a goodwill gesture, it seemed to me. I filled him in on our approach to the Archbishop and the latter's recommendation that we contact Dr Margaret Barker.

Allen was barely able to conceal his annoyance. I tried to reason with him that the experts we had consulted, namely Margaret and the Archbishop of Canterbury, were eminent scholars and good people, and that we needed their help, but he patently did not agree. I argued that selling the codices to collectors would set back the scholarship. However, he scoffed at my simplistic view, adamant that we should be the ones to translate and interpret them. To my surprise he suggested that we draw up a contract between Hassan and ourselves.

Casually over lunch, Allen told us that he had borrowed one of the codices to study at home, and that he had had it for several days. He would have known that I had never been given access to any of the books – in fact, no one had even told us there were any in the country. Feeling betrayed, we now believed that Allen must have been meeting with Ron and Shane behind our backs. Jennifer and I must have hidden our astonishment well, as he continued undeterred to tell us how a man who had introduced himself as Shabazi, a friend of Hassan's, had showed up at his house late one evening aggressively demanding that he hand over the codex. He did not know what to do, so he called Ron, who told him he ought to hand over the book. Allen then produced his camera and showed us a photograph of the man, who indeed looked quite menacing. The situation was growing more complicated and enigmatic by the day.

A couple of hours after arriving home, Allen phoned to thank us for lunch. Then in the next breath he told me that he was going to Israel to meet Hassan. After hanging up, I suddenly remembered the report. I scanned it quickly before settling in for more concentrated study. Looking briefly over the conclusion, something popped out at me that froze me in my tracks: it was the continuation of what had been omitted in Allen's summary: '… also the conclusion is consistent with the location site of the original discovery, *which was in Jordan, near the Israeli border* [my italics].'

Jordan! Why had Ron kept this from me and yet told Allen? Had he deliberately misled me about the provenance or was Hassan deceiving all of us? Meanwhile, Hassan had invited Jennifer and myself to visit him in Israel to take our own photographs for the purpose of analysis. Our trip was scheduled in a couple of weeks' time. We would have to wait until then to get to the bottom of it all.

## Double Dealing, Single Meaning

A few days later, Hassan rang to obtain his, by now, customary update and to tell me that Allen was also planning a trip to Israel, for a meeting with Schlomo Moussaieff, just as Noam had boasted to Jennifer that grim evening in the basement bar in South Kensington. The appointment was for 27 May and its purpose was the sale of some of the codices. Professor André Lemaire would also be there. Hassan was beside himself with excitement. It was only after I hung up that it registered with me that Hassan too was double-dealing. I chose to keep silent counsel for the moment. At least our trip was planned before Allen's. We had to do something to talk Hassan out of selling the codices – a tragedy we could not bear to think about.

Schlomo Moussaieff has a mixed reputation within the antiquities business. Although he is reputed to have an extraordinary antiquities collection, it is alleged that he also has fakes among the genuine. However, he has been an exceptionally generous donor to museum collections worldwide and has established the Moussaieff Centre at Bar

Ilan University. He is also credited with being an expert in Kabbalistic manuscripts.

Determined to get to Israel as soon as possible, we started to feel the stress of the situation etch itself into our lives. At the same time we received a lot of calls from Hassan, who was under pressure to sell the artefacts as soon as possible. The pressure was coming from Boaz, who was trying to carve out a deal. We too were suddenly placed under pressure, by Hassan, to bring with us to Israel a Heads of Agreement regarding the media agenda to announce the news. We were only too happy to provide this, as our intentions towards Hassan had always been honourable and we were keen to prove this to him.

In the meantime, our lawyers had strongly advised us not to go: they said it was too risky. Jennifer and I had a meeting with Eversheds in London just before we left to update them on the situation, because Charles thought that we should obtain legal counsel before making any hasty decisions. I looked at the polished young lawyer seated across from us. It was clear that he could not begin to relate to me or to the surreal facts of the situation. Who could blame him? Even I was fully aware how suspicious it all seemed. A wild Bedouin Arab with a hoard of priceless antiquities and his dubious accomplices. We were not comfortable with the way things looked, but someone had to do something to save the codices. If Jennifer and I did not go to Israel, we might regret the decision for the rest of our lives.

Hassan by this time had started to express disgust with Boaz. He spoke of his desire to get rid of him. This would have made things a lot easier for us, but we were not sure what to believe. However, there was a strong undertone of the political in everything Hassan said. We got the distinct feeling that we were being played as pawns in an ever-evolving strategic game of chess – both sides of which Hassan was playing out simultaneously.

Our next challenge was to borrow money and gather together the necessary equipment for our trip to Israel. I knew that, quite simply, I had to have the best. If the visit was going to be successful, I needed to have camera kit that was as high-definition as possible. The resolution of the photographs had to be such that the codices could be studiously examined and translated. This was an insurance policy in case, terrible though it was to contemplate, the codices should ever disappear. Much to our relief, believing in the importance of our mission, our patron Helena came to our aid, offering to fund the trip and the purchase of camera equipment.

### April 2009, Tel Aviv: A Journey into the Dark

A few days later, on 14 April 2009, we found ourselves at Heathrow, boarding a plane to Tel Aviv. The thought of Hassan's unpredictability made it a journey filled with foreboding, as well as excited anticipation. But it was Boaz we were particularly wary of. Hassan had told us over the phone that he did not want to have anything more to do with him, since all he thought about was money. He assured us that he would not be taking any more of his calls. He repeatedly said how eager he was for us to get over as soon as we could, since he was ready to sign our contract and was looking forward to working with us. However, we could not shake off the ominous feeling that all this was a ploy.

Helena had arranged for Shlomo Eyal, a translator and Israeli tour guide, to meet us at the airport to be an intermediary in clarifying the finer linguistic details of the contract Charles had worked on with the help of Eversheds. After collecting our baggage and sailing past customs, we scanned the crowd for a man with a red cap. We spotted him easily enough: a red cap among a sea of black yarmulkes.

When Hassan realized that Shlomo was with us, he was incandescent. Why had we brought him along, did we not trust him? Shlomo seemed unfazed by Hassan's belligerent outburst and tried to explain his role: he was here simply to help with the language barrier. Shlomo persisted in his friendly way until Hassan finally conceded. We went to secure a table in the airport café while Hassan went off to get cool drinks for everyone. It was at this point that my heart sank: out of the corner of my eye I saw Boaz approaching us. Obviously, Hassan had turned, yet again.

We hurriedly briefed Shlomo on our requirement of him: to take in what Hassan and Boaz were saying to each other and relay it back to us, discreetly. The two of them strode over and Boaz gave us a guarded welcome before launching into a tirade about the contract and the fact that we had not allowed them to see it beforehand. The fact of the matter was that our lawyers were still going over the finer details and would be emailing the final agreement to us within 24 hours. Admittedly, this was not an ideal situation, but it was not our fault.

Hassan started to yell, switching from one position to another on a furious whim: he *was* going to sign the contract; he was *not* going to sign the contract. He hurled obscenities freely. Boaz was playing him like a grand puppetmaster – Shlomo confirmed this to us through sideways looks and arched eyebrows. He complained of our supposed trickery, turning up with 'just a piece of paper with no meaning'. It was a game of wearing down the opposition. We needed to convince Hassan that we were genuine and determined.

It was an arduous couple of hours. Jennifer looked ill from the tension. After I had done my utmost best to calm him, Hassan stood up and said he had had enough: he did not want to do business with us, but he was going to take us to his house as friends.

* * * *

**The Essenes**

> *Of making of many books there is no end …*
>
> *Ecclesiastes* 12.12

Judaism began to emerge as an exclusive religion from out of the Babylonian exile (c586–539 BC). It was shaped fundamentally by its first prophet, Ezra. As a name or movement, the term refers solely to those who returned from Babylon, back to their homeland, Judea. The entity formerly known as 'Israel', the ten northern tribes, went elsewhere –

these people were the 'lost sheep' that Jesus spoke of. To the north the Samaritans, much adulterated though they were by outside influences, were to claim the identity of lost Israel. To the south a more conspicuous movement came together, within the geography of Judea, yet set apart from the everyday life of the Second Temple, which encapsulated the aims of the community of the Jews. The Temple that Zerubabel was to reconstitute c515 BC and re-dedicate had been 'cleansed' of all of its former affiliations: it was now the home of the only God that mattered, Yahweh. 'Thou shalt have no other gods but me,' said He, indirectly admitting that there *were* other gods. The centralized Temple became, once again, all-powerful and all-consuming. All other gods were banished.

The community that came together to oppose this view cherished a much older vision, one that came to be recognized as Christianity. For not only did these believers seek to preserve the life-blood of Israel, literally flowing through their veins, but also they sought to keep alive what was an extremely ancient belief – one that no amount of editing could expunge from the holy books. More remarkably still, they did not pay any heed to the Temple of Jerusalem: that was now lost to them for good. Instead, they continued to bow their heads at sunrise and sunset in the direction of Egypt – to Heliopolis, home of the oldest of the dying and rising gods. This community was the Essenes.

It is obvious now why the Temple Jews should be so opposed to the Nazarenes/Nazoreans and also to the Essenes: both were sects that had very good claims to pre-dating Judaism and, in the view of the opposition, they were legitimate targets precisely because of their legitimacy, and because of their connection with what was seen as old and, ultimately, pagan. Both, within the context of 1st-century Palestine, were to claim the moral high ground, but from different perspectives.[6]

Judaism was initially very radical in terms of both approach and application. During the tumultuous era of the 1st century it had become ultra-conservative. To the Nazarenes and the Essenes it seemed that Judaism, in being a centralized and altered belief system, was essentially corrupt: Law was placed above humanity.

Essene belief offers an intriguing link between the pattern of one emergent culture and the vast antiquity of another. From what little is known of them, the Essenes seemed to have formed a settlement near the shores of the Dead Sea around the 2nd century BC. The general consensus of scholarly opinion seems to be that they withdrew from Jerusalem in the reign of Jonathan Maccabee (d. 143 BC) to form a community in the area of Qumran. Apparently, the group opposed the appointment of the new High Priest, Jonathan, because he was not from the correct hereditary priestly family.

The exiled group was led by a prominent priest known only as the 'Teacher of Righteousness'. For obvious reasons Jonathan, it is believed, is a candidate for the identity of the 'wicked priest' mentioned in the community's surviving texts. These texts are the Dead Sea Scrolls, which remained hidden for almost 2,000 years until their discovery in the 1940s and 50s. The term *Essene* does not occur in the community's description of itself, as found in the Dead Sea Scrolls. It is very likely that the Essenes and the Nazoreans were, in fact, the same sect.

The Essene communities were to be found throughout Judea and beyond, not just by the shores of the Dead Sea. Intriguingly, there are many similarities between their faith and what we have come to recognize as Christianity. They shared communal meals, believed in the coming Kingdom of God, underwent Baptism, and partook in an early form of the Eucharist. Key among their precepts was the belief in a kind of semi-divine hero figure who would come to renew the Covenant with God. It was this that particularly interested me, as on the codices there are voluminous displays of eight-pointed stars, symbolic of the expected Messiah, as well as palm trees representing the line of David, from which it was hoped that the Messiah would spring.

The Essene communities scattered throughout Judea, and linked by common cause, were also the keepers of secrets. As Dr Margaret Barker puts it:

They kept alive the memory of the First Temple (Solomon's Temple) which had been heaven on earth, and of the anointed priest-king, who had been the presence of the Lord with his people. In their writings the rituals of the old temple became their descriptions of heaven and they remembered how the priest-king had entered the Holy of Holies as a man but returned as the Lord to establish his kingdom and judge his enemies.[7]

The Essenes-Nazoreans were harking back to the days of splendour. Furthermore, the codices seem to be intimating these factors very explicitly: had they been sealed in order to preserve those secrets?

It would seem that what we have at the outset is a breakaway movement from mainstream Temple-based Judaism, itself broken up after the death of Jesus; and that from this one movement a number of others emerged. In truth, there is little evidence at all that links the Scrolls with the Essenes. The connection is still a matter of dispute, although the general scholarly consensus is that it exists. The question is: who were the Essenes?[8]

There have been attempts by some scholars and writers to link them to a warlike, bloodthirsty sect called the Zealots.[9] This view is in large part based on conjecture. Philo of Alexandria (sometimes called Philo Judaeus, or Philo 'the Jew'), writing in AD c25, points out in no uncertain terms that they did not bear any weapons, nor were they to be associated in any way with the making of weapons or anything warlike. Josephus echoes this view, and also states that the Essenes nowhere had strongholds to defend, nor did they fight in battles. One of the most famous references to them was made by the Roman Senator and man of letters Pliny the Elder (AD 23/4–79), who stated that they lived on the western edge of the Dead Sea and that they had no women, no sexual desire and no money.

The Essenes seem to have been spread throughout the region of ancient Judea. They were called Polistae, meaning that they were 'of the city', so their connection with the settlement at Qumran sometimes seems questionable. Opinion has changed over the years, but the common consensus now is that Qumran was indeed inhabited by a religious sect of a non-violent persuasion. Certainly the idea that it was a fortress for anti-Roman rebels has been effectively disproven.[10]

It is known, mainly from the works of 1st-century writers, that there were aspects to the Essenes and their beliefs that, in time, would come to be recognized as 'Christian'. They practised baptism and the sharing of communal goods and participated in a ritual involving bread and wine, a meal that was held in honour of the Messiah, to prepare for his coming.

The Essenes are praised by Josephus, who was himself of priestly descent. He writes about them as follows:

> The doctrine of the Essenes is this: That all things are best ascribed to God. They teach the immortality of souls, and esteem that the rewards of righteousness are to be earnestly striven for … It also deserves our admiration, how much could they exceed all other men that addict themselves to virtue …[11]

Somebody else, whom we have already encountered, was rather partial to the Essenes. Writing in the *Antiquities of the Jews*, Josephus comments that Herod tried to enforce among certain parties in Judea an oath of fidelity to himself and his government (15.10.4). However, of all the parties concerned, the Essenes were excused this oath. Herod, apparently, held the Essenes in high esteem: indeed, he seemed to be in awe of them.

The existence of the Essenes raises some disturbing questions, not least among which is their apparent connection to what the Jews had come simply to call 'paganism'. It is very much a reactionary view, as they were actually following antique Temple practice.

The Talmud refers to certain groups of Essenes, possibly those who lived in the Essene quarter in Jerusalem, as *Kananaios*, or 'zealots'

– not in the sense of the term today, implying extremism, but Zealots in the priestly sense: people who were zealous in the service of God. This appeared in the Gospels as 'Canaanites',[12] which some scholars, particularly Professor Robert H Eisenman, understand as a term for the violent variety of Zealot, thus making the Essenes and the Zealots one and the same: fanatics. I believe, however, that, on the whole, New Testament translation, into Greek from a Hebrew original, is reliably accurate. Circumstantial evidence points that way. For the term 'Canaanite' links the Essenes with the northern realm of Israel, from where the Suffering Servant Messiah would emerge, the old religion that Jesus sought to restore, and this is reflected in Essene belief and ritual.

The Essenes saw themselves as the only true Israelites, the remnant of Israel, and in this sense it might be strongly inferred that they were not only Jews but, at the same time, a survival of the older royal bloodline, the House of David.[13] The Essenes, being the remnant of Israel, were also prophets; and, accordingly, they were descended from the ancient Kings of Israel and Judah.

Fundamentally, Essenism, through a combination of historical factors, has come to be seen as the 'larval stage of Christianity' – and when we look further at this enigmatic sect, we see very little difference indeed between Essenism and emergent Christianity: one seems to be a development *into the other.*

According to Josephus, Pliny and Philo, the Essenes were thought to have had some kind of a philosophical connection with the Pythagoreans, and it is possible that many of their beliefs derived from this ancient thinker. However, it is known that Pythagoras, in turn, derived much of his knowledge from a 6th-century BC Jewish source, believed by Professor Ben Zion Wacholder of the Hebrew Union College, Cincinnati, one of the leading experts on the Dead Sea Scrolls, to have been the prophet Ezekiel himself. Such a view, if correct, would certainly tally with the later acceptance of Christianity in northern Palestine in the late 1st century (there were well-established Essene communities in the north).

Things now begin to get very interesting indeed, particularly with regard to Josephus' use of the cognomen, 'Essene'. Josephus wrote in Greek but his works were translated into Latin early on. The term 'Essene' is one that has distracted scholars over the years. It is apparent that the Dead Sea community did not refer to themselves by this term; and as Josephus was writing in Greek, it has been extremely difficult to derive the original Hebrew meaning of the word. However, for what it is worth, I believe that it is a pun for what may turn out to be a very broad concept.

The English word 'essence' has its origins in the Latin *essens,* from the verb *esse,* meaning 'to be'. I believe that Josephus was aware of this pun. When writing in Greek, he would have been familiar with the original Hebrew word for 'Essene'. 'Essence' is a synonym for the soul, the 'light within': the community calls itself by such terms regularly in the Scrolls.

> Before the sun is up they utter no word on mundane matters, but offer to him certain prayers, which have been handed down from their forefathers, as though entreating him to rise … Before meat the priest says a grace, and none may partake until after the prayer. When breakfast is ended, he pronounces a further grace; thus at the beginning and at the close they do homage to God as the bountiful giver of life. … For it is a fixed belief of theirs that the body is corruptible and its constituent matter impermanent but that the soul is immortal and imperishable.[14]

The etymology that I have offered is in no way fanciful. It gives us a flavour of Essene belief. The Essenes themselves would have transmitted the knowledge, the *nous* of their sense of God, not by compiling books and treatises, as historians seem to expect of them, but by means of puns and philosophic association.

This was a period and a society wherein people learned by giving out the right question, in response to which they were given the correct answer – in contrast to the present day, when information is thrown at us from all sides.

Modern scholars have admitted their own exasperation with trying to formulate a reasonably accurate etymology for 'Essene'.[15] This led me to investigate less recent sources, and in my quest I came across the following, from Allen H Godbey, dating from 1930.

> *The Jewish Encyclopaedia* claims the Essenes as a branch of the Hasidim, of Maccabean times. No even semi-plausible etymology for the name 'Essene' has been found; but the ancient authors agree that the name had to do with holiness, piety or a special consecration to God. Philo of Alexandria explained that it meant *therapeutai theai* (Greek), 'ministers of God'. Without recanting a score of fanciful etymologies, all the evidence points to an ancient order of sun-worshippers from the Euphratean alluvium, some of whom were Judaized; others had become associated with the shrine at Ephesus. [This is curious given the later Christianization of the shrine to Mary.] The evidence points to the familiar Akkado-Assyrian cultus-term, *assinnu*, a 'devotee, Temple-servitor'. *Assinnu* is an intensive form and would imply 'very devout, assiduously religious'.[16]

This is remarkable in that it confirms the Temple-based perspective of the Essenes, that they were 'devout', implying that they were also preservers or restorers (the term *Nazorean* also means 'preserver' or 'restorer'). The fact that they were associated with the shrine at Ephesus, later to become famous as the shrine of the mother of God, Mary, is the 'cherry on the cake'. Then, from 1948, there is this passage from the late Robert Graves:

[The Essenes] appear to have been an offshoot of the Therapeutae or Healers, an ascetic Jewish sect settled by late Mareotis in Egypt; Pliny described them as the strangest religious body in the world. Though Jews, and a sort of Pharisees at that, they believed in the Western Paradise – of which precisely the same account is given by Josephus when describing Essene beliefs as by Homer, Hesiod and Pindar – and, like the later Druids, in the return of pure souls to the Sun, whose rising they invoked every day.[17]

Although these accounts are accurate in part, the scholarly view is now different, reflecting a belief that the community were Sadducees, from *Zadok* (meaning 'Righteous'), the High Priest of Solomon.

However, it might well be that the origin of the name of the Essenes comes from the Greek *therapon*, meaning both 'servant' and 'healer'. Philo Judaeus relates the term Essene to the Therapeutae, who were healers. The Suffering Servant Messiah, whose coming was expected by the Essenes, is most famous as a healer – the Rite of Atonement is about healing the sins of the nation and of the people.[18]

The Essene colours were blue and white: colours which in the great classical paintings before, during and after the Renaissance were associated with Jesus himself. The Essene novice wore a blue robe, the adept a white one. Everything about the Essenes seems to point in the direction of later Christianity.

The Essenes bowed their head towards Egypt at sunrise. But this in fact does not make them sun-worshippers, only worshippers of an *aspect* of the sun, which they associated with the hero who was God's Son.[19] Writing in 1969, Professor Matthew Black commented that 'the term "Essene" was acceptable provided we do not define Essenism too narrowly – for instance, by equating it exclusively with the Dead Sea group – but are prepared "to understand the term as a general description of this worldwide movement ..."[20]

The general impression I have sought to convey in this brief overview is that Essenism, in seeking to restore the lost rites and liturgies of the First Temple, the Temple of Solomon, was a kind of prelude to the rise of Christianity. This observation is borne out by the Church Father Epiphanius, who declared that those who were once Essenes went on to become the very first Christians.

\* \* \* \*

## April 2009, Tel Aviv and Um al Ghanam: Camels and Codices

After the farcical meeting we were hugely relieved to get away from Boaz, as we followed Hassan to the car park. His car was just as we might have imagined it: a flashy gold Land Cruiser with all the bells and whistles. We all piled in and drove off at breakneck speed to Hassan's village, Um al Ghanam in the north of Israel, just over an hour's drive away.

Hassan turned off the main road onto a bumpy dirt track. We had come to some kind of enclosure, stopping in front of what looked like a large dusty arena, built of pink sandstone. Upon closer inspection we saw that it was filled with camels, which came running towards us, making hilarious resonant noises from their vibrating lips. Hassan told us that he had wanted to start a camel-riding business for tourists, but the Ministry of Tourism had refused him permission – for no valid reason, as we later found out. Why should a Bedouin not legitimately earn a living for his family in the custom of his people?

'Come, I have something to show you. I would like to know what you think, David.' We followed Hassan, trooping across gloopy mud that made walking difficult – it had been raining quite heavily before our arrival. 'See all this land,' he said, 'it's mine. I bought it several years ago. People from my village help me to dig it.' It soon became clear to us that in this region this is exactly what Bedouin do: they buy land in order to dig for antiquities. In fact, 90 percent of antiquities discovered in Israel are found by Bedouin.

We piled back into the Cruiser and drove into Hassan's village on the slopes of Mount Tabor. All the houses were identical cement blocks with darkened windows to keep the heat out; electrical wiring was draped everywhere. There were few trees, but lots of children running around smiling and waving to the strangers arriving in their village.

Hassan's house was what one would imagine a modern Arab home to be: marble floors, lots of bric-à-brac, gilded fixtures, in eclectic taste. In the centre of the sitting room, together with a grandfather clock and gigantic twin imitation Sèvres vases, was the real *pièce de résistance*: a washing machine – the ultimate status symbol.

The table was beautifully laid. Ayda, Hassan's pretty wife, came down to greet us, with their four young children. Jennifer gave them a bag of presents she had brought. Shyly, they thanked us and ran off with the loot: we were charmed by them. Hassan encouraged us to eat, although hardly touching anything himself. Restive, he kept nipping outside for intermittent drags of whatever it was he was smoking. 'When you're finished you must come upstairs,' he said. 'I have something to show you.' We climbed up to the kitchen with him.

'Get your camera.' I did as ordered and we watched puzzled as he leapt onto the kitchen counter like an alley cat, straightened his body and lifted one of the Styrofoam tiles in the suspended ceiling with his head. 'No one will ever find these,' he said grinning, as he reached into the cavity and retrieved a little packet. Like a boy, Hassan was eager to show us the best of his treasures first. Carefully he unfolded layers of cloth from the first book, with reverence.

'Take pictures, David,' he urged. 'You are going to want to take pictures of this. I want to open this book tonight and see what's inside.' We were stunned into silence: the low-resolution pictures we had seen had not prepared us for such beauty. I had never seen anything like it. As I had known, it was made of lead, bound all around with lead rings reminiscent of the books in Orthodox iconography. The cover was delicately embossed with imagery that had been hard to make out from the photographs. On the front face of the book was a small rectangle outlined by one half of a menorah; the other had been worn down –

possibly by years of touching, in reverence by those who had held these precious books as holy. The menorah was nine-branched – seven plus a supplement of two branches. At the base of the cover there was a further menorah, seven-branched, surmounted by battlements; and within the rectangle, some text. In the top third of the front face was a group of palm trees – all of which appeared to be in fruit. At the base on the right-hand side, there was a series of Tau crosses – Crucifixion crosses. At the top of an inner rectangle, a palm frond ran horizontally, and running along the right-hand side were three eight-pointed stars. This was the book that I had initially seen in other photographs – it was the size of an average-sized modern hardback. But here, in the cold light of Hassan's kitchen, it was more wonderful than anything I could have imagined. Until, that is, he unwrapped a smaller book and here before us, at last, was what we had come for: the codex bearing the portrait of Jesus. It fitted exactly into the palm of my hand.

Hassan urged me on, but I was stressed and tired, and had a highly technical camera that I had yet to come to terms with. I had had the camera for only two days and the instructions for it were daunting. However, I worked as fast and as efficiently as possible. The initial results were poor: the tube lighting in Hassan's kitchen was terrible, and I had the devil's own job of positioning everything properly; but at last, after much manoeuvring, managed to get a few good shots.

'Now we will open it,' said Hassan. Some of the binding rings crumbled as we worked in turn. I kept a few bits as samples, since I knew that corrosion like this was a very good sign. Laboratory conditions would have been preferable, but all we had was this kitchen. The pages were compressed together and difficult to open. Hassan tried unsuccessfully, then I did the same, and finally Jennifer with her more nimble fingers succeeded.

Looking over her shoulders, as she delicately prised the first pages apart with tweezers, I was rendered speechless by what I saw before me. The silvery pristine beauty of the image was deeply moving: but what on earth was it? Most remarkably, among all the aged and corroded pages in the rest of the codex, this one was uniquely pure. It was totally unmarred by time and the external elements: it was a miraculous vision.

Despite being blank with shock – the vision was so completely unexpected – I set about photographing the codex all the same. Its ethereal quality suggested something supremely important; I just had to figure out what.

## In the Warm Light of Day

> '*My Mother the Holy Spirit took me by one of my hairs and carried me to the great mountain, Tabor.*'
> The Gospel of the Hebrews (in Origen, *Commentary on John*, 2.12.87)

Next morning we awoke early to bright sunshine. There was a great deal of work to do, photographing all the books and taking all the forensic samples. If Hassan insisted that we open up some of the books, I wanted, where possible, to collect proper dust samples and any other detritus that might be valuable in determining where the artefacts came from. After a couple of cups of potent Arabic coffee spiced with cardamom we were ready for action.

Hassan had already set up a table in the back of the house and a few cloth-bound packages were awaiting us. As we threw ourselves into the task, he meticulously pieced back together the lead binding rings that we had opened last night and replaced them exactly as they had been.

Throughout the day as I photographed the codices, new packages kept appearing, while the ones that had been photographed were neatly repackaged and returned to their hiding-places. Jennifer could not help observing a couple of them. She saw him remove a large electrical board from a wall in the foyer. And at one point Hassan appeared with a crowbar, loudly prising open two sheets of corrugated aluminium that formed the side wall of a shed close to where we were working: another package emerged.

During the day various youngsters appeared with packages that he obviously had stored with family in the village. One package, brought by his nephew, contained some especially stunning artefacts: a pomegranate plate, along with several tablets and scrolls. The pomegranate we were unsure of. A comparatively large piece, it had been precision-cut out of copper – or so it appeared. The edges were too sharp and perfect, and although the brickwork etching mimicked the pattern in some of the obviously much older books, the workmanship was clearly not of the same calibre and was suspiciously fresh-looking – and yet other pieces in copper seemed to be quite aged. Jennifer and I agreed that Hassan's collection was likely to be a mishmash of the genuine and the dubious, and that we would have to be circumspect in our appraisals: we could take nothing for granted. The 'art' of forgery was, after all, a big business in Israel. I was glad that at least we were able to collect scrapings for testing. The metals laboratory would be able to separate the wheat from the chaff.

The scrolls were of a different quality altogether. They consisted of very fine rolled lead sheets and were extremely fragile. I knew instinctively that they were the real deal. I reiterated my concern about the safety of the books – in particular, the book with the face. 'Don't worry my friend, that one I sleep with under my under my bed. If anyone comes,' Hassan said with a menacing laugh, 'I cut their throat with my knife.'

We were surprised by quite how much there was; but fortunately I was prepared for this possible scenario. Our method had to be quick and efficient, without compromising either the end-result of photography and note-taking or the integrity of the books. We set out the table like a production line. The books were individually unwrapped at one end, then transferred one at a time to a plastic sheet. We took dust samples of each with a brush before setting it against a white pillowcase to photograph it. The plastic sheet was then folded to enable the detritus to slide safely into sealable plastic bags labelled with a corresponding number we attributed to each book. Each book was then measured and photographed alongside a piece of paper, numbered accordingly, so we could track all details on each book separately, for easy reference later. Jennifer numbered and positioned the codices; I photographed them from every angle. It was a long, draining day.

As we worked, Hassan began to relax, fascinated with the process we were conducting. 'You know, it makes my wife crazy, but as soon as the family is asleep, I take out some of the books and rub oil into them. I love to touch them. Sometimes they speak to me, and the symbols jump out and I see things that I didn't before.'

I smiled at him. There was an innocent naïvety to his musing. Despite all this talk of selling, Jennifer and I could not imagine he could ever part with them, no matter what price he was offered. He was a man both obsessed and possessed by them.

It took five hours of work. The pressure to get the best possible shots, and as many as possible, was intense. We only stopped when the sun faded. I had managed to capture almost a thousand high-resolution images. I had never expected to get this far. Hassan had been good company, if sometimes alarming.

I set about transferring the images onto our laptop for safekeeping. I wanted to get this done as quickly as possible. Boaz was due to arrive that night and I needed to have a clear mind. As I was transferring in the bedroom, Hassan came in with a CD.

'David, do you need these? These are the photographs that Ron took of the cave. You can copy them if you want.' I could not believe how cooperative he was being. I had worked hard at gaining his trust and it was paying off. Ron, of course, had never admitted to us that he visited the cave site. Since his return from Israel he had been cagey about everything.

While we were waiting for Boaz's arrival, Khamis, Hassan's business manager, had come from Bethlehem to join us. Jennifer and I were actually quite glad to have another person, as Boaz and Hassan had proved to be a volatile combination and the last thing we wanted was a repeat performance of the airport scenario.

'You know, Hassan, you look remarkably like the face on the book,' Jennifer teased him. We had already remarked on the uncanny resemblance.

'I'm no Jesus!' he exclaimed, laughingly.

'Seriously, Hassan, do you want me to tell you a bit about your Bedouin ancestors?' I asked. 'Did you know that the Bedouin are sons of Benjamin, Bani Israel?' He looked delighted to discover this. 'What you should know,' I continued, 'is that the first Kings of Israel were Benjamites. The first King's name was Saul. However, for some reason that we can't be certain of,' I said, choosing my words carefully, 'the Benjamites disappear from this chapter of history, but they do appear again – for instance, in the Bible. St Paul and Mary Magdalene both described themselves as Benjamites – so you are in good company, my friend.' I patted him on the back as I said this.

Boaz finally arrived, full of bravado, refusing to look at us. I initiated conversation, as there was no point in delaying the inevitable. I told him of our discussion with Hassan and his readiness to sign our Heads of Agreement. As we anticipated, Boaz was adamant that there would be no agreement, unless we changed the document drafted by our lawyers. I was getting weary of his stubborn obstructionism: we had already agreed terms in principle. Realizing that we were not getting anywhere, I changed the subject, asking Hassan if we could see the document he had mentioned, validating his legal ownership of the codices. He left the room briefly and came back with a letter.

'It is from the Israel Antiquities Authority,' he reassured me as he handed the letter over. Indeed, it was a letter confirming that Hassan Saeda was the owner of a number of nondescript objects. It bore the stamp and red wax seal of officialdom. However, I was not convinced of its authenticity, particularly since I knew what a big business the trading of illegal antiquities is in Israel. The document did not specify how many artefacts there were, nor how precisely they were comprised, nor how or where Hassan had obtained them. Neither was this a document of authentication. A part of me wanted to believe Hassan, but I had grave doubts. For now, the only thing we could do was carry on, and see if I could extract any more information out of him. That would not happen with Boaz around.

'Did you show the IAA the book with the face?' I asked, afraid to hear the answer.

'No man! Are you crazy?' He laughed. 'No way, I just showed them a couple of books, not the good ones.' I was sure they would not have let that one go back home with him.

Boaz outlined his view of where things stood: he was determined to stick to the script. To avoid another tedious debate, I raised the curatorial issue again. 'Hassan feels very strongly,' I explained to Boaz, 'that the artefacts should be in a museum, where everyone can see them and gain access to a part of their history.'

'I think that before we can discuss these things, we need to look at the contract.'

Hassan seemed uncharacteristically quiet and unresponsive. He was exhausted from a long week of farming at the height of the season. He gestured to Boaz that he had had enough for one evening. Much to our great relief, Boaz took his cue and left.

As if to celebrate his departure, Hassan brought out a bottle of Tabor Vineyard, a local wine. It was just what we needed after the days of tension, although admittedly we had had some enjoyable moments as well. The wine loosened us all up, although we were never off our guard completely.

'Boaz is a good guy, you know,' Hassan said at one point. It was obvious that he relied on him. 'He helped to get me out of prison.[21] I was supposed to be in much longer.'

'What were you in prison for?' I enquired with trepidation.

'Some guy made bad things for me, so I hurt him,' he responded matter of factly. I did not press for details, but he seemed to want to talk about it. 'I never want to go back there again. It was really bad time. They tried to make me cut my hair, but I went crazy.' His refusal to cut his hair reminded me of the ancient Nazirite taboo. They believed, as in the legend of Samson, also a Nazirite, that spiritual strength lay in their hair. 'There was *no way* I was going to let them touch my hair, so they made me go in a hole in the ground. They kept thinking I would give in, but I refused. Finally, after 10 days, they let me out. They couldn't believe I stayed in for so long'. His pride in this was obvious.

Thinking it over, I could see that Hassan would have to choose between Boaz and me. He had known Boaz for 10 years. It was not going to be easy to wean Hassan away from Boaz's influence. However, I could not help clinging to the fact that Hassan seemed genuine in his intention to share the codices with the world. He was so interested in understanding and knowing their history. I realized that the odds were against us; but that night we gave Hassan our promise that we would do our utmost to secure a place for this amazing discovery in a museum. It was a promise that we were intent on keeping, with or without Boaz's cooperation.

### A Party in Jericho

We awoke on our last day relieved that the photography was behind us. Now our priority was getting the contract signed. 'Don't worry,' was Hassan's constant refrain, but worry we did.

Hassan decided to take a day off his farming to show us a little of Israel. As he was relatively close to the Sea of Galilee, Jennifer and I agreed we would very much like to see it. Hassan was a good host, considerate and generous. Unfortunately, the day was overcast, with occasional rain. We drove across from Tabor to the Sea of Galilee, called Lake Tiberias in Israel. Fed by the waters of the lake, the farmland all around was rich and profitable. We stopped by the shores of the massive freshwater lake – the scene of Jesus's most famous miracle, his walk on the water. This was the neighbourhood of Jesus, where he had gathered his disciples around him. Here the most senior of them, Peter, had plied his trade as a fisherman. Everywhere we went that day, in search of clues about Jesus and his milieu, we found a church or a monastery on the spot where he was said to have performed one of his miracles or where he had rested, or where some event had taken place. As a result of these associations, there are many churches in Israel, particularly in this area.

Shortly afterwards Hassan drove us up to the northern highlands and the border where Israel meets with Jordan and Syria. The region is a testimony to past and present political tensions, for in the narrow divide between two border fences is a minefield with warning signs forbidding entry. The panorama was spectacular. Looking back down into Israel, we had a fantastic view of the lake despite the dull grey sky. I stretched my legs and turned around to face the craggy, arid mountains of Jordan, dotted with parched green shrubbery.

'Hassan, are we anywhere near the cave site?' I asked. I had a sneaking suspicion that we were not there by chance. 'Yeah, we're only about 10 minutes away,' he said, 'but you can't drive this way. It's over the mountains and there are bombs around here, it's very dangerous.' He was referring to the landmines surrounding the border.

Upon our return to the house, we hastily packed our bags, as Hassan informed us that we were going to a party in Jericho that night, and since Jericho was closer to Tel Aviv we would spend the night at his friend Farez's house and leave for the airport the next day.

As we were packing, Hassan called to Jennifer: he had something he wanted us to take back to the UK. Despite our uncertainty and protestations, Hassan insisted that we take three of his small tablets with us, which were part of the same hoard. Two of them bore the recognizable symbols of date palms and eight-pointed stars. The third one was really special: it was full of writing. Hassan thought we should have them when we announced the discovery to the press. He wanted us to take other artefacts, but we declined: the notion felt uncomfortable. A seasoned expert, who had obviously done this before, he showed Jennifer how to slip the items in her wallet, between her plastic bankcards, which ironically were about the same size. The plastic, he reassured us, would prevent them from being detected by security checks. Nonetheless, we were nervous about having them. (See figure 14 in the plate section.)

It was a two-hour drive to Jericho on the Palestinian border, most of it in the dark. Jennifer and I sat on the back seat reflecting on all that had happened in the past three days. Hassan was singing along to the Arabic music he had cranked up to a crescendo on his radio. At the border, young soldiers with submachine guns lined the route. Little huts on stilts serving as watchtowers were scattered about and clumps of barbed wire were strewn across the barren landscape. Orange-hued spotlights cast an eerie light, heightening the sense of foreboding. What were the guards going to think we were doing? 'Don't worry, they all know me,' Hassan reassured us as a couple of soldiers at the gate flagged us down to check our passports.

Upon entering Jericho, we turned off onto a small road just next to the cable car station that takes tourists up to the Monastery of the Temptation, a Greek Orthodox church carved in the mountainside. We reached a large, plain, whitewashed house bedecked with glorious fuchsia and deep purple bougainvilleas. A stocky man with a shiny bald head approached the car and extended his hand. 'Welcome, I am Farez,' he greeted us. Hassan had told us on the way that Farez was a jeweller specializing in making jewellery using gold and bits of ancient glass found around the ruins of ancient Jericho. He had a warm manner and we immediately felt reassured.

In the meantime, we had been desperately trying to check our emails. Our Blackberry was supposed to serve as a line of communication in case we found ourselves in danger. We were also eagerly anticipating an email from Eversheds with the final contract for Hassan to sign (annoyingly, the document had not been ready in time for our departure). Much to our frustration, we found that we were completely unable to call or receive calls or emails from the UK. Farez and his family were very Westernized and fully equipped with modern technology, but their printer had broken down that very day. All of us were in a state of heightened emotion. We had to leave the next day. Hassan was in a state. Dialogue was tense and arms were flailing. Finally he came over to us with a smile. 'Don't worry my friends, we are going to buy a new one.'

Sure enough, less than an hour later Farez's son returned with a brand new printer. Where they had bought one at this time of night we will never know. Within minutes it was hooked up. Much to everyone's relief, we were at last able to download the contract sent through by Charles *and* print it off.

We handed the contract over to Hassan, who in turn gave it to Farez, who went through it line by line with Khamis. A few technical points were discussed, then Hassan announced that he was ready to sign, as long as we added the names of Farez and Khamis to the contract as witnesses. Knowing that Hassan was illiterate, we happily agreed to this. We were just relieved that Boaz was out of the picture and unable to interfere.

Then we all went back to the courtyard to meet the others. With the drama behind us, we were able properly to meet Farez's wife and three teenagers, who were thrilled to have English-speaking guests. As it turned out, the family had spent time in Sweden and had visited England and particularly loved London. Farez's two daughters were longing to go back there to study and bombarded us with eager questions.

Before we had arrived, Farez had set up his laptop on a ledge in the courtyard for a slideshow of photographs. Jennifer and I were casually glancing at the flashing images when one turned up showing someone we recognized: Ron. There were numerous photographs of him clearly enjoying himself against the backdrop of various landscapes. They were from his visit to Israel last year.

Jennifer and I looked at each other with raised eyebrows. Another photo came up that caught our eye. A woman too pale and uninhibited in her behaviour to be Middle Eastern appeared on the screen with her arms draped casually across the shoulders of Farez and Ron. Khamis was standing quietly next to us so I asked him who she was.

'Oh, that's Yvette,' he said. 'She is a journalist from London. She is the girlfriend of Shabazi.'

'Aren't they the ones who have one of the books?' I asked, remembering what Allen had told us. Khamis nervously confirmed this.

'She must also be the same Yvette who posted those photographs on the website,' Jennifer whispered under her breath. She obviously knows Farez from Sweden as well. They all must have some sort of dealings going on over there. I wouldn't mind betting they are also somehow involved with the discovery.'

## May 2009: In Israel for 23 Hours and 40 Minutes

We boarded the plane to Tel Aviv for the second time in two weeks, now with great trepidation. We had arranged for a cameraman to hop on a plane after us at a moment's notice, as Hassan had promised to take us all to the cave site to film. With the contract now signed and cooperation assumed, we were hopeful – despite the reservations that had been expressed by Eversheds. The first trip had been productive: God forbid that anything should happen to the artefacts, but at least we had proof of their existence, so the risk of that visit had been worth taking.

Eversheds had been useful in researching the validity of Hassan's ownership, on the basis of whether the discovery was determined to be in Israel or Jordan. On the last trip Hassan had been evasive about the location of the cave. Now he would only offer to take us at night, because it could be dangerous, as there were soldiers in the area. Apart from the fact that it would be virtually impossible to film in the dark, it crossed my mind that the site might not be in Israel after all.

It is a well-known fact among antiquities dealers that Israel is the only country in the Middle East where trading in artefacts is allowed – or at least overlooked. Eversheds had done some useful research for us on this. Much of the booty found in other Middle Eastern countries, including Jordan, is smuggled into Israel, where for the right sum of money offered to the right person, a 'letter of authenticity and/or ownership' can be bought with no questions asked. However, according to Jordanian law, we had been told, if the discovery did come from Jordan, it belonged to the Hashemite Kingdom of Jordan, not to Hassan. This would also mean that the trove had been smuggled out of Jordan and into Israel. Tricky though it would be to do so, I would have to try and get some straight talking out of Hassan. Jennifer and I were certainly not interested in working with criminals, but we knew that we were in the affair too deep now to just walk away.

Hassan was friendly but edgy when he met us at the airport. He immediately told us that if Boaz called we were to keep quiet, as he had been advised that we were not arriving until tomorrow. We were only too happy to oblige.

'So, David,' Hassan asked as we climbed into the Land Cruiser, 'did you bring me a disk with a copy of the pictures?'

I had decided that until I knew the provenance of the find, putting my images into Hassan's hands would be unwise. 'I'm really sorry Hassan, I forgot. I've had so many things on my mind.'

'That's not good, David. I am really not happy – you promised. You Englishmen are all the same. Lying dogs. You all lie. You say bad things about us, but you English are the worst.'

Jennifer and I sat there in the vehicle, determined not to respond in kind. Something had changed, but I was not yet sure what it was. Even if I *had* given Hassan a full CD of the pictures, I knew it would not have been enough for him. I tried to get him to support our idea of placing the codices with a museum, for the public good, but he was having none of it. He drove like a maniac, shouting, swearing and working himself into a frenzy. Jennifer and I wondered with great anxiety how this was going to end. It was the worst possible start to the trip.

Boaz, I suspected, had convinced Hassan that we were trying to trick him, which had wound him up to a state of high emotion. We knew the pressure on him was immense. But much to our relief, he started to calm down a bit as we approached his village. He must have worn himself out with his own tirade. Once again the table had been laid for dinner. Neither of us had much of an appetite but we dutifully filled our plates.

Hassan sat and watched us eat, excusing himself by saying that he had eaten earlier. We did not believe him. We were actually quite shocked at how he had deteriorated in the two weeks since we had last seen him. His face was gaunt, his eyes sunk deep into their sockets.

'About the trip to the cave site,' he announced, 'it is not going to happen.' Our hearts sank. We had borrowed funds to come out here. We would have to call our cameraman, who was awaiting our signal to hop on the next plane over, and tell him not to come.

'Hassan, we came all the way over here because you promised to take us to the site,' I reminded him. 'Now I am the one who is not happy.'

'Only one person can go. My friends said so. It is too dangerous for my friends – too many people. And besides you never paid me the money. I asked you to bring money. Did you bring me the money? Boaz said to bring 50,000 pounds. You lied again, David.'

I deliberately avoided the money issue. 'Who are your friends? Why is it dangerous for them?'

'My friend is a taxi driver. I met him and his family when I went to Aaqba for my farm business. He told me about the books and when I went back again he showed me the cave and offered for me to buy the books.'

'Aaqba? Isn't that in Jordan?' I asked, taken aback but trying not to show it. 'Why is it dangerous, Hassan?' I pushed, albeit gently. He completely ignored my questions.

'This cave, you should see it,' he said, suddenly going into a reverie. 'It is big, this cave, big as a city … about three to four hundred metres. No, seriously it is, it is a very, very big place, a lot of people must have lived there.'

I asked him what he had found there.

'Lots of things. The books were found in three caves. There are lots of them and other things too, some of them came out of metal boxes and others were found in graves.'

'Do you have the boxes?'

'No, my friend has one. He sold most of the books to me, but he kept some for himself. He sold four to some guy in Dubai, but I have the best ones.'

'How much did you pay for them?'

'I gave him 250,000 dollars for everything. It is a good thing for him and for the village – they are very poor. I helped him to buy a school bus for the children.'

'Why can't we go to the site? You said last time that we would go, and now you're going back on your word?'

Hassan's eyes narrowed. 'Because the cave site is in Jordan there are lots of military guys around. My friends could get into trouble.'

'How did you manage to get the books across the border?'

'It wasn't easy, my friend. It took me several trips.' Jennifer and I looked at each other, amazed: he must have even more than he showed us. 'On one of my trips back I was stopped at the border. I showed the guard the book with snakes on it and told him the books were magic. I said to him, "Come my friend, come to Mount Tabor and I can help you speak to your father. I make a fire and put my hand on the book,' he rattled on nonsensically.

'He probably thought you were crazy,' I could not help commenting.

He laughed uproariously. The guard had probably thought they were fakes – or was he bribed? It is likely that he knew Hassan from his cattle feed business. He had told us that he did a lot of business in Jordan; he would have routinely traversed the border at Allenby Crossing.

So. At last he had admitted it. Just as we suspected, the cave was not in Israel, but in Jordan. Where did that leave us? 'We cannot legally travel across the border on our passports from Israel without visas,' I pointed out to him.

'No way, we would have to travel at night and go across the mountains, avoiding the border. We cannot go with so many people. Your cameraman, he is the only one who can go.'

Naturally, this would not be possible. Not only would he be unable to handle the situation alone, but also they could not go without me there to analyse the environment and take the necessary forensic samples. However, eager as we were to see the cave, we were not prepared to sneak into Jordan like thieves in the moonlight.

This confession now changed everything, including the validity of our contract and any possibility of working together. From an official perspective, we would be dealing in smuggled illegal antiquities. We were not prepared to go down that path.

'I could be in big trouble if this ever comes out,' Hassan confessed.

'Not if we go about it in the right way,' I offered.

'No way,' he laughed. 'My friends would get into trouble. Anyway, I lied to you. The cave is in Israel.' But of course this naïve contradiction carried no weight.

'Well, I think we should go to Jordan and visit the site in broad daylight with nothing to hide,' I ventured.

He laughed again. 'You will *never* in a million years find it! No way!'

Jennifer and I had had enough for one evening and excused ourselves: we were exhausted. Hassan appeared relieved. The evening's tension had been dreadful. Hassan's confession, although not entirely surprising, was nonetheless a devastating blow, as we had not yet discussed the ramifications of this possible disclosure. It was hardly surprising than neither of us was able to sleep, only drifting off in the small hours of the morning.

We awoke to doors and windows slamming and loud angry banging. I jumped out of bed and into my clothes, ready to face the latest tempestuous episode.

'David, you did not tell me the truth!' Hassan, waiting for me in the living room, was in a rage. He had either been speaking to someone or he had allowed the previous day's thoughts to fester. The air of menace this time was fearsome. Hassan obviously felt he had been lied to.

Actually, I had never promised to bring copies of the photographs to Hassan: I had offered to do so only once the provenance of the codices had been ascertained. I remembered Ron's terrified expression, obviously unaware of Bedouin custom and tradition, as he told us that Hassan had knives and guns. How far would he go?

Hassan yelled at Jennifer to come out of the bedroom. She was acutely distressed. I did not like the feel of where this was leading. Much to my relief, Khamis arrived.

'Sit down, and do as I say!' Hassan commanded. He slapped a sheet of paper and a pen on the table. 'David, you will write what I say,' he ordered.

I stayed silent. The last thing I wanted to do was antagonize him further.

'If I do not return the three tablets belonging to Hassan Saeda, I will have to pay him for them,' he dictated. This was strange as he was the one who had insisted we take them in the first place. Why should he think we had no intention of returning them?

When at last he was satisfied that I had written what he asked, he made us both sign at the bottom of the statement and write our passport numbers on the documents. We felt as if a gun was being held to our heads. He took the signed paper and put it into a folder with other documents, including the letter purporting to be from the IAA.

'Call me a taxi, we are leaving *now*!' I yelled angrily. I was furious about the way he had treated us. He started to back down, shocked by my uncharacteristic fury. However, I was not in the mood for his pathetic attempt at appeasement.

We were greatly relieved to get a lift to the airport from Khamis – Hassan had asked him to take us there. Khamis was a kind man. His expression showed that he was sorry about the way things had turned out. We were able to secure a flight out that day, which meant that our visit to Israel had been for a record time of 23 hours and 40 minutes, although it had felt like an eternity. Hassan called me repeatedly as we waited at the airport, expressing all kinds of regrets. However, I was not interested. Jennifer and I vowed we would *never* go back again.

**Spring 2009: Academic Shock**

The first week after our return, we walked around in a stupor. Jennifer and I talked into the small hours of the night. Although we had hit a brick wall, we certainly were not ready to give up. The fear of letting the codices disappear into unscrupulous hands kept us going. To make matters worse, Hassan was calling several times a day with benign updates. He seemed determined to keep open the lines of communication.

However, being Hassan, he could not help himself. He was still entertaining visitors who had called him out of the blue to see his treasure. He never seemed to find it odd how these people managed to get his telephone number. He relished telling us about these visits, always eager to get our take on them. At least we knew what he was up to.

One day he rang, all eager like a schoolboy, and asked me to guess who had visited that day. 'The Vatican,' I suggested – it was the first thing that came into my head.

He laughed. 'Very good, David. You are close. Some lady named Rita Jahn from Germany came over and wanted to look at the books. She said she was a representative from the Vatican. How did you know?'

I was as surprised as he was, of course, although the disclosure made the hair on my neck stand on end. Bob had commented during that fateful lunch meeting that he was concerned that Professor Lemaire may well have taken this information to the École Biblique, the archaeological wing of the Catholic Church. I was anxious that the knowledge must not spread too far afield. I did not know at this time what the theological implications would be for the Church, and before they were told about the codices I wanted to have a grip on the situation myself.

Hassan rang me again a few days later with another update. 'Two men from the Church came to visit me today. They said they are from Belgium.' I said I hoped he had not shown them too much, and he reassured me that he had not. 'Next week Moussaieff is coming to see me,' he announced proudly. 'Don't worry, David. I am not going to show him all the books. Just a couple.'

As much as he seemed to enjoy being the centre of all this high-powered attention, he was also uneasy. The stakes were being raised. Boaz and Allen were beginning to take over, I suspected. Hassan was feeling his control slip.

I called Margaret and informed her of the situation. I asked her if it would be possible to speak with one or two of the experts she had mentioned in an earlier conversation. A week or so later, I found myself speaking to a professor based at a well-known American university in Utah. We had some interesting discussions over the course of a few weeks, and eventually I thought it would be a good idea to send a few images to the university to see what their reaction might be. Cautiously, I sent them copies of the original amateur photographs of the codices: good enough to get a view of what the artefacts were, but not good enough to glean much else in terms of detail or dimension. What I got back by way of a response was dismissive. As Margaret later astutely put it when I shared the email with her, 'they are obviously suffering from academic shock'.

Wed 20 May 2009

David,

I have heard back from some of the people whom I have asked to look at your images. I have received several comments.

Regarding the photo of the place where the books were found, one says, 'By all normal interpretations, this is a columbarium, or 'Dove Cote Burial,' for cremated remains. While Judaeans and Egyptians practiced inhumation burial, the Romans were largely cremators – like the Villanovans. Cremation burial - and Columbarii - are ubiquitous all over the Roman Empire. It is hard to believe that a burial site would be used as an ancient library or repository of Temple-related materials.'

Regarding patinas, 'FAKE PATINAS ARE APPLIED TO A SURFACE, AND DO NOT EMINATE OUT OF A SURFACE AS PART OF IT. So, the 'flake-off' feature we see here is VERY SUSPICIOUS ... WE SEE BRAND-NEW SURFACE AND NITCHEDLY NEW LETTER FORMS. In other words, THERE IS NO CORROSION on the surface, nor any deterioration of the letters we see: they appear new, new, new, perfect and sharp. SHARP is the key word. I have studied the raised letters on a Roman lead pipe. Those letters are corroded, and so there is more lead oxide there than pure lead. Any bump or scrape will crush away part of the letter, which is mostly oxide compounds with mineral. Examples of ancient lead with ancient water calcification patina build-up have a different appearance than the plates in these photos.'

Also, 'I have lived a lot in Egypt, as you know, and, Date palms there are seen by the tens of thousands – everywhere. As they were in ancient Judaea. Ancient Jews knew date palms. They knew that the dates cling close to the tops of the trunk. To see date bunches hanging like this from the middle of the frond is odd; it is to me untenable that an ancient would blunder this way, or, suddenly go Cubist and do a Picasso date palm.'

Another scholar who is very familiar with the history of Aramaic and Hebrew scripts is unable to recognize any ancient parallels to several of the letters in these inscriptions. He recommends that patterns of the letters be examined to see if any kind of code or grammar can be detected.

Personally, as I have looked at the full collection of images that you have recently sent, my main concerns are with the crudeness and the redundancy of almost all the images and features of these plates. You mentioned the 'face' on one of the plates as being a human face, but from the photos that arrived two days ago, it looks to me more like a lion's face than a man's face. Perhaps something different is evident looking at the plate itself. The lion could symbolize Judah, of course. However, I was involved heavily a decade ago in the examination of a collection of inscribed slate relics from Michigan, which we eventually found, conclusively, to be fabrications of about a century ago. Unfortunately, examining the photos you have sent reminds me more of those artifacts than of anything I have previously seen from the ancient Mediterranean world, I'm sorry to say, although I surely hope that further evidence will prove otherwise.

Perhaps you already have answers to these questions. I am
still waiting to hear from one other colleague in particular. I shall be
especially interested to learn what happens in the coming week.

The email roundly denounced the discovery, stating that it was
impossible for the codices to be genuine: they looked 'new, new, new'.
It went on to say that they appeared 'too polished and too bright' and
that lead, to be this old, 'must look corroded'. It was an emotional
response that was flawed in logic. My first thought was that all they had
seen were a few badly lit photos. But the email went on, inexorably,
as if the analyst could not help himself: 'The date palms are forgeries;
the fruit-bearing branches, if they were real, would never show the fruit
halfway along the branch, the iconography is very specific on this point.'
Out of curiosity I went online to hunt down other examples and found
over 600 exactly like our own 'with fruit halfway along the branch' – all
of them verified as antique. (See plates 2 and 6.) As for the point that
the books looked polished and 'new', I had taken care to explain that
Hassan in his eagerness to see what they were had scrubbed them with
basic bathroom cleaner followed by a generous coating of olive oil –
so of course they were shiny! I could only conclude that the analysis
had come from a junior researcher, as suggested by the language in its
enthusiastic rejection and the emotive emphasis based upon so little
evidence. As for the suggestion that the niches were a columbarium, this
was patently absurd. Columbaria were niches used for the interment of
the ashes of cremated human remains. They had to be deep enough
to contain such remnants. Our niches, as could easily be seen from the
photographs, were shallow. Unless Roman soldiery recruited dwarves,
this idea was beyond parody. This response, I suspected, was a first taste
of what was yet to come. Academe is a known minefield. I would have to
tread very carefully indeed.

\* \* \* \*

During the period of Jesus and the Apostles, Palaeo-Hebrew was more or less defunct – which makes the use of it on the codices remarkable. Hebrew was a sacred language, and would only have been used for holy ritual. This seemed to me to mean that the codices were very holy indeed, harking back to the period when Hebrew was still in use and was thought to hold sacred power, as the Language of God Himself. The Ten Commandments, given by God to Moses, were in Hebrew. I could not escape the conclusion that these books are trying to tell us something overwhelmingly important.

I was still trying to work this through in my mind, and the more I thought about it, the more a possibility came to mind. Given the uniqueness of the books, was it possible that they originated from, and were used in some way, inside the Temple of Jerusalem? There was, after all, Temple symbolism written plain as day all over them. Looking at these books, I could not help feeling that they were, to paraphrase Churchill, a mystery wrapped in an enigma.

I was deeply engrossed in the idea that Christianity was extremely ancient and that what Jesus was trying to achieve was not just a restoration of the Temple, but a restoration, in addition, of the ancient religion and theology. The codices afforded so many tantalizing hints and clues. The iconography was, as even the Israel Antiquities Authority had admitted in their letter to Hassan, just not Jewish. I had quickly come to the same conclusion. These codices were 1st- century in provenance, as the initial metal tests had concluded, but in their use of image and symbolism, as well as in their language, they seemed somehow older. (See plate 7.)

It is an extraordinary thought that the living Christianity of today should seem to be a survival that goes deep beyond the mists of ancient history, even before Solomon.

## June 2009: To Jordan to Meet with the Queen

Much to our delight we received a check-in call from Charles. He had accepted a high-powered job in the Middle East, which meant that we could not be in contact with him as often as we had been, although he had reassured us that he was available by phone or email. He was in London for a week and suggested we meet up. We found a quiet corner, and Jennifer and I poured out the latest news to him.

'Well, you two, my news,' said Charles, 'is that I've been in touch with Eversheds and they've informed me of the legal position. The bad news, I'm afraid, is that Hassan is no more than a common criminal who has stolen the artefacts by deception.'

'Even so, we can't give up now,' I protested. 'Is there anything we can do?'

'Yes, actually. I think a visit to Jordan is in order. You must prepare a solid dossier of information for the Royal Office and relate the entire story to them. The visit should be with the express purpose of working together with the Jordanian Government to make sure the artefacts are repatriated and protected.'

Just when we had slowly begun to accept this new position, Hassan rang out of the blue one day from Farez's house in Jericho. It was as if he had somehow sensed our withdrawal from the relationship. 'Hello, David, I am calling from Farez's house to tell you that I don't want anything more to do with you and neither does Farez. We do not want to do any more business with you. The contract is no good.'

I agreed, relieved that he had chosen to take this stance: he had unwittingly made the decision for us. Strangely, despite his new coalition with Farez against us, he still rang with compulsive regularity. However, as my trip to Jordan loomed ever nearer, Jennifer and I agreed not to take any more of his calls and to hold off on any further decisions until I had discussed the situation with the Jordanian authorities. As we had feared, the silence from us only made him more frantic, and the calls became more urgent, frequent and angry.

At Heathrow, in the departure lounge, I repeatedly opened and closed my laptop nervously, once more studying my photographs of the codices to reassure myself that all this was real. Helena had organized the trip through diplomatic channels. I could not believe I was off to meet the Queen of Jordan. I had no idea how Her Majesty would react.

Regrettably, Jennifer had to stay back and deal with some pressing issues on the home front.

Her Majesty was scheduled to take a flight to Egypt following our meeting, so the Queen Alia International Airport was the most convenient place to meet. As I entered the terminal reserved for Royalty, I was greeted by the Queen's secretary and followed her through the stately, marble interior into an anteroom, to take my place with several other people who were also awaiting an audience: two Americans and a professorial-looking older man. A few minutes later the Queen's secretary returned to escort me to the meeting room. She motioned to the older man to come with us, introducing him to me as Dr Abdul Nasser Hindawi, former Director of Antiquities of the Jordan Museum.

Her Majesty was perched regally on a gold damask sofa, and rose gracefully to greet us. It was a beautifully decorated space reflecting both Arabic and Western styles. I launched straight into the story of the artefacts, the evidence for their authenticity and an assessment of what it all meant.

'This is wonderful, but why are you doing this?' Her Majesty asked. I explained what an important discovery this was for Jordan and how we are anxious for the artefacts to be repatriated. I had so little time to say so much. I could only hope the photos could relay my message effectively.

The meeting lasted no more than 20 minutes. However, the Queen seemed suitably impressed. She expressed her appreciation and agreed that this was indeed a major discovery, one that should be dealt with directly by the King's Office.

Dr Hindawi and I were escorted back to the anteroom to finish our discussion. He was animated and excited. 'This is amazing! It is extraordinary that you are here,' he said warmly. 'I would like to thank you on behalf of the people of Jordan for this very generous gesture.'

'The codices are too important to be sold into a private collection,' I remarked. He nodded at me appreciatively and handed me his card. Before we went our separate ways, he clasped my hand again and wished me Godspeed with the project.

The Queen's secretary had told me to await a call from the Office of Protocol for the Royal Court within the next few hours. They would arrange for me to meet with the correct authorities some time within the next 24 hours with a view to gathering as much evidence as possible. The next morning a limousine was sent to collect me for a meeting at the King's Office. Arriving at the palace, I was greeted by Samih, a junior working in the Office of Protocol for the Royal Court. His approach was confident and smooth, as he ushered me into the palace and through to his office. On the way we walked through the gardens and passed the Throne Room: the atmosphere was relaxed and friendly.

Samih introduced me to General Abdul, the senior military attaché and liaison from the Royal Palace, who said: 'I am going to arrange an appointment for you to meet Major Mahmoud Al Hewayan and Colonel Mohammed Manaseer, who are top men at Jordanian Military Intelligence (JMI). They will help you in any way they can.' Samih promised he would call me when the meeting with JMI had been arranged. He said he would aim for late afternoon.

My car was waiting for me in the hotel lobby at 2.45pm to take me to my appointment with the JMI, which turned out to be less than 10 minutes from the hotel. A soldier guarding the gate lifted the barrier and we drove through, greeted by an armed guard.

'Mr David, we are very pleased to meet you. We are deeply honoured by your loyalty to Jordan,' Major Al Hewayan initiated. Colonel Manaseer smiled and nodded his head in agreement.

'I like England very much. I was trained at Sandhurst,' the Major said with obvious pride.

'I am impressed,' I responded genuinely. I was touched by the Jordanians' enthusiasm for all things British, but at the same time perplexed. The British had let down the Arabs in the aftermath of World War One – all the promises that T E Lawrence (of Arabia) had made on behalf of the British Government had been betrayed. Unbeknownst to the Arabs, who with Lawrence's guidance and expertise had been marshalled into a superbly effective fighting force, the British and French had divided the Middle East between themselves – as if they won the war. It was a betrayal that has never been forgotten, and a contributing factor in the difficulty of Western-Arab relations ever since. I mentioned this to the Colonel, but he just shrugged it off as an embarrassment, something that had happened in the past.

We talked about an immediate strategy. I showed the Colonel and the Major the photographs of the cave site taken by Ron in March 2008, and explained to him that Hassan's reason for not taking us to the site was that military manoeuvres were going on in the area. The Colonel and the Major exchanged looks. Suddenly the Colonel leapt to his feet.

'I know exactly where that is!' He said something to the Major in Arabic. 'If you could come back after a week or so, we can arrange to accompany you in reconnoitering the site. We will assist you to undertake all of the necessary analysis.'

## The Great Pretender

When I got back to the UK I put in a thank-you call to Helena, who had been supportive of the discovery since we had first confided in her back in February. Helena was extremely well connected and understood our need to approach people in high places to help us – without them there was a real risk that we would never achieve our aim. Her involvement had been paramount to our accomplishments thus far. There was no way we could refuse her request to involve her son Horace in our efforts.

As Charles was now away and very busy with his new job, and therefore compelled to oversee our project from a distance, Helena suggested that Horace could assist him. Much to our chagrin, however, we were concerned that Horace's interest in the project lay less in the historical value of the codices and more, it seemed to us, in the opportunity that they afforded him. In our desire to repay Helena's support we opened the door for Horace and he barged right in. Through a contact of his mother's, we had already managed to get an appointment with the Military Attaché at the Jordanian Embassy in London. We decided that putting up with Horace was a small price to pay.

Although not well versed in the intricacies of the project, Horace insisted he should handle the meeting on our behalf. I had to admit feeling a bit encroached upon. However, his background had trained him in proper etiquette and protocol, so I had no reason to be concerned. I agreed to let him go in our stead, and met up with him several times beforehand for a full briefing, giving him photographs of some of the codices, as well as of the area in Jordan where the cave was located from the disk Hassan had given us. I gave Horace Ron's telephone number, to see if he could persuade Ron to join him at the Embassy – Ron would not give out any details to me, but I was pretty sure he might succumb to the flattery of being invited to the Embassy to meet the Military Attaché. I was confident that under the subtle duress of the Jordanian authorities he would come clean and admit the cave site was in Jordan.

Horace rang me that afternoon to say that Ron had agreed to come along.

'I told him I was with Jordanian Intelligence,' he said, when I asked him how he had managed that. I was horrified. Dishonesty like that would get us into trouble. 'I know what I'm doing,' he countered with bravado. We had already begun to regret involving Horace, but it was too late to back out: the appointment had been made.

The meeting was at 12.30pm. He had promised to call straight after the meeting, and we sat around nervously waiting. Then at 2 o'clock we decided it was time to call him. He refused to speak to me until after he had slept off his hangover – he admitted to partying the night before. Jennifer and I were upset and decided to call Charles, who expressed shock at Horace's behaviour. Horace did not ring until after 4 o'clock.

He recounted what had happened. All the way through the meeting he had maintained his intelligence officer fiction. Ron had appeared on time at the Embassy, but would not speak until he was assured immunity from prosecution. He was informed that a pre-requisite of his immunity would be that he not sell the story to the press. After being given the necessary assurances, he admitted to having visited Jordan, but he denied that he had been to the cave site. The pictures that were shown to him were not his, he insisted.

Jennifer and I, though appalled at Horace's blundering attempt at diplomacy, felt that at least, thanks to the meeting, our cause had been alerted to the Jordanian Royal Office via the Embassy. We were finally getting somewhere. Nonetheless, after yesterday's farrago, Charles strongly advised that we sever all links with Horace. We agreed this was necessary, but were saddened by the effect this would have on our friendship with Helena. Regrettably, we were left with no other option.

Margaret called, keen to tell me about her evening at Lambeth Palace, where she had attended a dinner and met with the Archbishop of Canterbury, who had enquired about the discovery.

'David, I've had a closer look at the tablet that you left with me last Friday and have begun the process of transcribing it. My immediate thought is that it has a recurring, and sometimes backward, pattern to it, and that therefore it may be a kind of Essene identity card. My guess is that it would have allowed the bearer to enter other communities during his travels as an emissary and would have permitted him to partake in communion, as well as other rituals.'

A few days later the Jordanian Royal Office called to tell us about preparations for our trip.

### June 2009: Return to Jordan

We arrived late at the King Hussein Airport full of excitement and determination. I was eager to introduce Jennifer to the remarkable people I had met on my previous trip, especially the newly ranked 'Colonel', Mahmoud.

Early the next morning we were escorted to the Headquarters of JMI, expecting to go on from there to look for the cave site. After a careful look at the photographs and a quick glance at the Google Earth coordinates, which did not reveal much given that this was a restricted military zone, I was reasonably sure of the direction we should take. I was hoping that the Colonel would be able to help us further.

The Colonel greeted me like an old friend and I introduced him to Jennifer. He led us to the office of his superior, also newly promoted, General Manaseer. It was good to be back and with such high-level support. Pulling out photographs and maps of the area, the Colonel studied them with a furrowed brow. He left the room and five minutes later came back with a colleague, who was officially off duty and dressed in civvies except for a pistol in a holster around his waist. We were introduced to the Captain who greeted us warmly. It so happened that Hussein was brought up in the area of the cave site. The Colonel briefed him in Arabic. Then we showed him the photograph of the man in the cave that Hassan had given us, hoping Hussein might recognize him.

'I know this man, he lives in my village, Saham, in the north. His name is Nabil. He's a drug dealer.' He then turned to the Colonel and said something in Arabic.

'Hussein says that it may be a coincidence, but strangely enough, it is known around the village that he has all of a sudden become wealthy.'

We quickly produced more pictures on the laptop: image after image of landmarks and landscapes surrounding the site. Hussein recognized them all. We were well prepared for our expedition. The day was hot and threatened to get hotter: it was essential that we make a start. Soldiers were loading a big black SUV with munitions: grenades and rows of bullet cases to accompany the submachine guns.

'Should we be worried?' Jennifer asked the Colonel, who was busy overseeing the operation.

'No,' he chuckled reassuringly, 'there are always armed guards patrolling the area, as the site is a militarily strategic one, but we have been told to offer you protection. We take our orders seriously.'

It was a long drive, through fertile valleys and into up into the hills and mountains. As we headed north towards the city of Irbid, we encountered a vast crusader castle in front of us, high on a hill overlooking, from its vantage point, the whole of the territory around it. About 20 minutes beyond Irbid, the Colonel pulled over to the side of the road. There was no other car in sight – this was well and truly the middle of nowhere. We parked next to the sarcophagus that we had seen in Ron's photographs. As we opened the car doors, the heat hit us like a wall. We went over to inspect the great stone object. There was a head-rest carved into the stone as well as eight-pointed stars carved into its sides. Near by was a *mikveh*, a ritual bath that had demarcated the entrance point to the valley.

Not far into our descent into the valley we stumbled across the entrance to our first cave.

'Allah be praised, this is incredible!' the Colonel exclaimed. I looked around in wonder. The cave floor was a miasma of different smells forming a hot putrid stench, rising from an oily pool of water. A large white crab scuttled about (what on earth was a crab doing in such a place, 50 miles/80 kilometres from the sea?).

'I don't think this is exactly the spot,' I announced, 'but we seem to be roughly in the right place – this appears to be a 1st-century tomb.'

Ahead of us in the shadows I could make out four burial slabs, typical of the early Christian period. Each had been carved out of the living rock; archways had been cut out above them, an ancient foreshadowing of what can be seen in many a Western church and cathedral.

'What's that flat space to the left of each niche?' Jennifer asked, pointing to the slabs.

'That's for the laying out of the body,' I replied. 'Look to the right – that's where the unguents were placed for the cleansing and anointing of the corpse.'

'Would that not be the channel for the bodily fluids to run out of the chamber?' Jennifer asked, pointing to the spot where I was standing.

I glanced at the Colonel and Hussein. It was just after midday and if we did not get a move on we, would not get much accomplished. I was reminded of what the Colonel had previously told us: we were trekking through one of the most dangerous areas in the world. Back in the 70s and early 80s this was the main hideout of PLO terrorists and it was rumoured that Al-Qaeda and other militant groups had at one point also been here. Oleander bushes in full bloom guided our pathway down what was rapidly becoming a gorge.

The Colonel trailed behind us as we ventured downstream into thickening undergrowth. The walls of the gorge grew higher as we marched on. Growing from the cliffsides I could make out what I guessed might be olive trees or a desert species of oak, terebinth perhaps – a tree much spoken of in ancient times, and one dedicated to many of the Middle Eastern hero-gods, some of whom had been crucified and had risen from death. Suddenly I noticed something in the corner of my eye – pomegranate trees, lots of them.

The Colonel caught up with me. 'These trees,' I said, pointing at them, 'are all over the codices.' He grinned, as if taking pleasure in this interesting day's work. Pomegranates and pink acanthus were everywhere, but at least we had now left behind us on the dry ground the dry brush whose harsh spikes had covered our legs with bloody scratches.

We carried on walking, making our way gingerly through what had now become dense foliage. Suddenly, emerging from under the canopy of a low tree, the path divided in two. We turned left, and the spectacular depth and beauty of the valley unfolded before our eyes. Ahead of us appeared a steep crag, dotted with wide but inaccessible caves. It would certainly be worth investigating these at some point. However, in this intense heat that was unthinkable, and in any case we would have needed climbing gear.

Before descending into the valley we had noticed cave upon cave in the porous rock of the heights. Some of them on lower ground were being used as sheep pens; others were dumping grounds, as evidenced by heaps of festering sheep's bodies, with clouds of flies all around.

It was strange to think that we were not that far from Israel and the Sea of Galilee, the modern Lake Tiberias, which we had visited only recently, but in such drastically different circumstances. These mountains traced the border line between Israel and Jordan. The Israeli side is flat, running into the ancient bowl of a vast freshwater lake. Here, in stark contrast, was rugged majesty – rocky, forbidding, and guarding great secrets.

Yet there was fertility here too, in the depths. Soon the pomegranate trees gave way to a virtual garden of apple trees, banana palms, melons, cucumbers and other domestic food crops, in little terraced gardens jutting out from the steep sides of the valley. The scene was Biblical in its simplicity and charm – an environment that had hardly changed in 2,000 years.

Suddenly, out of nowhere, two shepherds appeared, surprised by the sight of two Westerners. They offered us mint tea. While the Colonel and Hussein sat talking to them, I got up and wandered off, to establish the lie of the land. Emerging from the groves, I was surprised to see two caves high above me, like the eye-sockets of a human skull – I knew now why the locals call this the Valley of the Skull. Looking around, I could see many other cavities in the mountainside. The valley got deeper and deeper, becoming a canyon. This was indeed a fantastic hiding-place. As I walked on, I had the eerie sensation of being watched, but quickly dismissed my uneasy feeling as superstition; nevertheless, I could not shake off the fact that these were historic resting places of the dead.

When I got back to the group, our escorts were still sipping tea with the shepherds. The Colonel beckoned Jennifer and me aside and told us that they knew the place we were looking for. They had confirmed that some of the caves had only just been discovered. They were going to take us to one of them.

We meandered through groves of short trees, bushes and small fruit orchards, which we tried our best not to disturb. We passed several citrus trees in fruit, heaving with large green lemons. The old shepherd picked a few and handed them to Jennifer, who accepted them with delight. 'Aren't these the *etrogim* depicted on the cover of some of the codices?' she asked.

Yes, that's right,' I confirmed, 'although your specimen is rather a small one compared to how big they can grow.' I can tell this surprised her: one large fruit she was holding filled the whole of her hand.

We clambered over rocks and got caught in thick thorny bushes that tore at our clothing. Suddenly, there was a cave, dug into the cliff-side, buttressed by man-made barricades of stone, with two 'windows' above the entrance. These again appeared to be skull-like in formation. From afar it was an eerie-looking place. Our two shepherd guides would go no further out of respect for the dead.

I clambered up. The entrance, gaping like an open mouth, was more than a metre above us in the cliff-face, accessible but a challenge. Jennifer had just managed to scale the last of a few makeshift steps into the mouth of the cave when she let out a loud shriek. Several bats flying out of the entrance had narrowly missed her, their wing-beats barely perceptible above the din of the flies. We both went in, followed by the Colonel and Hussein, our sweat catching the heavy swirling dust and making us sticky and grimy.

Directly in front of us was a rectangular rock-cut tomb filled with shale, with a tell-tale niche cut into the wall at one side. The Colonel glanced at his watch. We had been wandering around for a good five hours.

'David,' he said, 'the General has planned a special banquet for us and we cannot be late. But you have all day tomorrow.' The trek back to the car was gruelling. We were tired, hot and sticky. As we pressed upward, we saw a large black pall of billowing smoke in the distance, close to where we had parked our car. We looked at each other, fearing the worst. There was panic in the Colonel's eyes. It was our car!

Coming out of the gorge onto the higher ground, we stood there, stunned. There was a raging bush fire, no more than half a metre from the car. Grass and brush crackled loudly. The air was as hot as a furnace. Other, cracking noises came to us from slightly farther off, as the Colonel guided Jennifer around the inferno. Gunshots. The sniper could not have been more than metres away.

With great bravery Hussein ran towards the vehicle. His hand wrapped in a piece of dampened cloth, he opened the door. Smoke was billowing all around the car. Thankfully it started straight away and Hussein drove a few hundred yards to safety and cooler air. We ran towards the car and piled in, aware that we were being watched.

'Tactical retreats are the best part of battle!' exclaimed the Colonel, with wry amusement as we drove off at speed, all of us giddy with relief.

We arrived back at JMI in the late afternoon, exhausted yet excited. The General had organized a wonderful feast. Afterwards we repaired to his office for some Turkish coffee and a debriefing. 'David,' said the General, 'if we are to continue to help you, you must contact the King's Office, as we will need their permission to interrogate Nabil. You must understand that this is not a Jordanian issue. It is an international one.'

### Ever-decreasing Circles

We had agreed to meet the Colonel for drinks at our hotel before going into Amman for dinner.

'I have some very good news for you both. We have just been granted permission to detain and interrogate Nabil, our chief suspect. Tell me, David, do you think we are doing the right thing?' The Jordanians are peaceable people, and he genuinely seemed loath to apply coercion unless really necessary.

'I appreciate that this might be uncomfortable for you, Colonel, as you've got to question someone based on second-hand information. Perhaps you aren't totally convinced that what he has done warrants such strict treatment. My take on it is that through an act of selfishness, a whole community has been denied the right of access to some of the most important relics ever to be seen by humanity. That community is local, international – the world.' The Colonel listened intently as I continued. 'By being in private hands, these artefacts will remain the playthings of people who might decide on a whim if scholars or outsiders can see them. Furthermore, by rights they should be in Jordan, where the tourism that inevitably will result from this discovery will turn the site into one of the most important places of pilgrimage in the Christian world. Everyone will be a winner, but most importantly the local community of Saham will harvest the rewards.'

'You are right, my friend. I will bring him in. The truth starts from the day of his birth until now.'

We were brought to Reem Albawadi, or 'Gazelle of the Desert', a traditional Jordanian restaurant full of old-world romance, chosen by the Colonel. It was an imposing old sandstone fortress that had been gracefully converted. Waiters in traditional dress were bustling about, carrying trays piled high with flatbread directly from clay ovens.

'So David, what was it that we saw today?' the Colonel asked. 'Did you find what you were looking for?'

'What we discovered today may have profound implications for our understanding of the origins of Christianity, and possibly Islam too.'

The Colonel's eyes widened. 'I really want to help you. I agree that what you are saying is very important and should be shared. But you will realize it is awkward for us, as you know, dealing with Israel … very delicate.'

'I do appreciate that. What do you think would be the best way to go about it?' I was eager to handle this in a way that the Jordanians would be comfortable with.

'Well, the best way would be if *you* could bring the discovery to the public. That would ease things considerably for us. We will support you. It will be much easier to approach Israel with everything out in the open. We have a good relationship with them and want to keep it that way.'

'Jennifer, you couldn't hand me the tweezers, plastic bags and stuff out of my camera bag could you?' I asked excitedly. Despite yesterday's harrowing experience, we found ourselves back at the cave site. The Colonel had been concerned for our safety, but we were adamant about the work we had to do. Hussein shuffled around at the entrance while I inspected the dark recesses at the back of the cave. Suddenly something that really caught my eye and brought me into direct contact with the world of the 1st-century Bible. There on the floor in front of us was a huge, carved, round stone, big enough to have covered a tomb, which is what I suspected lay behind it. I made a mental note to consult with the Colonel about getting a Jordanian archaeological team together to excavate here. For some reason this tomb had remained untouched.

As I peered into the dark depths of the open grave below me, I felt an intuitive foreboding. I reminded myself of what Theophrastus the ancient Greek philosopher had once said: that superstition was cowardice in the face of the Divine. It occurred to me that what might possibly be happening was a kind of inner monitor picking up on the sheer antiquity of the place and the presence of the past. I had heard about this sensation from others, that there is an innate human ability to tap into the primeval self that informs the power of the place, making such archaeological sites so special. Put simply, it is the interaction of humanity and environment.

I jumped in. The dust in the grave was moist and stuck to my hands. I realized that it could be organic, and a shudder ran through my body. I spotted a bone partially hidden by some shale at my feet. I tried to rationalize this in my mind, by thinking it was likely to be an animal bone, but it reminded me of something much closer to home.

'Hey, can someone poke your head outside and tell me where the sun is?'

'Why do you ask this, Mr David?' Hussein replied, understandably curious.

'Just point,' I said, after he gone back out into the light. He did so.

'This place is oriented east–west,' I said. 'These are Christian tombs all right.' (See figures 20, 21, 22 and 26 in the plate section.)

*Figure 1.* The Face (of Jesus?), the Man of Woes. The face is encapsulated within a nimbus or cartouche. There are four seals at the top, four at the bottom and three on the left-hand side – and where the book is to be opened there are seven seals.

*Figure 2.* Limescale, detritus and corrosion on display around
the Davidic Palm Tree (the Tree of Life) and eight-pointed stars,
which indicates the coming of the Messiah.

*Figure 3.* The seal rings are surprisingly fragile and all too easily fall apart upon attempting to open any of the codices.

*Figure 4.* There are variations of thickness throughout the hoard.

*Figure 5.* Corrosion holes where impurities have broken through the metal matrix – the fragile and corroded metal of the codices is unique, leading to problems of dating through a lack of other comparable examples.

*Figure 6.* Interior close up showing palm trees and eight-pointed stars. Along the spine there is a build up of corrosion products and crystalline mineral deposits.

*Figure 7.* One of the larger codices, approximately the size of a hardback book. Note the balustrade at top with inscription and eight-pointed stars.

*Figure 8.* Open book demonstrating further watermark corrosion and coloration. Note how the page rides up around the sealing rings.

*Figure 9.* The smallest of the books are just over an inch square. This one exhibits the flowering pomegranate, symbolic of the High Priesthood.

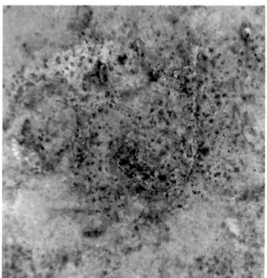

*Figure 10.* As work progressed we were surprised at the interior state of the books.

*Figure 11.* Micrograph exhibiting pitting both in and around the lettering: demonstrating that the letters cannot have been added at a later date.

*Figure 12.* Crystalline surface deposits can be seen in the lettering around the Menorah.

*Figure 13.* A micrograph showing linen fibres caught in the limescale and detritus.

*Figure 14.* Etrogs, a species of citrus, seen here on one of the Lead Tablets from the Hoard – the sheen is the result of being coated by olive oil.

*Figure 15*. A large inscribed bowl found in the hoard. It is one of the few items made from copper that we were witness to.

*Figure 16.* The *mikvah* or Jewish bath with descending steps on the side of the road parallel to the valley.

*Figure 17.* A sarcophagus next to the mikvah

*Figure 18.* Arid landscape on the upper part of the valley of the cave site.

*Figure 19.* The Oleander bushes on the way down into the valley site.

*Figure 20.* Jennifer and Hussein outside the first tomb cave, discovered on our descent into the valley.

*Figure 21.* The interior of the first century cave-tomb depicting the slabs of stone used to lay out bodies.

*Figure 22*. A *piscina* or font immediately outside the first century cave-tomb.

*Figure 23*. A pomegranate grove near to where we took tea with the shepherds.

*Figure 24.* One of the shepherds in the valley site.

*Figure 25.* The eye sockets of a skull can distinctly be seen in the face of the valley cliff.

*Figure 26.* David inspecting the cut tomb in
the cave shown to them by the shepherds.

*Figure 27.* View from Jordan to Israel overlooking the site of the
Battle of Yarmouk, just a short distance from the cave site.

# PART III

# OPENING THE SEVENTH SEAL

*This is the kind of divine enlightenment into which we have been
initiated by the hidden tradition of our inspired teachers, a tradition at
one with Scripture. We now grasp these things in the best way we can,
and as they come to us, wrapped in the sacred veils of that love toward
humanity with which scripture and hierarchical traditions cover the
truths of the mind with things derived from the realm of the senses.*

Dionysius, *On the Divine Names*, 5992B[1]

## The Fatal Vision

*I made known to you brethren, as touching the Gospel which was preached by me, that it was not after a man. For neither did I receive it from a man, nor was I taught it, save through the revelation of the Christ known revealed within me.*

St Paul, *Galatians* 1.11

Two thousand years after Jesus, Christianity is based almost entirely on the influence of St Paul; and on St Paul's experience of Jesus in a vision that he had on the road to Damascus. To scholars the Christianity of Paul has become known as Gentile Christianity, because Paul came to preach that Jesus had superseded the Law of Moses. Circumcision and various other practices were no longer a requirement of faith.

Paul is one of the most controversial characters of religious history, a man of almost pathological extremes; and yet all we have to base our knowledge on are the Acts of the Apostles and the oldest documents of the canonical New Testament, the letters of Paul himself. The first we hear of Paul is when he appears in *Acts* as Saul of Tarsus, a man in the service of the Temple, a trusted confidant of the High Priest. The *Acts of Paul*, an apocryphal text from the 2nd century, describes him as a squat, balding man with bandy legs. The post he held was a prestigious one, and this has raised serious questions regarding Paul's origins. Certain scholars, Hyam Maccoby among them, have taken from much later anti-Pauline writings the idea that Paul was either a Gentile from a Gentile family or was a convert to Judaism. There is even a possibility that Paul was a northern Gentile – in other words, a Benjamite from the region of the old kingdom of Israel. It is to Paul himself that we must turn to address the enigma of his origins. He testifies that he was Jewish, and emphasizes this fact. He speaks explicitly in his letters (*Philippians* 3.5) of his leanings towards the philosophy of the Pharisees. But the crucial point is that he was very high in the employ of the High Priest of the Temple as an officer of the guard. This would have required a level of access to areas of the Temple that were strictly forbidden to anyone perceived to be even partly foreign. Paul's job description is at odds with the possibility of Gentile origins.

In the *Clementine Recognitions* we first learn of Saul throwing James down the Temple stairs. This single act provoked vicious riots and a general outpouring of anger over the mistreatment of a good man. From early on we get a strong impression of Saul's antipathy to James – even after his conversion to James' way of thinking. Paul's letters convey the enigmatic sense of a man who has put the past behind him, and does not wish to discuss that past in any detail.

From *Acts* we glean that the early Hebrew-Christians were causing the Temple authorities a great deal of grief. Saul was given a commission to pursue and persecute certain members of the early Church. We also see Saul presiding over the martyrdom of Stephen. A Hellenized convert whose views of the Temple brought him into confrontation with the Temple authorities, Stephen was stoned to death for blasphemy.

It is easy from reading the New Testament to picture a lonely Saul wandering the northern highlands, falling off of his horse at the sight of a splendidly bright and blazing vision of the apotheosized Jesus; and then being so overwhelmed by the vision that he ceases the pursuit and becomes one of the pursued. The big question, however, is what did he actually see?

Paul stresses that he was in pursuit of early Christians when he had his vision – and it is curious that they both happened to be in the precise area where the discovery of the codices was made. Paul makes it clear that the story of *Acts* is not entirely accurate. What he saw was the 'Risen Christ' – a revelation of Jesus the Messiah. Paul, ever after, can only mean the Risen Christ: he never knew the physical Jesus. It was a vision of such profundity that it wrought change in him almost instantaneously: the scales fell from his eyes as he was confronted by what he could only recognize as 'the truth'. His statement in *1 Corinthians* 15.8 is telling, for here he describes himself as 'born out of time'. This is an accurate description of the most holy place in Hebraism: the Holy of Holies inside the Temple at Jerusalem. When crossing its boundary, one passed into a timeless zone.

Paul's emphasis on the Risen Christ shaped Western theology, prompting us to question the precise character of the vision a little more closely. He speaks of Jesus as 'Son of God, the Lamb', 'the sacrifice for our sins', 'the salvation of our souls', but he seems to make little reference to his life as a human being, even though it is highly unlikely that he was ignorant of the facts of Jesus's life.[2] He is writing only 10 or 12 years after the Crucifixion, but does not mention the family of Jesus, nor any of the episodes in his mission, nor any of the usual details we might expect to read about. His Jesus is purely theological. Furthermore, in Paul's letter to the *Galatians* (1.10–17) there is a marked rivalry between the author and certain members of the Jerusalem Church, as Paul's Christ seems at odds with their actual experience of him: Paul appears to be pleading with them, his frustration clearly felt in the text.

Close reading of the description in the Acts gives us the impression that Saul was accompanied by few men, and in search of even fewer: Christian communities at the time were still rather small, and could easily be picked off by their persecutors. It therefore comes as a surprise to read (in the *Clementine Recognitions*, 1.71–2ff) of James' exile to Pella and the revelation that he had been joined by as many as 5,000 on the road, only to be opposed by a further 5,000 (for it must be assumed that Paul's remit to pursue the early Christians meant that he too had had many followers.) Somewhere on the road to Damascus 10,000 men encountered each other. This little-known fact somewhat alters our perception of the early Church.[3]

Paul declared in *Galatians* 1.11–17 that he had had a 'revelation of Christ', 'not of human source'. The implication is that the Christ he is talking about is not the actual physical Jesus known to the Apostles but the Apotheosized King who had entered the Holy of Holies in Jerusalem – and had become incarnate as the Son of God. Literalists might assume that Paul had seen the ghost or spirit of Jesus. However, the actual encounter is likely to have been less supernatural. With its haunting exterior image of a man encapsulated within a halo, could it have been the sight of the main codex of the hoard, and in particular its bright shining interior with its extraordinary mystical images, that transformed Paul? (See plate 1: The Face of Christ.) In *2 Corinthians* 3.18 Paul refers to the Glory of the Lord, explaining the radiance as an element of the Christian hope: could this be confirmation that he saw the bright, shining interior of the Book? (The Greek *katopritzo,* meaning 'beholding' or 'reflecting', also translates as looking into a mirror.) When Jennifer and I saw the face depicted on the front cover of the codex, we were amazed; when we saw the interior image with its bright shining face, we were rendered speechless. Given that the codices were found so close to the road to Damascus, Paul's encounter with them seems like a plausible explanation of his vision and his conversion.[4]

In the *Wisdom of Jesus Christ* (*Coptic Gnostic Library* III.4.91), an ancient Egyptian Gnostic Coptic text from the early Christian period, we have a description of Jesus's appearance: 'like a great angel of light,' the writer says, 'and his likeness I must not describe.' In fact, there is a similar description of the Teacher as 'the light' in the Dead Sea Scrolls: 'Illuminated with perfect light' are the words from one of the scrolls (*1QH XXI*); while another says, 'Thou hast enlightened me through thy truth in thy marvellous mysteries' (*1QH XV,* formerly *VII*). A reasonable inference here is that Paul's vision was not unique. Paul's language bears comparison with both the Dead Sea Scrolls and with the Gnostic and Apocryphal texts, which until now scholars have not regarded, for the most part, as first-hand evidence.[5]

*Acts* goes on to describe how, immediately after his terrifying experience, Paul was left blind: he was accompanied to Damascus 'by the men he was travelling with'. These same companions, who had not seen the vision (they only heard the accompanying sounds), had foresight enough to introduce him to a man called Ananias, who happened to be a disciple of Jesus and had been commanded in a vision to seek Paul out (*Acts* 9.7–17).[6] In interpreting this text, we must remember that *Acts* was written from the point of view of Luke, not of Paul himself, who only alludes to this episode in his Epistles; and Luke is writing for a Roman audience, and therefore telling the story in an exaggerated way in order to get his point across and impress his readers.

Along with his community on the flight to Pella (as told in the *Clementine Recognitions*), James brought all his records: the very books that would reveal the true nature of the earliest Christianity. Paul's letters have thus far been recognized as the oldest books of the New Testament. So logic would suggest that if, as Saul of Tarsus, he pursued the followers of Jesus to this place, then the books of James and his community would have been the oldest books of the New Testament. What was revealed to Saul by the hand of James, brother of Jesus, lay at the very heart of the early Church.

Since Paul (formerly Saul) was a man of devout and strident opinions, the presence of Christ's face on the front cover of the codex must have shaken him profoundly, particularly as such graven images were forbidden under the reformed Law of the Second Temple. The idea of actually *seeing God* must have been at once extremely shocking and traumatic. The fact that the books were sealed and then placed in a cave in the middle of nowhere informs us of their exclusivity, with the implication that they were possibly perceived as dangerous.

*The Book of Revelation* mentions the Risen Christ as the sun. The sun, of course, is a bright blazing light – it is a metaphor for the vision of God by those considered pure enough to see it. Throughout the Old and New Testaments, visions are always associated with the idea of shining brightness. When Moses descends the mountain, his face is shining; when Jesus is transfigured he is shining, brilliant, full of light. It is curious how *Revelation* also uses these metaphors in association with sealed books.

We are told elsewhere that Paul knew 'a man in Christ' who was 'caught up to the Third Heaven' (2 Corinthians 12.2–4), and the man is generally taken as a disguised reference to Paul himself. The idea of being taken up into heaven could well be an attempt to capture the intensity of the vision that Paul had experienced. Heaven, or Paradise, is imagined in architectural terms as the Temple; and our codices are full of Temple symbolism. Like Heaven, the Temple was divided into seven sections, from its entrance right up to the Holy of Holies. Paul's ascent is a reference to the mysteries of the third stage.

In his letter to the Corinthians, written originally in Greek, Paul, in reference to his vision, uses the term *ophthe*. This word means 'visionary seeing': in other words, Paul saw something objective that led to his having a subjective experience. The first syllable of the term ophthe means 'optical; that which is seen'. Paul saw something, and it was this that inspired his inner vision, his revelation. At no point does Paul actually state that what he saw was the *physically* resurrected Jesus.[7] In fact, what he describes is having witnessed something that provoked a crisis in him: it is a moment of pure insight, as if he has been struck by lightning.

As if to confirm the point, Paul states in *1 Corinthians* 15.8 that he was the last to see the vision of the Risen Christ; in other words, he had been preceded in this experience of the divine. What he is saying is that he was not the only person to have seen the image – and this chimes with the testimony of the *Clementine Recognitions* that tells the story of the flight of James to Pella. Paul is not as specific in the details. It is almost as if he is admitting that he has witnessed an apotheosis, the divinity of Christ, but in terms more real than any mere vision. This time he had seen something real and solid – and it had shaken him to his very core. The fact that he rose to the Third Heaven is indicative that he had seen something and been transformed by it. Paul has become an initiate; he has been let in on particular secrets, to a specific level. And in order to appreciate this, he would have needed guidance from someone already admitted to the inexpressible truth.[8]

Paul is a great one for speaking in hidden terms. For example, when he says he was blind, the implication is that he was *spiritually* blind. Acts tells us that he was cured of his blindness, by Ananias in Jerusalem. Paul then states explicitly that he left the region and spent three years in Arabia. Exactly what is meant by 'Arabia' is not immediately obvious, because Arabia in the 1st century was a general term for what today we would call the Middle East. However, when we look at Paul's letter to the Galatians, we see that he means the area in and around Pella.[9] Needless to say, upon his return Paul was every inch the enthusiastic convert who had placed himself under the leadership and guidance, however temporarily, of the Jerusalem Church – that is, under the aegis of James.

By the time that these events came to be written down (AD c51–8), Christianity had become a more substantial movement; and the schism between the Hebrew-Christians of James and the Gentile Christians of Paul had already occurred.

Paul does not want to displease the Jerusalem Church. He has therefore written his story in a way recognizable to his Roman audience, and in tune with Roman sensibilities. For Paul himself does not write of his conversion: he merely makes enigmatic references to it. However, the distinctiveness of Paul's message, its divergence from the beliefs of the Jerusalem community, is clearly conveyed by the author of *Acts*.

What offended the 1st-century Jews about Paul was the fact that he had deliberately started to preach that the faith of Moses had actually been superseded. What Paul did next was electrifying. He began preaching his message to a wider audience, beyond that of Judaism. Much to the annoyance of James and the Apostles, he began preaching to the Gentiles, informing them that the dietary laws and circumcision could be abandoned. Furthermore, in his idea that good works serve little purpose, since it is by the grace of God that salvation comes, Paul had radicalized the original message, much to the horror of the community back in Jerusalem. Writing only 10 to 12 years after the Crucifixion, he has become the prophet of a theological construct.[10]

Paul wrote his first letter, to the Thessalonians, 20 years after the Crucifixion, in the early 50s AD. In his subsequent writings Paul, who was to become profoundly mistrusted by the Jerusalem Church, speaks of mysteries and of things that cannot be told. For example, in *2 Corinthians* 12.3–4 he states: 'I know this man who was caught up into Paradise...and he heard things that cannot be told, which man may not utter.' Some have said that this is a sign that Paul actually deserted Christianity and turned it into a Greek mystery religion. However, there is another possibility, and a thought-provoking one: that the teachings of Jesus were not all preserved in the New Testament Gospels. Some were lost; but others were deliberately kept secret and never written down – or so many scholars who take this view have often been inclined to think.

At the end of the 2nd century AD, Irenaeus, Bishop of Lyons, wrote a long work, *Against Heresies*, which is often quoted by scholars and writers alike. However, it is in his lesser-known work, the *Demonstration of the Apostolic Preaching*, that he wrote about the essentials of Christian belief. As Dr Margaret Barker relates:

> The first part of the book describes the seven heavens, the powers and the archangels, the relationship of the cherubim and seraphim to the Word and Wisdom of God and the role of the sevenfold spirit. Furthermore he knew that this teaching had been encoded in the symbolism of the Temple. For Irenaeus these things were the fundamentals of Christian teaching. They are similar to the material in the Book of Revelation, alluded to elsewhere in the New Testament, but not recorded in full. Is it likely that what Irenaeus regarded as the first fundamentals of Christian teaching had not come from Jesus? *And if the teaching about heavenly powers had come from Jesus, why is there nothing, apparently, in the New Testament Gospels?* [my italics][11]

Mosaic Law was still the moral and spiritual foundation of Christianity and Judaism in Ebionite eyes: Jesus was the Messiah, but in this role he was an *angel* of the Lord, the Great Angel, one who had apotheosized as the atonement sacrifice of the people. However, the idea of Jesus being wholly divine was anathema in Jewish eyes, and dangerously so. In a sense, the differences between Paul and James were not over Jesus, but over Jewish Law. The genius of Paul was in seeing Jesus as wholly divine, but in fact this was a small step from the original belief of the Nazarenes/Ebionites.[12]

Given that the situation back in Palestine was extremely tense, most of the Apostles could not quite bring themselves to believe that their former persecutor was now one of their own number, and they treated him with all of the disdain that they could muster. Paul, for his part, decided to do what Jesus himself had urged the Apostles to do – that is, to preach to the wider Israel. Except that Israel in the Pauline sense became a metaphor for common humanity.

However, what was truly disconcerting for the Jerusalem Church, back in Palestine, was that Paul went much further – a step too far, even. He referred to Jesus as God. Not even Peter, the founder of the Catholic Church as designated by Christ, had gone this far: he only ever referred to Christ as a man. Paul's vision had more or less presented him as a super-charged prophet. Paul was making the terrible mistake, in the eyes of the Jerusalem Church, of giving away their secrets to all and sundry without the necessary understanding of precisely what these secrets meant: Jesus was divine, but not as Paul was inclined to see it. Paul, for his part, speaks despairingly of the Church as 'grievous wolves'. However, delving further into the situation between Paul and the leaders of the early Church, we start to see how Paul must have come across to them. Here he was, the new kid on the block, but they suddenly realize that he really has no interest in Jesus as the Messiah, only as the Son of God, eternal and pre-existent. Then, much to their chagrin, he tries to convert them to his view. The thought of Paul telling James, a holy and devout man of significant reputation, that his sibling was divine is really too precious.[13]

Paul was born a freeman and a citizen of Rome. An educated man of his time, he was a speaker of Greek, the lingua franca of the Eastern Empire. That he was a sensitive and intelligent man is easily discerned from his letters, and also from some of the distinct differences that were to arise between him and the Apostles in later years. Although the Apostles too were most likely educated men, their education would, by comparison with Paul's, have seemed mean, and impressive only by the standards of Judaism. Paul, by contrast, was cosmopolitan. He held a wider view of the world, beyond the sharp confines of the Jerusalem Temple. Paul's knowledge and use of Greek were central to his worldwide view.

This is important to remember, because it was under the influence of Paul that the Gospels would later come to be transcribed into Greek, and *out of the context of their original Jerusalem Church settings.* Paul is insistent upon his being Jewish, 'circumcised on the eighth day, a member of the people of Israel, of the tribe of Benjamin, a Hebrew born of Hebrews' (*Philippians* 3.5).[14] What Paul is affirming is not so much his Jewishness as his wider Israelite blood – connecting him with Israel, the old northern kingdom: Israel the patriarch; Israel, *which comprised the tribe of Judah, amidst the other eleven tribes, in the glorious days of David and Solomon.* It was a mite eccentric to pronounce your 'Jewishness' during the worst possible period of relations with Rome, of which Paul was a citizen. To have been an Israelite would have been different: the Romans were sympathetic to the Samaritans, the old community of Israel, and to other scattered former tribes elsewhere; but the Jews were a different matter entirely. What Paul is declaring is his affiliation to what would become a widespread belief – a belief in the Risen Christ.

To understand precisely what this means, it helps to return to the actual nature of Paul's vision, and to the realization that the story, as told in *Acts*, is not unique – and therefore is not as it seems. The name of Jesus means, 'God is Salvation'. As the Son of God, Jesus *is* salvation. To Paul the physical presence of Jesus had apotheosized into the purely divine.

\* \* \* \*

### June 2009: Pulling in a Suspect

The next morning I rang the Colonel. Hassan was now calling several times a day: the harassment was getting intolerable. I had hoped that the

Colonel could assist us with the relevant authorities in the UK to secure some sort of protection. He said he could not make any promises, but would see what he could do, promising to get back to me next week. I sensed the Colonel was angry with Nabil for making him look a fool. He assured me he was going to pull him in again over the next 24 hours. This time they were going to take a firmer hand.

A voicemail message from Hassan interrupted the long afternoon of the summer solstice. He was livid, having finally cottoned on to the fact that we had been to the cave site in Jordan. Just before he rang I received a call from the Colonel informing us that they had held Nabil in custody for three days, but had not been able to get much out of him, except that he had admitted to finding a few coins and other objects from the area, all of which he was willing to give up. Unfortunately, there was not enough proof to make this an international incident. It was while I was on the phone to the Colonel that I noted another missed call from Hassan. This time he had really flipped. I handed the phone to Jennifer and replayed the message Amidst his angry ranting we were just about able to make out: 'You are stupid because you are wrong. The cave is not in Jordan, it's in Syria.'

\* \* \* \*

## Across the Jordan: Nazarenes, Essenes and Ebionites

In the *Infancy Gospel of James* (also called the *Protoevangelium of James*), an apocryphal text, there is the following description: 'A great light appeared in the cave so that eyes could not bear it, and then when the light withdrew a baby appeared.'[15] In *Luke*, Christ is born in a cave, and elsewhere a bright shining star heralds the Nativity (*Matthew* 2.1). Given what we know about Paul's vision, the emphasis on bright light is revealing (cf *Luke* 2.8). The Infancy Gospel would appear to be telling us that the main codex of the collection, along with others, was deposited in a cave. According to the details given in *Acts* and in the *Clementine Recognitions*, the cave must have been located somewhere on or near the road to Damascus. The *Clementine Recognitions* tells of the flight by the early Christian community to Pella in the region of the Decapolis. The Decapolis, on the other side of the River Jordan, was a vast area including within its boundaries the city of Damascus, well to the north in Syria. Both Josephus and Philo tells us that Essene groups were situated throughout the region,[16] and it is likely that the Dead Sea Scroll found in cave 4 at Qumran, the *Damascus Document*, refers to an actual settlement in the region of the cave site – it is references to 'Damascus' within this text that have given the book its name.[17] Long thought to be a code for Babylon or Qumran, it is now becoming quite clear that the 'Land of Damascus' actually denotes the region of the Syrian metropolis.[18]

The *Damascus Document* talks about a character now known to history as the Teacher of Righteousness. The Dead Sea Scrolls tell us that the Teacher was killed – some translations even speak of him being 'pierced', as if by nails. The *Damascus Document* first came to light in the form of two manuscripts in a Cairo *genizah* collection – a *genizah* is a room adjoining a synagogue in which fragments of sacred documents no longer in use have been stored. Fragments of multiple copies were then found at a later date in the caves at Qumran. The texts do seem to be markedly explicit in the details and directions of this region: they speak of a 'new covenant in the Land of Damascus' (following the intimation of the prophet Jeremiah, in *Jeremiah* XXXI.31). The region concerned is the neighbourhood of the Syrian city and the area within its approximate vicinity, even as far south as northern Jordan. In *The Pentecost Revolution*, Hugh J Schonfield gives us a few more details:

> Through the territory, which embraced a fertile belt of country, ran the River Dan, a tributary of the Jordan ... Anciently this had been Amorite country ... to this country, called by the Zadokites the land of Damascus and 'the wilderness of the peoples', had migrated a body of the Jewish Chasidim seeking

refuge from the persecutions of Antiochus IV... This migration
took place in 159 BC after the death of Judas Maccabeus.[19]

This is interesting, as this is precisely the area in which Paul was said to
have had his famous vision – and is also the area in which the codices
were discovered. It is remarkable that the Dead Sea Scrolls should point
not to Qumran, the region where they were believed to have been
composed, but to this more northerly region where so much seems to
have occurred in the early years Christianity. (See plates 25 and 27.)

The 10th-century commentator al Qirqisani, a Karaite scholar,[20]
wrote of a group of people who had hidden their books in a cave. He
mentions that the group, known as *Magharians*, meaning 'cave people'
(Hebrew/Aramaic), lived at or just before the time of Jesus. It is how
he characterizes them that makes them stand out from other sects of
the time, although little is known about the group. The distinguishing
factor is that they believed that the *theophanies* (visions of God) described
in the Hebrew Scriptures refer to a Great Angel, rather than to God
Most High. This angel is said to have created the world. This is
remarkably similar to the doctrines of the Gnostic groups in the first
few centuries AD.[21]

It is curious that perhaps the more important evidence is given in
another of the Dead Sea Scrolls, the Copper Scroll of Qumran (*3Q15*) –
the only one of all the scrolls discovered that is *made of metal*. A reading
of this text suggests that a branch of the Essenes came into more regular
contact with this northern community.

The thing that stands out in the *Damascus Document* in relation to
this group is the expectation of only one Messiah figure – whereas other
communities scattered throughout Palestine had shown an expectation
of two or of dual messianic figures: one priestly, the other kingly:

None of the men who enter the New Covenant in the Land
of Damascus, and who again betray it and depart from the
fountain of living waters, shall be reckoned with the Council

of the people or inscribed in its Book from the day of the gathering of the teacher of the community until the coming of the Messiah out of Aaron and Israel.[22]

However, it is the mention of images, sealed books and books of the Law that really strike us in this text. 'But David had not read the sealed book of the Law which was in the Ark of the Covenant,' we read.[23] The Scroll becomes even more explicit:

> ... but all who held fast escaped to the land of the north, as it says, 'I will exile the tents of your king and the foundation of your images beyond the tents of Damascus.' The books of the Law are the tents of the king [for the 'tent' is the tabernacle, the presence of God in the midst of the people], as it says, 'I will re-erect the fallen tent of David.' The king is leader of the nation and the 'foundation of your images is the books of the prophets whose words Israel despised.'[24]

The site of the community is also made explicit in the *Damascus Document*, which mentions the star prophecy to be found in one of the oldest books of the Old Testament, *Numbers*. This is very similar in style to the way in which the certain of the Gospels (*Matthew* 2.1, *Luke* 2.8) have been composed, giving us a location and then details of the various messianic symbols that appear. In *Numbers* 24 we read: 'I shall see him, but not now: I shall behold him, but not nigh: there shall come a Star out of Jacob, and a sceptre shall rise out of Israel. [...] Out of Jacob shall come he that shall have dominion ...' (*Numbers* 24.17,19). 'Jacob' is a reference to the north. The Gospel sources make it clear that, given the tense atmosphere in Jerusalem, Jesus had to make forays into the city, and into Judea, on a temporary basis – and from a distant location. From *John* 10.39–40 we know that when the threat of his enemies drew close, Jesus took refuge across the Jordan, sometimes for as long as six months at a time.[25] Jesus is also said to reside from time to time in Bethany. The place name Bethany translates as 'house of the poor', and is quite possibly a reference to the Nazoreans. Perfumed oil was said to have been kept there, and if the house was truly poor this single factor would have been highly unlikely – perfume was an expensive commodity at the time. Although the one Bethany we know is across the Kidron Valley in Jerusalem, it is very likely that there were other locations of the same name.

All the elements are here: a close community expecting a single kingly Messiah, whose Books of the Law were sealed. All clues points to the site where the codices were discovered. The area is north of Pella, not far from Lake Tiberias on the Jordanian side. It now becomes clear that Paul's remit was to seek out and harry those groups dangerous to the Temple authorities; it is also clear from other scholarly studies that there were many such groups in this area.

The Dead Sea Scrolls' *Thanksgiving Hymns* (*1QH 7–9*) celebrate the eagerly awaited Messiah.[26] These same hymns speak of the mysterious figure of the Teacher of Righteousness who sees himself as the irrigator in the garden: again this seems to be an explicit mention of the *wadi* (valley) where the codices were discovered, and indeed the codices themselves have scenes of gardens on them. The area some way down into the valley is lush and fertile, with pomegranate groves, olive trees and other fruits. Near by, in a cave, we saw an olive press. However, what immediately strikes the eye upon entering the valley is that a *mikveh*, a ritual bath, guards the opening – the implicit message being that one had to be ritually pure to enter the valley. Just beyond this feature, as we have seen, there is a 1st-century-style sarcophagus.

Equally interesting is the fact that the New Testament mentions all the relevant parties concerned, with the exception of the Essenes.[27] Is this because the authors took it for granted in their readers the knowledge that the Essenes too were waiting for the Kingdom of God,[28] that they were included in the appellation 'Hebrew-Christian'?[29] Epiphanius (AD c315–403), the early Church Father and Bishop of Salamis, wrote that 'They who believed in Christ were called Essenes before they were called Christians.'[30]

Professor Israel Finklestein is also clear on the subject when he says that the Nazorean movement and the Essenes are one group.[31] In the *Book of Judges*, Samson, the great Old Testament hero, emerges from out of a cave. Samson was a Nazirite, so the implication is that Nazarenes (Nazoreans/Nazirites) are associated with caves. Samson was also semi-divine and shone like the sun: in other words, he was full of the Glory of God.

Epiphanius (AD c315–403) in his *Panarion* speaks of Ossenes (Essenes). He also states that the original Judaean Christians, who were generally called 'Nazoreans', were known as *Jessaeans*. (For more on these potentially confusing variants of the word 'Nazarean/Nazorean', see below.) Now, *Jessaean* might translate as 'follower of Jesse', and there is an implication here of the name of Jesus too.

King David, we might recall, was the Son of Jesse, and the Essenes, being the remnant of Israel, saw themselves as the remnant of David's house – that is, of the Kings of Israel. The Greek name for the Essenes was *Essaoi*. Philo Judaeus refers to them as *Essaeans* and makes it clear that this was not originally a Greek word. *Essa* was the Coptic Egyptian for *Jesus* in the 1st century AD. Since this name is cognate with the classical Arabic *Essa* or *Issa* (which occurs in the Quran as a translation of the name Jesus), we have a connection that points to *Essaeans* meaning 'followers of Jesus'. The Essenes and Nazareans are very closely related, if indeed they are not the same sect – for the term Nazarene comes from the Hebrew root *nazar*, meaning 'Followers of the King'.

In Hebrew the term is *nazor* (meaning 'protector' or 'guardian'), which was the title of the King. Another version of the word is *nezer*, meaning 'branch' as in 'branch of the Tree of Jesse'. This tells us that both words are connected: they are puns of each other.

While Jesus, in the Gospels, is reported as being *the* Nazarene, *John* is the only Gospel that mentions that the notice on Jesus's cross included the words 'Jesus of Nazareth, King of the Jews': the other three Gospels say only 'King of the Jews'. What John actually says is: 'Jesus the *Nazoraios*'. Nazareth has an *a* as the second vowel, but this form has an omega, *o*, just as in *Acts* 24.5, where Paul is accused of being a member of the sect of the *Nazoreans*.

*Nazoraios* is most likely to be a Greek word taken from the Hebrew *notzer*, meaning 'the one who keeps/guards the old ways'. This became the general Hebrew term for Christians. In *Revelation* 12.17 the Christians are described as the other children of the woman clothed with the sun (her Son was Jesus), and they are the ones who keep the commandments.

It is highly likely, given the way in which John presents Jesus in the rest of his Gospel, that the notice on the cross meant 'Jesus the *Nazorean*, King of the Jews'. The Hebrew-Christians who settled east of the River Jordan (that is, in codices territory) were called the Nazoreans.[32]

Many commentators believe that the various terms, 'Nasareans', 'Nazarenes', 'Nazirites' and 'Nazareth', were purposefully used by the early Roman Church in order to conceal its true history and confuse seekers after the facts. This has a conspiratorial odour to it – the smell of a strange plot to turn the historical Jesus into the purely theological Christ. However, despite all the different terms, there may in fact be no difference between them. Some scholars might argue that this hypothesis is an exaggeration, that some of these sects are older, and therefore different, from others. The truth is that all these sects stem from a much older, common source; and this would appear to confirm exactly what Epiphanius is saying: that all who believed in Christ were called Essenes. At the time of his writing in the 4th century, the Essenes no longer existed as a sectarian movement. Scholars have assumed that this was because they were utterly destroyed by the Roman legions in the first of the great revolts. However, this view may be only partially correct: there is no reason why they should not have disappeared simply as a result of conversion to the new Messianism. The fact is that they had been awaiting the coming of the Messiah: in his acclamation they had become his first followers – Nazoreans of the Jerusalem Church: the original Apostles.

The Nazoreans (or Nazarenes) and the Nazirites are surely one and the same sect. The Nazirites, whose most famous members include Judah, Samson, Samuel and John the Baptist, kept themselves separate from the community of Israel. They were dedicated to God under the other holy name of Adonai, meaning literally 'My Lord'. The 'Lord' is, of course, a title often applied to Jesus. The Nazirites recognized no prophets after Moses and claimed that the first five books of the Hebrew Scripture, the Pentateuch, were not written by Moses as some claimed.

Further confirmation that Nazarenes and Nazirites stem from the same source comes again from Epiphanius, in AD 367. He writes of a sub-sect of Nazirites called the Sampsaei, whom many scholars and authors, including the 1st-century Josephus, regard as Essenes, who were themselves separated from the Judean community. Furthermore, in a reflection of the persecution of the early Christians led by Saul himself, the Sadducean establishment of the time put a symbolic curse upon the 'separate ones': 'Oh God, send thy curse upon the Nazirites.'[33]

(James too, as the leader of the Jerusalem Jewish believers in Yahshua [Jesus], had taken a Nazirite vow at the beginning of his adult life. He was a Nazorean or *Nazir*, and a High Priest, and therefore entitled to enter the Holy of Holies.)

The Essenes believed that, in entering the community, they were entering into a New Covenant with God (*Essene* being the Greek term for the sect, it would be more accurate to call them the *New Covenanters*). In both *2 Corinthians* and *The Gospel of the Hebrews* (as well as *Hebrews* 8.6) we find the same concept of the New Covenant, an understanding that goes back to Jesus himself. When Jesus poured the cup of wine at the Last Supper, he declared: 'This cup that is poured out for you is the new covenant in my blood' (*Luke* 22.20).

It is curious that one of the Dead Sea Scrolls should mention 'The Cup of the Wrath of God' (1QpHab, XI4–XX12). However, of more interest is the fact some of the codices bear actual representations of the Cup of Wisdom. This points to the feminine quality of Wisdom, as expressed in the Solomonic *Song of Songs* – a concept that we again encounter in the Temple of Jerusalem.

The Essenes called themselves the 'Sons of Light'[34] but according to Epiphanius one of their sub-sects was called the 'Sampsaei' or 'Sampsaeans'. Sampson or Samson is the famous hero of the Old Testament who wreaks terrible things upon the Philistines. In fact, he was a kind of Hebrew Hercules, his myth being the classic story of the hero. Samson was also a Nazirite; and like all Nazirites, he refrained from washing and cutting his hair or beard.

One characteristic aspect of Essene belief is the preservation of the names of God through the angels:

> They swore 'to preserve the names of the angels'. Gabriel, Michael etc were taken from the Hasidim (*Daniel* and *1 Enoch*). There were good and evil fallen angels. The workings of nature were explained by various angels, the lowest classes 'represented little more than personified natural forces'. There were also stars 'heavenly watchers': 'The Essenes also shared with apocalyptic and the whole Hellenistic environment the widespread conception of a *sympatheia* between earthly and heavenly events.' The stars were thought of as living beings and the angels were essentially foreign gods stripped of their power. They became intermediaries for a distant god, and were most influential. Jewish and Hellenistic views could easily be combined.[35]

In 1972 Dr José O'Callaghan, a Jesuit priest, Professor of Papyrology at the Biblical Institute in Rome and Biblical scholar, published his analysis of a fragment of a scroll from the Dead Sea hoard known as *7Q5*, which tells the end of the story of the feeding of the five thousand. He did not set out to find a papyrus of the New Testament from Qumran, but that is how things turned out. In brief, scholars had found it difficult to identify the fragment at all, until Dr O'Callaghan realized that the only thing it could be was a fragment of the Gospel of Mark – the earliest fragment of any Christian literature. His findings were dismissed as 'impossible' until the intervention of the Reverend

Professor Carsten Peter Thiede, who supported the controversial claim.[36] Until this time, it had been considered absurd and even naïve to imagine that the caves of the Dead Sea could hold documents of the early Christian communities.

If the identification is correct, then it raises the issue of the probable conversion of the Essene community to the new Messianism as well as the wider community at large, just as mentioned by Epiphanius.[37] The circumstances begin to tally with certain aspects of the story raised in the Clementine literature, which is now largely seen as the writings of the early Ebionite community (*Ebionim* translates as 'Poor Ones', bringing to mind the mysterious words of Jesus, 'Blessed are the poor in spirit', in *Matthew* 5.3); also with certain of the Hebrew texts, such as *Esdras*, which were composed at around the same time by the same community.[38]

It is interesting to realize also that the various problems that have arisen about the timing of the Crucifixion, especially with regard to when the Last Supper was celebrated, may be resolved if the Essene calendar is taken into consideration: they celebrated their own Passover meal on a Tuesday evening, not on a Thursday, as was the tradition outside Essene rule. Beyond this, there is a strong possibility that the Last Supper and the first Christian Pentecost were celebrated in an Essene guesthouse in Jerusalem. As Otto Betz and Rainer Riesner have made clear, it is exceedingly likely that the first Christians and the Essenes were living next door to each other in the city.[39] Moreover, the likelihood is that there was an overlap in cultural and religious communication. As Betz and Riesner say, 'Both Philo (*Apology* I) and Josephus (*Jewish War* II, 124) agree in attesting that there were Essenes throughout Palestine.'[40]

The Essenes, Nazarenes and Ebionites, if they were not one and the same thing, were at the very beginning of the Jerusalem Church pretty much of one voice, and had yet to split into their disparate elementary sects.[41] Epiphanius was writing over 200 years after these events and by his time these sects were already at each others' throats – with even Epiphanius taking the odd pot-shot. In the opinion of Petri Luomanen of the University of Helsinki, his description of the Nazarenes as a sect apart from the Ebionites is a complete fabrication, one invented to put a gloss on an otherwise inconvenient fact: that the original Church still existed. Such a view ran counter to the generally accepted history of the Church. The evidence resides in the lack of any mention by Epiphanius' great friend, St Jerome, of the two sects being divided.

Jerome in fact makes a very interesting observation about the Nazoreans:

> The Nazoreans understand this passage [*Isaiah* 31.6–9] in this way: O sons of Israel who deny the Son of God with a most vicious opinion, turn to him and his apostles. For if you will do this, you will reject all idols which to you were a cause of sin in the past and the devil will fall before you, not because of your powers, but because of the compassion of God. And his young men who a certain time earlier fought for him, will be the tributaries of the Church and any of its power and stone will pass. Also the philosophers and every perverse dogma will turn their backs to the sign of the cross. Because this is the meaning of the Lord that his will take place, whose fire or light is in Sion and his oven in Jerusalem.[42]

Jerome is reflecting the early restoration aspect of Jesus's teaching: that Israel has long gone astray, that the Nazoreans represented the true Temple. The idea that many of the Essenes may have converted to Paul's version of Christianity is reflected in the fact that *Acts* was written from a largely Pauline perspective. However, as Professor R P C Hanson points out, in *The Acts in the Revised Version*, 'we cannot be absolutely certain that *Acts* was recognized and used widely by Christians before AD 170'[43] when *Acts* is first mentioned by Irenaeus (AD 130–202), Bishop of Lyon and early Church Father. The gap between the writing of *Acts* and its eventual use by Christians has led scholars to conclude that the book was subjected to much editing in the 2nd century. There are two extant copies of it: one, from Alexandria, dating from the 5th century; and the other a later Greek text. Textual differences between the two reveal the extent of later editing.

It is thought that the Ebionites/Nazarenes used an altered *Gospel According to the Hebrews*. Their text was the original text of Christianity: it is rumoured to have been based on an original Hebrew version of the Gospel of Matthew,[44] but what is of interest is the fact that this Gospel, from an assessment of its theology, is based upon the very ancient tradition of Wisdom, in the original Israelite sense of the term, with its references to the Garden of Wisdom – the subject of many of the images to be seen upon the codices. Yet again the story of Jesus is harking back to the days of the First Temple where Wisdom was present as the feminine dimension of God.

In Hebrew the term *nazor*, as we have seen, means 'protector' or 'guardian', which was the title of the King. The Nazoreans were protecting something, by concealing it – in caves, away from the polluted Temple. *Nasaraia* means 'keeper of secrets', while *nazar* means 'truthful'. The Nasareans were keepers of secret truths, and we now know that Jesus himself shared may of those secrets with the three pillars of the Church: James, John and Peter.

In *The Apocryphon of James* we find the following passage on the subject of secret knowledge:

> Since you asked that I send you a secret book, which was revealed to me and Peter by the Lord, I could not turn you away or gainsay you. But I have written it in the Hebrew alphabet and sent it to you and you alone, but since you are a minister of salvation of the saints, endeavour earnestly and take care not to rehearse this text to many – this that the Saviour did not wish to tell to all of us, his 12 disciples. But blessed will they be who will be saved through the faith of this discourse.
>
> I also sent you ten months ago another secret book which the Saviour had revealed to me …'[45]

This 'James' is the brother of Jesus, the one who led the Christians out of Jerusalem and settled them 'beyond Jericho'.

In *2 Maccabees* (2.2, 2.4, 2.5), written late in the Maccabean period (c176–37 BC) and edited in the 1st century, the prophet Jeremiah describes the hiding of the Ark of the Covenant not far from Mount Nebo). This is in the region where the 1st-century cave settlement was located and the codices discovered. The implication in terms of the dating of *Maccabees* and reading between the lines is that the Covenant was somehow renewed, reformed or rewritten (I owe this insight to a private communication from Dr Margaret Barker, June 2011). This is confirmed in the writings of Epiphanius, who in his *Panarion* states:

> But by now some will have replied that the Gospel of John besides, translated from Greek to Hebrew, is in the treasuries at Tiberias. It is stored there secretly, as certain converts from Judaism have described to me in detail. And not only that, but it is said that the book of Acts of the Apostles, also translated from the Greek to Hebrew, is there in the treasuries. So the Jews who have been converted to Christ by reading it have told me.[46]

Epiphanius was no fan of the Ebionites, denouncing them as heretics; however, he states that the Ebionite *Acts of the Apostles* was different from the canonical one. It is likely that the 'treasuries' he is talking about is actually the cave site, which is quite near Lake Tiberias. It is unlikely to have been a solely Jewish treasury: in the first place, such a treasury would have been located in Jerusalem or in another major centre. Secondly, Epiphanius is writing here about Jewish converts to the new faith, a faith that still adhered to the Mosaic Law. This has to be a Hebrew-Christian site – and the only one that fits the required geographical coordinates is the recently discovered site of the codices.

Epiphanius speaks of Josephus of Tiberias, a Jewish convert to

Christianity, referring to a treasury as a *gazophylacium* (*gaza* is Hebrew for 'treasure'):

> As many had different notions about this treasury because of its seal, Josephus plucked up the courage to open it unobserved – and found no money, but books money could not buy. Browsing through them he found the Gospel of John translated from Greek to Hebrew, as I have said, and the Acts of the Apostles – as well as Matthew's Gospel, which is actually Hebrew. It was for this reason that Joseph converted to the new faith – and became a count on the orders of the Emperor Constantine – the most famous convert of them all.[47]

\* \* \* \*

## Codices and Scrolls

The most powerful and defining moment in the entire corpus of the Old Testament is the moment when Moses ascends Mount Sinai and meets God. The Lord gives Moses the Ten Commandments – twice. The first set of tablets is smashed by Moses, angry at the sight of his people worshipping idols in his absence. Then Moses ascends the mountain again to collect two more stone tablets.

The description of the stone tablets is intriguing. In *Exodus* 32.15 we have a description of them being written upon by God Himself *on both sides*. This is odd. In the period concerned, as well as in the circumstances, the idea of two stones tablets being written upon on both sides is unlikely, although not unprecedented.

If we take the Mount Sinai episode literally, and try to imagine Moses carrying the tablets down the mountain, in realistic Charlton Heston fashion, one thing strikes us immediately: one stone tablet would be very heavy, and two would be doubly heavy, as well as extremely ungainly. The thought of Moses struggling with them down the mountain is faintly ridiculous. Unless, like our books, they were 'little'. The image of Moses, descending Mount Sinai, with his face shining and the look of wrath in his eyes, is iconic. If we reduce the size of the two tablets of the Law, we suddenly make him look diminished.

Quite why the Christians used codices for their secret wisdom, and not scrolls, remains a mystery; but perhaps this episode of the Commandments offers us a reason. Moses brought the old Covenant down from the mountain in a form not too far removed from a codex, or rather the pages of a codex. Jesus brought in the new Covenant to supersede the old. It is when we look further at the stories of Jesus and his parallel in Moses that we begin to see that one follows the tenet of the other, even when it comes to the Covenants, old and new.

*Deuteronomy* 5.22 tells us that the two tablets, though engraved by the hand of God himself, actually came 'from out of the fire, the cloud and the deep darkness'. This is revealing, for these are exactly the conditions that describe the smelting of ore. Tablets so described seem more likely to have been made of metal than of stone – and of course metal, in its natural state, comes out of stone.

Sinai is well known among Egyptologists as the place where there was copper aplenty, as well as silver, lead and other minerals. There are ancient metal mines and metal workings all over the mountain, which raises another question. While Moses was encamped atop Sinai, the people down below became restless and decided to make a golden calf. Given that the Children of Israel were believed to be former slaves and therefore poor, where did they get the gold from? Furthermore, if they did have access to gold, where did they smelt it? *How* did they smelt it? From just a few observations it is easy to see that the ancient story is incomplete: it is no more than half a story.

At this point, another thought comes to mind. To these peoples, it was the Word of God that held the true power. This is what the experience of Mount Sinai is all about. The Word of God was final, non-negotiable. To people at the end of the 2nd millennium BC, or the Bronze Age, there cannot have been many, if any, examples of a word or words cast in metal. Hence, like Saul of Tarsus seeing the Book of the Face for the first time, such a sight would have seemed miraculous: the phenomenon would have appeared awesome, unalterable, divine. Stone was malleable: any markings on it could be chiselled away; or, as Moses had already proven, stone could be smashed. Metal, however, was a different proposition altogether. It was cast in a molten state, possibly into a stone mould, where it was then set. The word could not be altered, scratched out, or chiselled out. It was immovable: it could not be edited.

The Word of God came down from the fiery mountain, ablaze with the wrath of God. This was just the kind of thing to unify a collection of disparate tribes – in this case, 12 of them, on the run from the King of Egypt.

Jewish scrolls, like those from the Dead Sea, are one-sided, not two-sided. It is books that have a tendency to be double-sided throughout. What we have here, arguably, is another convincing connection between our documents and the famous Tablets of the Law. The books could easily be seen as being a continuation of the Law as passed to Moses on the mountain – except that in this case it is not the old Covenant but the new that is affirmed. Both Covenants, it would appear, originally came in book form.

There is a strange and intriguing echo of this in the story of the discovery of a cache of manuscripts in AD 819 in the area of Jericho, not far from the shores of the Dead Sea. Timotheus, the Bishop of Seleucia, tells how a group of Jews from Jerusalem sought, in the light of the discovery, admission to the Church.[48] This episode tells us that such texts, once found, could be read at the time, and also that the effect of them was to confirm the early role of Jesus not only in the early Church but in the general life of the Temple as a whole. We are beginning to find confirmation that Jesus was thought of as the prophet predicted by Moses, the original Law-giver.

According to *1 Maccabees* (14.18), a book considered apocryphal by the Protestant Church, metal, particularly bronze, was the material of choice for important and official Temple documentation: the text refers to writing on bronze tablets in the mid-2nd century. A small number of scrolls were found among the cave-site hoard but they are far outnumbered by the codices. The use of scrolls and codices together suggests an early date for the settlement – a date when there was still a preference for using both of these media, as opposed to just one. By the end of the 1st century, Christians were almost exclusively using the codex format for their texts. However, with the exception of the Copper Scroll of Qumran, metal scrolls or codices have rarely if ever been found. A search of academic libraries worldwide in the months after the hoard came to light revealed no suitable comparator against which the codices could be analysed.

That leaves us with the question, why lead rather than copper? Because lead was easy to use and malleable; and, if you were on the run or an outcast, the turn-around from raw material, no matter what shape it was in initially, to finished product was swift. Lead requires a lower melting point. It was symbolic of poverty.

Lead is called a base metal, and was primarily used in the ancient world for piping for water ducts and the lining of sacred mortuary caskets. The ancient Egyptians used lead in the manufacture of glass and also in make-up, particularly in eye-liner. The Phoenicians too were well versed in the ways of metallurgy, and passed on their secrets to the Greeks, Romans and ancient Hebrews. *Job* 19.24 tells us that lead was inscribed upon with iron tools. Lead really came into its own with the Romans: there was a super-abundance of it.

Lead is found in ore along with zinc, silver and copper. Galena, the main lead source mineral, can contain up to 86.6 percent lead; most lead ores also contain significant concentrations of silver. This last point fascinated me, as our find also included a few copper items and, as we shall see, silver too. It is perhaps ironic, given the context, that the vernacular term for an ingot of lead is a 'pig' (and, indeed, raw iron is 'pig iron'). I wondered whether perhaps this usage was derived from Roman anti-Semitism, as a slang term hinting at origins in the Middle East.

The primary use of lead was to prevent the decay of bodies or sacred artefacts. Perhaps our artefacts were cast or beaten onto lead, and not on papyrus or parchment, for a number of reasons. Foremost among them, conceivably, was the preservation of something of extreme importance.

> 1 Behold, I will send my messenger, and he shall prepare the way before me; and the Lord, whom ye seek, shall suddenly come to his temple, even the messenger of the covenant, whom ye delight in: behold, he shall come, saith the LORD of hosts.
>
> 2 But who may abide the day of his coming? and who shall stand when he appeareth? [see *Revelation* 6.17] for he is like a refiner's fire, and like fullers' soap:
>
> 3 *And he shall sit as a refiner and purifier of silver* [my italics]: and he shall purify the sons of Levi, and purge them as gold and silver, that they may offer unto the LORD an offering in righteousness.
>
> *Malachi* 3.1–3 (*King James Version*)

Nine separate analyses on the metal of the codices have revealed that it is riddled with impurities – to such a degree that it is, in the words of one analyst, hardly worthy of the name 'lead',[49] although these impurities do point to a possible Roman-period origin. Moreover, further analyses have revealed that in some cases the metal of the books had had most, but not all, of its constituent silver removed – there is still a very tiny but telling amount remaining. In the 1st century the Romans developed techniques to extract most of the silver from lead. It was only in the 20th century that technology was created to remove *all* the silver. However, although the tests revealed that at some point, possibly in antiquity, the metal had been re-melted, it is too early to say whether the extraction process was performed by artificers within the early Romano-Christian period. But the important question was, from whence did it come?

One of the analysts, named Mark, who investigated the surface corrosion of the metal, was also a top-level civil engineer working in the defence industry. (See plate 5.) Mark's observations have been critical in assessing the appropriate direction of analysis. Commenting on the various metal reports, Mark told us that the tests had analysed the sample from the viewpoint of pure lead: this was a grave error, since the radioactive half-life of various of the other impurities present would have blocked a proper reading of the lead. In other words, the assessment of the date of the metal has been obscured not by the samples taken from the codices but by the technique used to assess them.

Mark told us that he is almost certain there are plenty of heavy metallic elements present in the lead of the codices, and it is these that we should be assessing – not the lead itself, as testing and dating lead are extremely problematic. Unfortunately, no tests have yet been developed whereby a specific date could be gleaned. Any dating will come almost solely from the analysis of language and iconography. Mark believes that what is needed in order to demonstrate the antiquity of the codices is not a metallurgist but a nuclear physicist: he thinks that the tests thus far have been too one-dimensional.

At the very time he was making this observation, the Department of Antiquities in Jordan was undertaking atomic tests. In late 2012 samples were taken to the Jordanian Atomic Energy Commission by the Director of Antiquities, Professor Ziad al-Saad. The results, in so far as he was given access to them, were very positive indeed. Unfortunately, owing to internal politics, he has since been barred from receiving any further results.

Further to this, Mark also said that the place from where the metal was sourced would also most likely demonstrate significant factors not seen in the samples tested so far, thus supporting its antiquity. A sample of metal from the site, before its preparation into lead sheeting, would be far more useful than samples from the codices themselves at this stage: the radioactive aspect could be viewed properly, and the impurities and carbon content too could be correctly assessed. Working with a group of scholars and experts, he concluded that the books demonstrate too heavy a corrosion to be anything other than 1st-century in origin. At a conference in Oxford in 2011 a comment was made to the effect that metal could easily be corroded by the simple expedient of camel urine and sand. This created much merriment on the part of Mark, who assured us that such deep corrosion could not have been caused by camel urine: uric acid, if present, would have been picked up in the other analyses; that and the fact that the calcium carbonate on them is far too severe for this even to be taken seriously as a proper question – unless the camels in question were drinking a lot of hard water. Mark said that the samples when taken from different places on the books would show different results because the balance of impurities would not be evenly scattered throughout the metal plates comprising the books.

Further to this, the analyses of the samples so far submitted to testing demonstrated all the characteristics that would come from metal obtained from deep within the earth, in volcanoes. Any metal sourced in this way would be a lot more radioactive than smelted ore, and would show in the tests as such. Isotope 210 would almost certainly be still active, as it decays over a longer period of time than other isotopes lower down the range – indicating that that metal may well have had its origin in volcanic emissions deep in antiquity. Analysis continues. When in 2012 tests were performed at a university in southern England, the presence of isotope 210 was marked, suggesting an origin within the last 100 to 150 years. The problem with this analysis was that it tallied neither with the evidence of the cave site environment nor with the assessment by scholars of the iconography and language, which both suggest great antiquity. Both these aspects are unique, but within the boundaries of possibility for the 1st century. Until further excavation and analysis are carried out at the cave site, where organic remains from the 1st century remain to this day, we must wait for further confirmation.[50]

In the early stages of scholarly debate, over wine and conversation, the era of Moses had been mentioned – the 2nd millennium BC.

Mark referred to the chapters in *Leviticus* about Moses being both *on* and *in* the mountain when he received the Ten Commandments, and a thought struck him as obvious and yet important. He said that a cursory trawl through his research and the metal analyses to date drew his attention to particular bunches or globules of pure but highly radioactive metal, mostly comprising lead found inside or at the rim of volcanoes, left there after the metal had been spewed out in volcanic eruptions – these pure globules then coalesced with bigger bunches of other metals and mixed together to certain degree as they cooled down. *Leviticus* seems to be describing this very process. Such clumps of metal would have been accorded a higher status, as being extremely holy in themselves – to fashion books out of them would make the books even more awesome in the eyes of all concerned. This was a significant point. Meteoric metal, or metal that was volcanic in origin, was held to be a most priceless commodity in early-late dynastic Egypt (c4000–c500 BC). This idea translated to Israel and Palestine in the early 2nd millennium – the time of the exodus of the Israelites from Egypt.

A further point to mention is the fact that rock-based ores have already lost part of their radioactive half-life, by virtue of already being in the rock: whereas molten metal from *inside* the earth is still very much active.

This raises a further point: that the silver content in the lead is at Roman levels – the evidence being that most of it was removed in the refining process.[51] This suggests that either the lead was re-used and then refined, or was refined at source. What is the likelihood of the lead coming from the crater of an active volcano and then being refined to the point of having its silver content removed?[52] The evidence so far would suggest that it was indeed refined at the later Roman date (as the volcano was by this time dormant) or that the artisans who created the books were the ones who worked also for the Romans, and that it was they who made the books, having taken the lead from its mountainous source and refined it at the place of extraction.[53]

If the lead *was* refined after its original smelting, to make codices that were intended to express the New Covenant, then the first time around the lead expressed the Old Covenant. The metal was already deemed inestimably sacred. It cannot have been any old metal, but must have been specifically 'holy' metal. Pots, pans, cooking utensils and old lead coffins, used as a source of the lead, would have stigmatized the books and the community that made them: such a history of previous use would had left a stain on what they had become. Furthermore, given the stigma attached to such origins, we can conclude that the metal was very probably non-Roman in origin. To the Hebrew-Christian community, this would have been a paramount consideration. The fact that the books are holy strongly suggests that in their primal incarnation they were something very considerable indeed.

In the summer of 2013 an analysis by Tim Blades raised some further interesting points. (See figure 13.) Tim has appeared on the acclaimed British archaeological TV series Time Team. He is a professional jeweller and artificer in metals for specialist markets; but he also has a sideline in challenging received academic opinion, particularly with regard to practical issues of jewellery and metal-making in antiquity. Tim was able to describe exactly how the codices had been made. Molten lead, when poured, will have a uniform thickness, but few of the codices were cast directly into moulds. They were beaten into pre-created moulds. Lead is very soft, and although the metal of the codices is extremely brittle and fragile, 2,000 years ago it would have been quite malleable. Tim used an old mangle from pre-washing machine days to demonstrate this. Each mould would have been created either in wet clay or even in solid rock, and then sheets of newly processed lead applied to the mould and hammered in. Such a process could only have produced three copies of each artefact at most, since the mould would have become quickly worn down, even in rock. Apparently, this 'printing' process came from jewellers, whose application of mould and metal was able to produce a limited 'print run'.

At the end of the process, the lead sheets would have been cut to shape, and this is very much evident in the codices. The signs of wear on the surface of some of them was a result of a secondary or even tertiary impression being made in the same mould. Each hammer blow would have brought great stress upon the forms incised in the mould, thus wearing the mould away with the repeated impact. The incidence of higher carbon ratios within the sealing rings used to bind together the thin sheets of the codices was indicative of the lead used for them being hardened over an open fire and then beaten into shape. The carbon would have been residue left over either from the fire or from the hammers with which each sheet was beaten.

Later that day, at home, we tried to hammer a coin impression into lead. It was extremely difficult, as the coin kept moving in response to each hammer blow – the result being ill-defined and fuzzy on account of accidental movement or slippage. The impression was *not* deep – the conclusion being that a coin impression would need either very soft lead and a good grip or clamp to hold it in place, or else a coin with *very* deep marking. These ancient metal-workers were clearly very expert indeed. My work with Tim showed that the codices were well planned in the preparation and well made: this was not the work of desperate amateurs.[54] With this in mind, the symbolism of the codices becomes all the more significant: almost nothing on them is the result of haphazard design.

Some additional remarks on the symbolism of lead are now called for. In alchemical terms, lead is famously transmuted into gold. This reflects neither pure science nor pure spirituality, but a world-view that saw no clear separation between the two. Every single jot (from the Greek, *iota*) of the world's phenomena had meaning and significance. What we are looking at here, in our consideration of the lead, is a language, one that illustrates the text to a greater degree than even a modern book illustration could hope to achieve. Therefore it has to be of significance that lead in the ancient Jewish world was symbolic of the god, Yahweh (sometimes misspelled 'Jehovah'). Perhaps the use of the metal here represents an element of transformation – spiritual and perhaps cultural. Could it be that the community that created the books was implying this?

It is curious that in the Roman Catholic Church, Papal Bulls too were made of lead. Obviously there was a highly ritualistic purpose in the use of such a metal, quite apart from its convenient malleability. In the private apartments of His Holiness the Pope there is a considerable collection of books comprised of lead from varying periods. Certain Gnostic groups also made books from lead, continuing what must have been a long-established tradition.[55]

\* \* \* \*

## July 2009: Closer to Home

After his latest noxious barrage, we had been deliberately avoiding listening to Hassan's messages, leaving them sitting in the message box of our cell phone. However, we had been advised that we should keep a permanent record of them as evidence, in the event that he actually followed through with his acts of intimidation, which at the time we still doubted. We bought a cheap cassette recorder and listened to them for the first time. The last one, however, was startling: 'David, you must know that the fire was started on purpose.' He seemed to be referring to the fire near our military vehicle in Jordan.

It was time to put in another call to the Colonel. Following Hassan's latest string of messages, we had contacted Charles for advice. He said it was really up to the JMI to intervene on our behalf, and recommended that I put more pressure on them, pointing out that it could be very embarrassing for Jordan if anything were to happen to us. I thus informed the Colonel of Hassan's latest batch of messages, as we were worried that some of his Bedouin friends, who we knew lived in London, might be recruited to track us down – whether rational or not, this was our personal fear. Although non-committal, the Colonel promised again to see what he could do, adding that it could be complicated.

I then told him that Hassan had referred in one of his voicemail messages to the fire by our vehicle. The Colonel asked if we could send him a copy of the recordings. He promised to call us as soon as he received the recordings, as he thought this latest testimony just might provoke a reaction.

\* \* \* \*

## The True Gospel

In 2009 images of the codices were sent via Dr Margaret Barker to a colleague and former member of the Dead Sea Scrolls team: a very eminent professor and former president of the Society for Old Testament Study, based at a university in the north of England. (Owing to the political nature of religious archaeology and the controversies surrounding other Hebrew and Christian discoveries, we have agreed to maintain the professor's anonymity.) His initial response was extremely encouraging, confirming initial suspicions that the language of the codices was indeed Palaeo-Hebrew.

His letter of 25 June 2009 outlined his support for the discovery and gave a preliminary assessment:

Dear Mr Elkington,

Thank you very much for sharing with me some of the images that you have of the objects from the Jordanian cave. The items are very striking, but their very unusualness exposes my ignorance in certain respects. However, here are some comments for what they are worth.

First of all, dating. On several objects there is use of alphabetic script. Several of the letters have good counterparts in the Palaeo-Hebrew alphabet of the period from approximately 200 BC to AD 200, though some of those forms also persist into later times. Sadly, several letters have shapes that are unknown to me, though they have affinity with a few of the shapes used in the Qumran cryptic and Nabataean alphabets from roughly the same period. Because of the sealed notebook format of some of the materials, I would be inclined to think that these items are from the later part of the period when such formats might be more common. A date in the 2nd century AD would not seem out of line, but would need verification from other sources; a slightly later date cannot be ruled out at this stage. The existence of the Qumran Copper Scroll, engraved in the 1st century AD, and many Roman documents engraved on metal, especially manumission texts, means that there is no problem with the use of metal, at this relatively early date, though the way the letters are made from metal rather than engraved is distinctive.

Second, deciphering. It must be remembered that in several Semitic alphabets of the time several letters can be confused with one another: *waw* with *yod*, *dalet* with *resh*, *bet* with *kaph*, and some others too. The uncertainty in interpreting some of the letter shapes combined with the possible confusion between some of the letters makes for great difficulties in deciphering the texts. The letters on the image of the large menorah possibly read *'-l-y k-the-m*; the first letter is possible, the second and third just about likely, the fourth possible, the fifth and sixth more certain [*sic*] [...] The sooner some of the inscriptions can be put in the public domain, the sooner we may know what some of these objects may be about. Palaeo-Hebrew was used consistently by Samaritan Jews from the Second Temple period onwards, but it was also used as a nationalist symbol by the Hasmonean rulers on their coins in 1st century BC, as also slightly later by Jewish rebels in the first and second Jewish revolts; in addition it appeared in several manuscripts found at Qumran, mostly for the books of the Pentateuch and Job. However, in all those instances the scripts are normal and fairly easy to read.

Third, the symbols. From what I have seen so far, it is clear that the symbols of the Jewish cult loom large. These symbols may relate the objects to the temple in Jerusalem, or to Mount Gerizim, or some other cultic site. One of the objects seems to have both the *lulab* and *ethrog* on it and so may be associated with the Jewish feast of Sukkot (Tabernacles). Another seems to have depictions of the temple architecture, walls and a portico or some structure. The use of such symbols does not necessarily mean that the temple to which they refer is still standing. The Samaritan temple was destroyed at the end of the 2nd century BC, the Jerusalem temple in AD 70. It is entirely possible that some 2nd century AD group used these symbols as a way of recollecting the significance of the temple. Those assembling such symbols could be Jewish, Samaritan Jewish, Jewish Christian, or Christian. *The apparent absence of any Christian symbolism might suggest that the items, if Christian, were early, before any Christian iconography had become fixed. Or that they are copies of early items.*

*It is well known that forgeries of various kinds abound in the region where these were found. However, to my mind the strange character of these items would seem to indicate that they are not forged. It is important that images of these objects and the circumstances of their discovery are made public as soon as possible so that a wide range of experts can offer their opinion, so that we can be more secure about whether these things are really from the period that they seem to belong to.*

*I commend your work in trying to have these things published expeditiously and all your endeavours with the Jordanian authorities.* [my italics]


Yours sincerely
[name withheld at author's request]


This initial assessment was understandably cautious, but it was very positive and offered significant clues. (See plate 14.) The expert confirmed, for example, that the script is definitely alphabetic script. In Semitic languages there are no vowels; therefore good educated guesswork has to be called upon, in order to begin the decipherment.

This is such a specialized field: the number of people in the world who can translate these specific dialects is very small indeed.

> ... from what I have seen so far, it is clear that the symbols of the Jewish cult loom large. These symbols may relate the objects to the Temple in Jerusalem or to Mount Gerizim, or some other cultic site. One of the objects seems to have both the *lulab* and *ethrog* on it and so may be associated with the Jewish feast of Sukkot (Tabernacles). Another seems to have depictions of the Temple architecture, walls and a portico of some such structure. The use of such symbols does not necessarily mean that the Temple to which they refer is still standing. The Samaritan Temple was destroyed at the end of the 2nd century BC, the Jerusalem Temple in AD 70. It is entirely possible that some 2nd century AD group used these symbols as a way of recollecting the significance of the Temple. *Those assembling such symbols could be Jewish, Samaritan-Jewish, Jewish-Christian or Christian. The apparent absence of any Christian symbolism might suggest that the items, if Christian, were early, before any Christian iconography had become fixed.* Or that they are copies of early items.' [My italics]

In order not to complicate the assessment, and because of his extremely busy schedule, the professor had not been shown the face of Jesus on what we think of as the 'central codex', the Book of the Face (or the Book of Seven Seals): so he was not to know that the codices definitely were not Jewish, even if they did have certain recognizable Jewish symbols on them. In later discussion with Professor Philip Davies, we came to the realization that there was another, very significant clue. The Temple depicted was not that of the Samaritans on Mount Gerizim – it was, quite simply, never *that* elaborate. None of the other factors seemed to tally with Gerizim as well as they do with the Jerusalem Temple: particularly the idea of Sukkot.

Sukkot is fascinating. It was known as the Feast of Booths or the Feast of Tabernacles, but its most ancient form was the Feast of the

Messiah. Dr Margaret Barker informed me, shortly after I received the professor's letter, that the nature of this feast was rewritten a very long time back by anti-monarchists in the years after King Josiah's reforms, c600 BC, no doubt fed up with Jewish misfortunes under the monarchical system. (Sukkot is the plural of the Hebrew word *sukkah*, which was a booth or hut reminiscent of the type of booths used by the children of Israel during the 40 years of the Exodus. Associated with the Sukkot are the four species which according to *Leviticus* should be waved during this festival, including *lulavim* (palm branches) and *etrogim* (as we have seen, an *etrog* is a species of citrus akin to an outsize lemon).

The Hebrew-Christians recognized Jesus as the one whom Moses predicted would come and supersede the Law of Israel. This gives the Feast of the Messiah an extra-special significance. For it more than confirms that Jesus was a King.

The book *2 Esdras* was considered to be in origin a Hebrew-Christian text, primarily on the basis that the writer or writers assert God's rejection of the Jews and go on to describe a vision of the Son of God. However, what is of particular interest is the fact that it describes a series of books, 94 in all, which God has commanded the elders to make: 24 books of the Tanakh (the Hebrew Canon) plus 70 secret works. It is the 70 secret works that contained the real wisdom – and they were to be hidden away (*2 Esdras* 14.37–47). Now, 70 books were rumoured to have been hidden away by James and his community – in the region of Pella.

Why should we believe that these books were metal? As we have seen, *1 Maccabees* tells us that all Temple documents were in metal. Further confirmation of the use of metal for texts came from a Professor of Greek based in Germany. Apparently members of the Greek mystery cults were given little metal plates that acted as a kind of identity card or entrance ticket. Is it not plausible that the credit-card-sized lead tablets inscribed with a Palaeo-Hebrew text might perhaps have served this purpose, or some other similar purpose?

Palaeo-Hebrew in the 1st century was a liturgical language, rather like the use of Latin in certain institutions today. Latin confers a sense of history and thus respectability, even though it is (sadly) long past its sell-by date for ordinary purposes. The Palaeo-Hebrew on the codices tells us that the documents are liturgical, and therefore important. They also, through this language, forge a link with the past – the original stone tablets in the Ark of the Covenant are likely to have been written in a related form of archaic Hebrew.

Analysis confirming the nature of the script was sent to me by another eminent professor, also a former president of the Society for Old Testament Study, in late 2010:

> Dear David,
> ... I think the script is probably Hasmonaean Hebrew, in particular the script they used on coins (2nd–1st century BC), and the six-letter inscription beside the Menorah I think reads אלך בתם, *yelek be-tum*, 'He will walk uprightly' from *Proverbs* 10.9.[56]
>
> How is the menorah related to the other inscriptions? Is it all one big design?
>
> Hope that helps. It's a start anyway.
>
> All good wishes
> [name withheld by mutual agreement]

*Hasmonaean* is another name for *Maccabee*, after the kings of the 1st and 2nd centuries BC.[57] The passage in *1 Maccabees* about writing on metal is spot on. *Yelek be-tum* is a direct reference to the Resurrection.

According to the late Dr Hugh J Schonfield, resurrection 'is not the same thing as spirit or soul survival of death. It has nothing to with wraiths, ghosts, or spirit materializations. Resurrection means the "getting up" of one who has been lying down as a corpse, the reanimation of a dead body ...'[58] On this point, Jewish resurrection teaching is quite blunt. However, there is another situation to which the term 'resurrection' might be applied. Given that God is the main force behind the idea of resurrection, and the principle that is held to re-animate the corpse, and indeed the maker of the body in the first place, it might seem surprising to discover that there is another form of death: the kind that comes when confronting God, *tête à tête*. This is what almost happened to Moses atop Mount Sinai – except that God decided that he would turn his back to Moses, allowing him to see only a portion as he passed by. And yet Moses still came down from the mountain with a shining face, owing to his extreme close proximity to the Holy One.

It is immediately after this episode in *Exodus* (33.23) that the Ark is built, a portable tabernacle, to accompany Moses' people in exile towards the Promised Land. Upon entry into the Promised Land, a temple was constructed to give God a permanent home, a place where the Ark could be stored and where God's eternal presence could be felt.

Following in the footsteps of Moses and Aaron, the first High Priest, the officiating High Priest at the Temple confronted the presence of God once a year, on the Day of Atonement, Yom Kippur. One other person did this too: Jesus, the last King of Israel, who also happened to be the Great High Priest. Parting the curtain, he would have entered the most terrifying place in Israel, encountering the dreadful presence of God in the Holy of Holies. The self-command to 'walk upright' in the terrifying presence of God was a reference to the offering of the physical body as a sacrifice for the people; as well as the rising of that body and its standing tall in the presence of God. What *Proverbs* 10.9 is telling us is that the High Priest was fearful before the sight of the Holy One. We can almost see him muttering the phrase to himself as he makes his obeisance and leaves with just the correct amount of haste.

The *Damascus Document* tells us that the Teacher is to 'walk in the Laws' until the 'standing up of the Messiah of Aaron and Israel in the last days' (*CD XII*). In this instance, *standing up* is synonymous with 'coming', 'return', 'rising' and 'resurrection'. According to this account, the Messiah of Aaron and Israel will (or did) 'atone for their sins' (cf *Hebrews* 4.14–5; 5; 67.11; *et seq*).[59]

In another Dead Sea text, *The Manual of Discipline* (as well as in the *Damascus Document*), the Teacher of Righteousness is associated with 'the time of the preparation of The Way in the wilderness' by the 'teaching of miraculous mysteries' (compare *Isaiah* 40.1–3). *The Way* is a term used frequently in the Gospels to describe the teachings of Jesus, particularly in *John* 14.6. 'I am the way, the truth and the life,' says Jesus. As for *wilderness*, this brings to mind the area where the codices were found.

In the years since the discovery of the Dead Sea Scrolls, much has been made of the similarities as well as the differences between these texts and the Gospels, as well as the letters of Paul. Scholars have been understandably cautious about confirming a positive link between the two. Now, however, with the discovery of the lead codices, and because we have common statements with reference to 'standing uprightly' and clear references to the symbols seen all over the codices, there is more than a shared similarity. And then there is the face of Christ on the front cover of the main codex – a clear link to the identity of the expected Messiah.

This last point is underscored by a reference that Paul makes in his letter to the Galatians, when he complains of double standards within the Jerusalem Church brethren. Paul adds revealingly: 'I saw that *they walked not uprightly* according to the truth of the Gospel' (*Galatians* 2.14) [my italics]. This is the language of the inner Temple and its mysteries: Paul is referring to Christ's actions inside the Holy of Holies as the King/High Priest of Israel. Much more was revealed to him on the road to Damascus than the vision of Jesus on the main codex. (See plate 1.) At the heart of the revelation was the fact that the Resurrection had taken place deep inside the Temple, in the Holy of Holies itself – the extension of the incident with the money-changers described in the Gospels (*Matthew* 21.12–13; *Mark* 11.15–19; *Luke* 19.45; *John* 2.13–17 ) but taken no further by the Gospel authors, for fear of discouraging their Roman audience, as well as inciting Roman antipathy. The fact was that the Resurrection was a purely spiritual affair, not something physical. It was an event of profound spiritual importance – more so than the Crucifixion which would take place *after* the Resurrection.

There is another telling echo of the Dead Sea Scrolls in the letters of Paul. In his second letter to the Thessalonians (*Thessalonians* 2.7–8) Paul states: '… the Lord Jesus will slay him [the deceiver] with the breath of his mouth.' This closely echoes an expression to be found in another of the scrolls: 'He shall slay the wicked with the breath of his lips.' (*The Great Isaiah Scroll*, 1QIsa). Given that the Dead Sea texts existed in Paul's day, he must have been well aware of their existence, or at least of the sect that produced them. He possibly understood their implications too – he was in the act of persecuting the people who wrote them after all. And he must also have been in possession of the fact that, ultimately, what was stated in the Dead Sea text we call the *Damascus Document* derived originally from Scripture. Did he go in pursuit of James already suspecting the truth of the Resurrection – its true nature and the location where it actually happened? Was the fact that Jesus's Resurrection was remembered as a historical and theological event in the main codex the straw that broke the back of Paul's resistance to the inevitable: that Jesus truly was the Messiah of *all 12 tribes* of Israel?

If so, this might explain a reference Paul makes that has become familiar to us in Christianity. The following words were found on a fragment of manuscript from the Dead Sea Scrolls discovery (Cave 4): 'And Thou didst renew for them Thy Covenant, founded on a glorious vision and the words of Thy Holy Spirit.' That the codices originated *during* the life of Jesus and not *after* is clear: they use Old Testament texts and references to show who Jesus is; whereas, if they had come later, they would have referred to him more directly and in the past tense, and this would have given them a testamental feel. Instead, what we have bear all of the hallmarks of messianic documents.

Looking back at the reference to *Proverbs* (see above, p182), the *tum* of *yelek be-tum*, meaning 'uprightly', is an important part of the Solomonic Wisdom tradition. On the codex in question the letters appear under a seven-branched menorah. There is an allusion not only to *Proverbs* 10.9, as we have seen, but also to *Daniel*. The first three letters under the menorah are a third-person verb: 'They shall shine with righteousness' ('in integrity', which is why it is around the menorah, symbolic of Wisdom, the lost feminine figure from the first Temple: 'righteousness', 'integrity' and 'uprightness' are three interpretations of the Hebrew word *tum*, meaning very much the same thing). The 'V' shaped letter is actually a 'G'. This reflects the prophecy at the end of *Daniel* 12.3. 'Those who are wise, who shine' (*nogah*, 'to shine'). This is Qumranic – and is to be found in the hymns of the Dead Sea texts.[60]

*Daniel* is the last book of the Orthodox and Catholic versions of the Old Testament, and certainly the most messianic of texts.[61] In *Daniel* 12.4 secret words are kept in a sealed book. This is reflected in *Revelation*, where the Book of Seven Seals is described in terms of the secrets it contains. The passage from *Daniel* is revelatory:

> Those who understand shall shine like the brightness of the firmament, and some who are righteous, like the stars of heaven forever and ever. As for you, Daniel, close up these words and seal the book until the time of the end, until many are taught and knowledge is increased.
>
> Then I, Daniel, looked and behold, there stood two others, one on this riverbank and the other on the other riverbank. One said to the man clothed in fine linen who was above the water of the river, as he held up his right hand and his left hand to heaven and swore by Him who lives forever that it would be for a time, times and half a time. Thus when the dispersion is ended, they shall know all these things.
>
> Although I heard, I did not understand. So I said, 'My lord, what shall be the end of these things?' He replied, 'Go your way, Daniel, for the words are closed up and sealed until the time of the end.'
>
> *Daniel* 12.3–9 (*Orthodox Study Bible*)[62]

This is a description of the Davidic Messiah: the linen dress is that worn by the Messiah on his entrance into the Temple. The fact that the passage also refers to being 'over the river' is very significant in terms of the early Christian community who lived across the Jordan – at the cave site. And then of course there are the words 'concealed and sealed up until the end of time', a clear reference to sealed books.

The word *tum* is also used in *Psalm* 101. As Dr Margaret Barker puts it, 'This Psalm, which many scholars regard as the "manifesto" of the Davidic kings in Jerusalem, is a statement of how the king would rule: "Only they who walk in uprightness shall serve me." *Tum* is a very significant word for the Messianic kings to use.'[63] The Davidic king was the model for the Christian Messiah, and so for Jesus.

The texts in question are: *Psalms* 101.2, 'I will give heed to the *way of integrity* [Hebrew *tum*] and 'I will walk with *integrity of heart* in my house'; and *Psalms* 101.6, 'He who walks *in the way of integrity* shall be my servant.' This is an important indication of the context of this inscription in terms of Jesus being the Suffering Servant Messiah.

The express use of Palaeo-Hebrew script has some precedents in the Old Testament. As Professor Robert Hayward writes, 'Melkizedek uses the holy tongue, Hebrew … "the language of the house of the Sanctuary".'[64] However, in 2 *Esdras* 14.42 specific mention is made of scribes using characters and a script that *they did not know*.[65] This can only have been Palaeo-Hebrew. Before looking at this in detail, it helps to recollect a comparable passage from *Revelation*. 'In John's vision,' in the words of Dr Margaret Barker, 'twenty-four elders with their incense joined with the four living creatures and myriads of angels to worship around the throne (*Revelation* 4.2–5 and 14). The elders must have been priests, because, in the temple tradition, only a priest was allowed to offer incense – and they stood among the angels ...'[66] These 24 elders are to be seen in 2 *Esdras* 14.42. They had been commanded to make 94 books, 24 to be given to the elders and 70 to be hidden away in a cave.[67]

A late 1st-century text, *The Shepherd of Hermas*, also makes reference to a *little book*. Hermas was a Christian prophet in Rome around AD 100.

Twice in the text the little book is described as a feature of Hermas' visions. In the first vision a woman dressed in shining garments reads from the book. In the second she gives Hermas the book, so that he is able to make a copy. It is during the copying that he makes the following statement: 'I copied it all, letter by letter, but I could not work out the letters of the alphabet, *sullaba* ["syllables"].'[68] Was this because the lettering was liturgical Palaeo-Hebrew?

In response to an email sent to another eminent authority in May 2009, I received the following:

David,

These images are extremely interesting. Are they the front and back covers of the same book? I can't quite tell for sure.

One thing I noticed right away is that there is a total of 24 sealing rings on the three opening sides, with 6 rings on the top, 12 on the long side, and 6 on the bottom (the other two being binding rings). It is unlikely that the number 24 would be accidental, especially in a Jewish-Christian setting. One thinks immediately of the 24 elders in the book of *Revelation*, who are mentioned by name exactly 12 times in the book of *Revelation*! These 24 elders sat around the throne of God in the heavenly Holy of Holies (as these rings are placed around the sides of these plates). The 24 elders testified that the Lord was worthy to open the eternal book with its seven seals (*Revelation* 4.4, 5.5), and these 24 also seem to perform the functions of approving entrance into the holy space (7.13) and announcing the time of judgement (11.18), which would be official functions associated with their roles as official witnesses in the place of glory. Each seal would normally be associated with one witness.

Speaking of numbers, I suppose it might also be significant that each of these 2 plates has 6 fruit-laden palms, for a total of 12.

Margaret has told me a little about the current situation. Let me know if I can be of any small help to you with these very intriguing artifacts.

(name and university withheld by mutual agreement)

Perhaps the most unexpected source for the random quality of the lettering on the codices comes from *The Gospel of Truth*, a non-canonical Gospel believed to have been written by Valentinus in the 2nd century (AD c140–80).[69] Dr Margaret Barker puts it clearly in a private communication of June 2013:

Dear David,

I am so pleased that you have had a chance to look at this text [*The Gospel of Truth*]. I needed to consult it for the passage towards the end, on the Name, and I confess that I had not read the earlier part of the text for some years, and certainly not since the codices were found.

The *Gospel of Truth* is a title given by modern scholars since the work itself has no title in its Nag Hammadi text. 'Gospel of Truth' is simply the opening words of the text.

It is generally attributed to Valentinus, born in Egypt in the early 2nd century but most famously a Christian teacher in Rome who had hopes of being chosen as the next bishop. It was only later detractors who condemned him as a Gnostic. There is certainly nothing Gnostic in the *Gospel of Truth*.

Much of it reads like an exposition of the Last Supper teaching given by Jesus and recorded in *John* 13–17.

The problem is that *John* is a Greek text, and Jesus would have given this teaching in Hebrew; and the *GofT* is in Coptic although Valentinus would have written in Greek.

This means that a lot of technical terms have been transmitted from Hebrew to Greek to Coptic and almost certainly suffered in translation.

That said, the *Gospel of Truth says that the book is the face of the Father* [my italics], and the mysterious book is a deposit of truth that is not read as consonants and vowels but as letters that convey the truth. The *GofT* says this book was also taken and opened by Jesus after he had been put to death, which means that it is the little sealed book depicted in *Revelation* 4–5 and then as an opened little book in *Revelation* 10.

This is all very interesting.

M.

Of *The Gospel of Truth*, a senior Roman Catholic Cardinal, Jean Daniellou, said: 'When the Gnostics made these statements they were imitating something that actually existed – they were imitating secret books that were known to have existed.'[70][71] This is really quite astonishing in its relevance to the codices. We now have a perfect description of the random nature of the lettering: they reflect the situation of scribes who were transmitting the most sacred secrets, beyond their own understanding.

The Gospel goes on to reveal that we can be saved by a book – the Book of the Living:

> For he revealed it as a knowledge...of the living book...Each letter is like a complete truth, like a complete book...the Father having written them for the aeons in order that by means of his letters, they should know the Father...[72]

This suggests that Valentinus knew that Jesus's secret teaching had been recorded by means of a code, such that only initiates knew what each letter stood for. *The Secret Book of James*, written in Coptic around

AD 100–150, suggests that this writing was a Hebrew script – certainly Valentinus' insistence on distinguishing the consonants from the vowels could imply this. Conceived as a repository of secrets, in a sense the book is a symbol of knowledge, *gnosis*.[73]

Jesus is mentioned in *The Gospel of Truth* as enlightening those who need enlightening 'because of forgetfulness'. We have to ask: forgetfulness of what? First Temple practice perhaps? 'Jesus appeared, put on that book [that is, he wrote in it], was nailed to a tree…'[74]

To be considered alongside the codices are other artefacts found at the cave site: bowls, cups, linen wrappings and amulets, one of which Hassan wears. This amulet is beautiful, with a clear depiction of the seven-branched menorah on it, surrounded by letters. The letters seem to be of the archaic Hebrew alphabet, but many are hard to identify, owing to both the condition of the artefact and the apparently random positioning of the lettering. One remarkable reference the amulet carries, in Palaeo-Hebrew, is *MSTN*, which means 'of Satan.' This is interesting, since the Book of Revelation makes reference to the same term. The word is quite specific: we do not find reference to 'Satan' all that often in the Christian Scriptures. The passage in *Revelation* describes the 'synagogue of Satan'. However, the synagogue reference may well be the result of a mistranslation into Greek (*Revelation* 2.8). The original term in Hebrew is *quhal*, which is the word for 'Temple', and this too appears to be in the inscription on the amulet. *Quhal* is also mentioned in the Dead Sea texts. This would appear to tally with the cry of Jesus during the episode of the money-changers: 'My house shall be called a house of prayer for all nations  but you have made it a den of thieves' (*Mark* 11.15–18). It is a cry against the corruption at the Temple, against the perceived blasphemy of allowing money, the root of all evil, to be exchanged in the environs of the holiest place in Judaism.[75]

\* \* \* \*

## Fake, Forgery, Accusation, Evidence

*The ignorant man sins with a clear conscience.*

Rabbi Hillel (1st century AD)

The question is: if the codices are fakes, then what are they fakes of? The official stance of the Israel Antiquities Authority (IAA) is to instantly dismiss a discovery as fake until more evidence is brought to light (unless it is an officially sponsored archaeological excavation). This is a practical approach and thoroughly understandable, as the market is flooded with false antiquities. Policy wins out over appraisal: such was the case with the codices. However, there was a further difficulty, in that we were led to believe they had been smuggled across the border from another country[76]: under international law the hoard belongs to the King of Jordan.[77] In dismissing the find, the IAA undertook no analysis and did not take any samples from the codices with which to come to their conclusion. Certain of the items were apparently shown to 'experts', but they were not well versed in this particular, highly specialized field. The experts were not named.

In an initial report on the codices,[78] the IAA stated that 'there are cases in which forgeries are carried out on antique materials. In the instance under discussion, it is possible to make use of lead slabs that originate from ancient coffins or similar items. In this manner, laboratory tests may determine that the material is indeed ancient while the find is in fact a forgery.' In a separate communication[79] they added that the books 'are a mixture of incompatible periods and styles, engraved on lead and tin plates.' There are a number of problems with these opinions. One is that the organization does not give any examples of which lead slabs had originated in ancient coffins, because no laboratory tests, of the kind they describe, were conducted. The IAA have pronounced on the codices without having taken any samples from the books and tested them. No information was offered as to how any 'ancient lead slabs' in Hassan's possession might have undergone a process of modern forging.

No guidance is given on such matters to inform archaeologists ever on the lookout for fakes. As for the remarks about the way in which the codices were made, it hardly inspires confidence when quite obviously the items concerned are *not* engraved, and the material is not, *and never has been*, tin. This is a major error for an institution with the reputation of the IAA. At the conclusion of their brief report, the IAA declare that they wish to have no involvement with the hoard. This struck the group of scholars as somewhat bizarre.

The conclusion that the IAA has been premature in their remarks is borne out by the corrosion analysis on certain of the codices: they demonstrate that the specific patterns of corrosion can only have been produced over very long periods of time. All this suggests that the books are not modern forgeries – and that they are certainly worthy of further study.

Professor Philip Davies has written:

> The necessity of such a default arises because most forgeries have the purpose of claiming to be something valuable, of assuming the identity of a plausible ancient artefact, such as a royal or tomb inscription or a pomegranate decoration. Bible-related forgeries usually have the aim of verifying or supplementing information provided in the Bible ... And of course forgery is rarely (and where technical expertise is applied, never) devoid of the profit motive.
>
> The so-called 'Jordan codices' are not, in the sense just defined, forgeries, because there is no genuine equivalent that we know of that they can be said to replicate.
>
> It is perhaps inevitable that the word 'forgery' has been widely employed, but disappointing, because it is an inaccurate description, and because many of those who use it know that but do not care.[80]

In other words, why fake something unique? If someone were manufacturing an artefact with the intention of selling it, would it not make more sense to make a copy of something already in existence, something known and verifiable?

When the discovery was first brought to light, an immediate check was carried out of various academic libraries across the world, both physical and on the Internet. The result was that the lead codices were found to be entirely unique. It would seem to be an odd forger who would conceive of creating something almost completely unknown and unique. This leaves the question of whether they might be copies of existing artefacts. A look at the thriving black market suggests that, in virtually all cases of discovery made by Bedouin in the district, recently discovered objects were already on the market at the time newly minted forgeries appeared – and in many cases the discoveries in question had already been authenticated by scholarly authorities. The fakes had copied the originals. Exceptions to this rule are the cases of both the James Ossuary and the Jehoash inscription. With regard to the former, many eminent and experienced scholars have stated on record that they believe the James Ossuary to be genuine. It is the inscription that is in doubt: this is an antiquity that has been added to in order to derive a false impression.[81] The Jehoash tablet was widely believed to be a forgery until, sensationally, the Israel Antiquities Authority recently decided that it wanted to keep it for the state after all. The legal wrangling continues.

Some of the codices have been found in the marketplace of Amman, capital of Jordan, and handed in to the Department of Antiquities because people did not know what they were: hardly the response that forgers would require to sell their merchandise.[82]

To create an artefact that implies a Hebrew-Christian origin when there are no other documents of this kind in existence would be foreign to the mentality of a forger. If someone did 'make' the codices with the intention of deceiving, then it must be recognized that their knowledge of the Palaeo-Hebrew language is world-class, professorial even. Only a handful of people in the world can speak or read this archaic language: so how were they able to get it grammatically correct if the inscriptions are unique? Could they have copied it from an pre-existing document?

If so, then such a document is in itself entirely unique and would be extremely valuable. So why has it not appeared in scholarly circles or on the market before now?

As a matter of course, a worldwide search of inscriptions was undertaken and the end-result, after a year of waiting for the results to be collected, was that nothing could be found that demonstrated that the script on the codices had been copied.

On another point, as scholars will attest, the Temple symbolism is such that only an expert with knowledge of the latest academic papers could have created it. To take one example, the depiction of the menorah alone has created controversy since we announced the discovery of the hoard: the two lower branches have been mistaken for eighth and ninth branches, whereas they are in reality the branches of the almond tree, implying the menorah's role as the Tree of Life. In terms of Temple symbolism, this is very specific knowledge: the association of tree and candlestick is an important link to the archaic past, little known until now. The codices depict a demonstrable schemata in their symbolism. This is unparalleled in the records. Certain early references speak of sealed books and of Temple symbolism, but these references are few and, with the exception of the *Revelation*, obscure. Although mentioning sealed books, *Revelation* in any case does not make it entirely obvious that such sealed books would contain Temple symbolism – nor could anyone have expected them to be made of lead.

In *The Gospel of Truth* we find the following lines: '[the] living book [was] revealed to the aeons, at the end, as [his letters], revealing how they are not vowels nor are they consonants, *so that one might read them and think of something foolish,* but they are letters of the truth which they alone speak who know them...' [my italics].[83]

One scholar of early Christianity instantly dismissed the hoard as fake, even though he had not studied or even seen any of the items. Others have stated with confidence that the language is 'gibberish' – one self-appointed expert even appeared on the US radio programme *Coast to Coast* to give precisely this view. The problem for him was that he was unable to recognize the script as Palaeo-Hebrew, let alone read it. Others (including a commercial Aramaic translator) have stated, with skewed logic, that in their view the writing is Aramaic, and that because they cannot decipher the script, the content must be nonsensical. Hebrew is very different from Aramaic, and the difference is easy to see. Vociferous condemnation has come from those least qualified to offer an expert opinion; vested interests have rushed to lend their support.

From the outset Hassan paid a lot of money to have tests undertaken to help him to understand quite what the codices were – and what date could be ascribed to them. This is not behaviour one would expect of someone out for a fast buck. In the summer of 2011 we were informed that 500 forgeries of the codices were going to be released into the Jerusalem market. Some months later, one of these came to light, and images of it were sent to the group of scholars working on our analysis. In their view, even at a cursory glance, this was an obvious fake. The lead was still very blue and exhibited a sheen indicating newness. The limescale stains were concentrated only in areas where the raised lettering and illustrations were to be found. The lettering was unintelligible. The symbolism was modern and stylized. There were no signs of corrosion in the lead.

There is also the question of provenance. The cave where the hoard was originally discovered was tracked down and, following a preliminary survey, has now been declared an official archaeological site dating from the early Christian period: proven archaeological features back this up.[84] The valley is very extensive and will take many months to survey. An initial assessment by the Department of Antiquities revealed a number of caves that have yet to be unsealed and excavated.

When Hassan came under pressure, he tried to justify his possession of the hoard by relating the story of how the artefacts belonged to his grandfather, who conveniently found them before 1948 – before the foundation of Israel – thereby implying that the ownership is his by inheritance. The story changed many times: one version was that the find was made in northern Jordan. To his credit, Hassan's main objective had been to see the books safely ensconced in a museum. His attitude to the cave site was less impressive: he viewed it as a place of profit and buried treasure – which potentially it was. He was at pains to point out that the caves have organic remains in them – and bodies. He was specific about the state of the bodies and described in minute detail the grave cloths they were wrapped in – for example, one of them, held apart from others in the cave, was wrapped in the skin of a crocodile. Hassan and his friends were careful in their approach to the bodies: anxious not to be obtrusive, in awe of who and what they might have been. Hassan also mentioned that the codices, when not found in niches, were wrapped in linen cloths and placed in sealed lead boxes – which were discarded when the artefacts were removed from the cave.[85] All in all, this attention to detail, some of it verifiable, does not strike one as the testimony of a forger.

There have also been confident claims that all symbols on the codices are to be seen elsewhere, that they are crude copies made by forgers. This assertion is inaccurate. As one of our experts puts it, 'the most complex pattern, which appears several times and seems to have been the main symbol of whatever the codices represent, has not been found elsewhere.' One commentator has stated that the seven-branched menorah on all the codices is uniquely wide and semi-circular and that, as comparable examples have not been seen anywhere, it must be a forgery. Such tortuous reasoning seems to be *de rigueur* among those who are seeking to condemn the discovery. Many of these voices have been challenged and the gauntlet has yet to be picked up by them in response to a whole range of specific questions.

The question of the manufacture of the hoard was raised in another conversation with archaeo-jeweller Tim Blades. Accusations had been made that certain motifs on the codices demonstrated that they had been stamped into the metal, that such a practice illustrated how easy it would be to fabricate the collection. Tim was very dismissive of these comments, pointing out that they were typical of those who had not put their thoughts into practice. As we have noted earlier, if the codices were 'stamped', then they would show that. To stamp a piece of metal is easy, but the stamp would have to be of quite some depth in order to leave a deep imprint, as on the codices. The image of the face has been confidently identified as a 'stamped coin imprint' but, as Tim and others[86] have pointed out, there is no coin in existence that has such a deep relief of an image upon it. (See figure 1.)

We have already looked at Tim Blades' comments on how the metal was cast in moulds (see p174). Beyond this, the faces are larger than those on any known coin from the period. As Tim was at pains to point out, 'each page has been individually made as a whole and then the lead beaten into it'. His observation is borne out by the slight differences in the writing of the script and variations in the quality of the symbols: they are similar, but not the same. Tim stated that he had never seen metal, let alone lead, in this appalling condition before. He too had performed a brief search, and saw nothing to confirm the accusation of forgery. Reflecting Mark's comments, he could see that the bleed-through of impurities was something that no forger could possibly fake even with modern techniques.

The metal on some of the codices is in a very fragile condition – especially that of the binding rings. These have been found to contain more carbon than the metal plates of the books, which has served to make them more brittle as the years have gone by. Corrosion analysis has revealed that impurities in the metal have, over many centuries, escaped from the metal matrix and chemically reacted with the surrounding metal: with the result that there are corrosion holes in many of the books, as well as many cracks and crevices. Some of the pages have flaked. At a macro level, crystalline growths can be seen. Where iron has emerged, rust stains are detectable. Significant levels of iron, copper, tin, zinc, manganese as well as silver, antimony and other elements were present in the samples taken for analysis at a number of laboratories.

The Jordanians have performed a number of tests, metallurgical and atomic, that have had positive results, though the results have been suppressed. In an independent report written specifically for the

Government of Jordan, by a private analyst hired by us, the following comment is made:

> There are many impurities in the metal and evidence of iron and copper from visible corrosion products ... Dendrites and crystalline growth ... show the grain formation within the metal as the objects cooled from the molten state. Various effects are visible across the collection but are most obvious on the reverse of the cast images of the face [...]
>
> Many types of corrosion have been at work during the life of these objects. These include standard oxidisation of lead to produce a grey oxide that makes the metal inert and almost prevents further corrosion. There are also many complex examples of different corrosion products that have built up to varying thicknesses across the objects.[87]

A curious observation made in this report is that there is a surprisingly large quantity of iron in the material, which is indicative of particles of solid iron trapped within the molten lead. This 'is more difficult to explain because of the substantial difference in melting points of lead (327°C) and iron (1,535°C).' The report makes it very clear that the quality of lead differs from sample to sample, from pure to very impure. This indicates a variety of different procedures in the creation of the books.

In some instances where binding rings had been applied, the pages had over time been compressed. There was also evidence that the books had been piled up in a small confined space – the lead boxes that Hassan described. In one example, observed at the Department of Antiquities in Amman, such was the compression that stress had more or less torn the front page from the spine at the front. (See figure 4.)

> In the case of the Main Codex the sealing all around was so tight that between the pages there are areas where air was completely excluded and the pages have stuck together. The

freshly opened book showed bright shiny lead across the centre of the inner pages and impressions of the designs from the facing page having been pressed into the reverse of the pages with faces. Areas of corrosion and patination around the edges show where air and possibly moisture has penetrated between the pages. Photographs of the edge of the sealed Main Codex confirm how tightly crushed together the pages were.

There are many types of corrosion present on the books: galvanic, crevice and stress corrosion. We were shown a piece of lead by our analyst: he asked us to test its malleability. Pure lead is soft and not unlike plasticine. Having bent it back to and fro, it was easy for us to see that it was in good condition. At this stage we were told that the piece of lead had come from the roof of a local church: it had been there for at least 200 years if not more, yet there were no cracks, no flaking and certainly no holes. Looking close up at the images, we could easily make out star-shaped cracks, particularly in the region of the binding rings, and some in the centre of the pages.

Galvanic corrosion has occurred in some of the pages of the books. This is occurring within the microstructure of the metal and is caused by impurities and different metallic elements having different potential. When there is an electrolyte present, such as moisture or water, this sets up miniature electrical circuits within the object itself, with one metal becoming an anode (positive side) and the surface corrosion layer, impurity, or other metal becoming a cathode (negative side) within the cell. The electronic circuit then migrates ions of the metal and eats away the parent metal over time. This has occurred with areas where iron is present in the structure, but is also evident with the lead and copper within the structure. In some areas there are many small holes formed, whilst in others the whole thickness of the metal has been completely eaten away.

Lead does not corrode quickly. It corrodes slowly – the reason it has been used for many centuries for roofs, guttering, plumbing and cooking pans.[88] The report continues:

> The erosion of lead through drips of water takes several hundred years, as evidenced by church roof material. Georgian and Victorian lead does not show anywhere near the level of hardening, cracking, flaking and corrosion as these, which suggests the objects to be much older than the 19th century. The mineral deposits, calcification and concretion show the same features as are found inside broken limestone and within limestone caves – which are known to build up over thousands of years. Similarly the crystalline oxides of lead in the thicker lead tablets look like they have come straight from the earth's crust – in mineral form, rather than this being refined (smelted) lead. Bi-metallic corrosion and galvanic action between the different impurities and components (pages and wire bindings), which are very slow processes in lead, also indicate that the objects have aged over centuries.

To corrode copper and iron is relatively easy: a forger can use acids to create a false patina. However, in the case of lead, corrosion is a much more time-consuming process. Furthermore, the application of acid to the metal would also have erased any crystalline traces from the surface, presenting a more uniform appearance. The report goes on:

> The corrosion within this collection of objects has built up over time resulting in extensive loss of material and build-up of significant hard and layered oxidation and other corrosion products. ... The stability of lead oxide and its ability to create a thin protective layer on the surface that prevents further corrosion mean that it would be exceptionally difficult to artificially re-create the range and extent of corrosion witnessed in this collection of objects.

In conclusion the report states:

> The main reason that it would be exceptionally difficult and expensive to fake these items is the sheer variety, density and disposition of metallic and mineral substances, corrosion products, erosion, accretion, hardening, cracking, flaking, crystallization and rejection of impurities from deep within the metal matrix.

The initial outlay required in order to age-falsify lead in terms of patina, corrosion and cracking, while at the same time retaining the crystalline deposits on the surface (thus ruling out the use of acids), would be, in simple terms, massive. As Tim Blades pointed out: why would a forger bother?

\* \* \* \*

### June 2009 – 2010: The Year of Dread

It had been two weeks and I still had not had a response from the Colonel. I put in a call to the Royal Office and spoke to Samih, only to be informed that his office was just an intermediary in the process: 'I'm afraid it is the JMI who you need to speak to regarding security services.' Neither side would take responsibility. I put in another call to the Colonel, who was decidedly reticent. For some reason, our request for a simple letter, asking for confirmation of the fact that we were working with them, seemed to have become a complicated issue. The Colonel promised to approach the General and call back tomorrow evening his time. Bureaucracy, it would seem, was the same the world over.

Following further upsetting messages, Jennifer and I were unnerved enough that we agreed it was time to contact the police, with or without the support of the JMI. Two heavily armed Special Branch liaison officers arrived at 7.30 the following evening to be briefed. We were offered round-the-clock security for 48 hours and advised that the local police should take our metal objects for safekeeping. Trustingly, we handed them over.

Just five minutes before the police were due to arrive to discuss the case further, another message was received from Hassan: 'David you must never mess with the Pope or with Jesus.' It was curious terminology coming from him. He was obviously still receiving his clerical visits.

Jennifer and I spent a good part of the day giving statements. There was a SWAT team ready in the event of our receiving a visit. This time the police took our cell phone to monitor incoming calls, as well as record any possible voicemail threat that may occur. We were informed that a bulletin had been issued to all port authorities to stop any attempt by Hassan to attempt to enter the UK.

In addition to Hassan's continuing stream of messages, we received an email from Boaz, via Noam, in legal jargon threatening 'severe action' if we continued to be active on the codices front. The email stated that we had no permission to use their property for any purpose, asserting intellectual property rights. We were also asked to pass their instruction on to others who might be working with us on the find. Boaz was positioning himself as a co-owner of the codices, knowing full well that neither he nor Hassan had any legal right of ownership.

In the ensuing months we learned a great deal about Israeli jurisprudence and its anarchical procedures: disregard for evidence, judges easily swayed by highly paid and often corrupt defence lawyers, seemed to be all too typical. Moreover, the IAA is closely aligned with the District Court of Jerusalem, as well as the Shin Bet or Israeli Secret Service and the police. We felt despondent about the chances of anyone in authority in Israel ever taking us seriously over one of their own.

Meanwhile, as a mother, Jennifer was starting to get worried about Alex. Hassan had mentioned him in some of his ramblings. How far would he go? I tried to reassure Jennifer that Hassan and his posse had no idea what Alex looks like, but she was not convinced and reminded me of the photographs Allen requested to take of her and Alex when he came to lunch. I called the police and Jennifer urged Mr Jolley, Alex's housemaster, to warn the school to be on its guard. It was surreal.

Then we found out by chance there was a rumour running through Melksham police station that I was a fantasist and a fraud. I could not understand this, given that the police had heard the messages themselves.

Meanwhile, a police officer leading the enquiry had taken the tablets, without my knowledge or permission, to the British Museum. Dr Irving Finkel, the specialist with whom he consulted, deemed them to be forgeries. Dr Finkel is a well-respected historian in his field: Mesopotamian cuneiform. These books were written at least 2,000 years *after* the emergence of cuneiform. Without rigorous metal, linguistic and historical analysis provided by experts in the field, one can only speculate.

Hassan also targeted Alex when he answered the phone at home. We did not bother reporting these calls to the police; however, I did retrieve the artefacts from their custody.

When I arrived back home, I opened the envelope and inspected the tablets. One of them had been damaged. There was a distinct bend, forming a ridge on the upper left-hand corner. Deemed to be fakes, they had been treated with disdainful irreverence: as valueless pieces of scrap metal.

By early December, there was a definite sense of a finale being played out. We had for a long time been wondering what Hassan and his cohorts would get up to next. However, the next incident came from an entirely unexpected source. Without our knowledge, going against a signed non-disclosure agreement, the publishing house that had commissioned my research on the discovery had contacted the OMSC lab that compiled the metal analysis. Unwittingly, a can of worms had been opened. The metallurgist who compiled the initial report contacted Allen. Word flew around in double-quick time. Shane, now living in eastern Europe but still in constant contact with the others, emailed our UK editor claiming that I had no right to publish a book and that I did not even know what the discovery was. He made his own claim on the intellectual property, saying: 'we would like to approach the open market with world-class authors and filmmakers attached. We will be seeking to sell the rights for these either as a package or separately.' He had our own publishers in his sights, but fortunately they saw through the pretence, particularly when they tried to phone him and reached a defunct number. However, there was a definite sense that our publishers now wanted to back out.

After a week of silence, the telephone messages started up again. Boaz joined in, mentioning our book and threatening to sue. The last message, although muffled, sounded to us like: 'I am on my way over.' The DC had assured us that Hassan could not enter the country and that he was under tight surveillance in Israel. Nevertheless, we were not entirely confident.

The next morning we received a call from a neighbour. He and his wife were out walking when they had spotted a taxi with two Arabs in it. One of them had got out and was overheard asking for our address – they had succeeded in tracking us down. Our friend photographed the taxi licence plate on his cell phone. Later, the police followed up on our report. They approached two dark-looking men outside a local pub delivering leaflets for an Indian take-away. They were convinced they had found the 'culprits'. Jennifer had shown photographs of Hassan to our neighbours, who confirmed the resemblance, categorically denying that the men they had seen were Indian. Meanwhile, Abbey Taxis confirmed that one of their cars had indeed picked up two Arab men from Chippenham station and had taken them to our village.

Our book was on course for Easter publication. We had been quite up-front with our publishers on both sides of the Atlantic about the controversy and shenanigans surrounding the project. At the publisher's request, Jennifer compiled a comprehensive report of everything we knew to date of the circumstantial evidence. Instead, the knowledge we shared was used against us. Much to our dismay, we received a call from our agent saying that the publishers were pulling out following a report from the SDEMA, a private investigation agency in Israel that had been commissioned by them. The investigation was ordered despite our earlier protests that it would be a waste of money. A copy of the email from the CEO was forwarded to us. The email informed us that independent research had been commissioned into the background of the codices, causing the publishers to be very concerned by what they had discovered. The investigation, in their opinion, had cast doubts on the authenticity of the codices. They reassured us that they believed we had acted in good faith, but in their opinion we had been misled. The email went on to say that the report was devastating in its conclusion, destroying any credibility the artefacts might have; therefore, regretfully, they would have to withdraw.

'Misled'? We had provided a comprehensive metallurgical report from one of the world's leading laboratories, as well as detailed confirmation and analysis by a number of the most eminent Biblical scholars in their field. All the scholars had supported the authenticity of the codices and had written detailed accounts of the language, theology and history, according to their special expertise.

The report itself turned out to be nothing more than a two-page criminal records check on Hassan. Moreover, there was nothing new in it: in his honesty, he had already told us most of it. What did, however, come as a surprise to us was Hassan's alternative name: Khila. But what did any of that information have to do with the authenticity of the codices? Also in the report was a statement from the IAA denouncing the codices as fakes. We were not surprised by this, as Hassan had already told us they had not been interested in them when he had taken a few to their offices to be assessed. There were also references to his crossing the border into Jordan at Allenby Bridge crossing, which he routinely did for his cattle feed business. The report mentioned confiscating a few artefacts, which backed up what Hassan had told us on our second visit. The only reason we could think of for this absurd attack on the authenticity of the codices was the politics of the situation.

Swiftly, we swung into action with a devastating rebuttal delivered a few days later. The publishers pleaded for more time, which meant an agonizing wait over Christmas. It was not until 6 January that we heard back. Despite being 'terribly disappointed', they had to decline, as the project was too 'fraught', even with the IAA finally backing down under pressure of our evidence. Not only had there been a significant breach of confidentiality that we felt put our security at risk, but also they had alerted the very people we had been fighting against to protect the codices. There was no apology, no acknowledgement of our rebuttal and no response to any of our questions, from either the publisher or the IAA.

# PART IV
# DÉNOUEMENT

*'When the legend becomes fact, print the legend.'*

The Man Who Shot Liberty Valance

## 2 February 2010: Corporate Deception

Our friend Anne rang to tell us the lead codices, and my involvement in the discovery, were all over the web. On taking a look, we were horrified by what we saw: The Lead Codices on Amazon, The Lead Codices translated in Spanish, The Lead Codices translated into French, Portuguese … It went on and on, pages of listings with various online booksellers. The incomplete manuscript had not even been turned in, and at the time this went live on the Internet our contract had not even been signed, yet here it was on a multitude of sites, due out on 5 May 2010 and available for pre-order. So much for our non-disclosure agreement. This did much to explain the frenzy of opposition over the past months.

A few weeks later the phone rang. Much to our surprise, it was Hassan. We hadn't heard anything from him in months, not since we had been tracked down to our village. 'Listen David, I want to apologize to you. I want you to know how sorry I am – I have been under a lot of stress.' He said I had made him angry, but now he was truly sorry for his behaviour. This turn of events completely wrong-footed me – I was not used to Hassan saying sorry. Hassan knew about our forthcoming book, and was keen to talk about it, but I gave little away. As an olive branch, he offered to send us some images of codices that he had not shown us before.

Were Jennifer and I being taken for fools again? Was Hassan's atonement genuine or was it a honey trap? Despite the unbelievable stress he had put us under, strangely we still felt compassion for the man, and wanted to help him out of the hole he had dug for himself. The Colonel had assured us that, given his cooperation, he would be granted immunity.

## August 2010: The Forming of the Codices Scholars

We gladly accepted Margaret's invitation to host a meeting at her home so that we could finally meet Professor Philip Davies, one of the leading scholars of the Dead Sea Scrolls team – in my mind, and in academic circles, he was a living legend. In a field rife with Christian agendas, Philip is renowned for his pragmatic and sceptical approach, believing that religious faith and historical truth are not a recipe for objective scholarship: in his own words, 'doctrine in effect dictates the agenda.'[1]

In 1989 Philip, along with his colleague Professor Robert Eisenman, sent a letter to Professor John Strugnell, Head of the International Team of scholars selected to study the Dead Sea Scrolls, with a request to study certain fragments. Prior to this approach, no one had dared to challenge the almost 40-year exclusivity imposed by the Team. The two scholars duly went public via the American and Israeli press when their reasonable request was refused. A firestorm of publicity followed, making the Dead Sea Scrolls a household name.

Margaret was in high spirits as we sat around the table bringing her up to date with the latest intrigue regarding the discovery. She had been in academe long enough to have seen and experienced more than enough bad behaviour in her many years as a Biblical and theological scholar. Since our introduction, Margaret has been and continues to be the lynchpin that has held the whole project together. There is no way we could have succeeded in our efforts without her valuable wisdom every step of the way.

Philip arrived half an hour later, looking like he had just been called in from fieldwork in the Middle East. He was tanned from years of overseeing digs, and looked every inch the image of a British archaeologist. He had a friendly, down-to-earth manner, despite his redoubtable reputation as a scholar.

'You've been lucky to have Margaret on your side. There are people you can trust and people that you definitely cannot trust,' Philip said.

Margaret agreed. 'I told David and Jennifer that they would attract dubious and ruthless people like bees to honey when working with something of this magnitude and importance: treasure hunters, jealous academics – anyone out to profit from their struggle.'

'Not to mention the Israeli side of things,' Philip added. 'I hear you have had a bit of a run-in with the IAA?'

Following this prompt, I took out of my bag a letter addressed to Hassan and Boaz from the IAA. 'In accordance with our meeting at the Israel's antiquity authorities office dated 6/7/2009,' it said, 'I hereby notify you that the antiquities authority has no interest in the objects.' The letter had been signed by the 'Manager of Antique Robbery Prevention Unit'.

Philip read the letter and smiled knowingly. 'You know what this means don't you? Either one of two things: that they believe the codices to be Christian and therefore of no interest to them or, and I think this is probably the more likely reason, that they know that they were found in Jordan and have deemed them too politically sensitive to get involved in.'

I put to him the question I had been longing to ask right from the beginning. 'What is your personal opinion Philip? Do you think they are genuine?'

'Well, my own conclusion is much the same as yours and Margaret's. If the codices aren't genuine, they are certainly good forgeries, and I would be a bit surprised if anyone took the trouble to forge this kind of thing. The slight deviations from known materials of the period – and there is not that much – in my opinion tend to favour them being genuine.'

'What do you make of the linguistics?' I asked.

'My own scrutiny of the images suggests to me, and to several of my colleagues whom I have conferred with, that the form of the archaic Semitic script, in use for nearly 3,000 years, corresponds well to what was used at the turn of the era. Likewise, several of the images on the covers reflect the iconography of that period, say 200 BC to AD 100. However, much of the writing appears to be in code, and many of the images are unlike what we might expect from Samaritan or Jewish artefacts of this period: either our knowledge is defective, or we are confronted with something rather different. The possibility of a Hebrew-Christian origin is certainly suggested by the combination of imagery that these artefacts exhibit. If this turns out to be correct, these codices are likely to bring dramatic new light to our understanding of a very significant but so far little-understood piece of history.'

I was thrilled that Philip too, albeit cautiously, was considering the possibility of the codices being Hebrew-Christian.

'Now, I have something to show you all that I just discovered quite by accident,' Margaret chipped in excitedly. I'll just pop in my study and get it.' She returned moments later with a weighty book on iconography. She opened directly to the page that she had marked with a scrap of paper: the image of Christ Pantocrator from St Catherine's monastery at Sinai, the oldest-known icon in existence. In this particular image Christ is not only holding a sealed book, but his visage bears a remarkable resemblance to that on the Book of the Face.

'I know you are all familiar with this icon,' said Margaret, 'but what I want to point out is the eight-pointed stars on the upper corners just above Christ's halo – they are identical to the ones on the codices!'

The rest of the afternoon passed by all too quickly. It was enormously rewarding to be debating academic points with two of the most prominent scholars in the field. Thick tomes covered the long oak table: Hebrew dictionaries, Greek lexicons, *The Oxford History of the Biblical World,* the Babylonian Talmud, books on the Old Testament, beautifully illustrated books on icons, and dusty out-of-print books on theology. Margaret thumbed through them rapidly, intimately familiar with their well-worn contents. We left the meeting with a renewed sense of purpose and motivation – this was what it was all about.

True to his word, Hassan sent through a series of images depicting more codices – this time made from what appeared to be copper or bronze. However, they were as baffling as they were striking. One in particular featured what appeared to be Alexander the Great's portrait with a crocodile beneath him. There were the familiar eight-pointed stars and a chariot on the upper left-hand corner, matched by a rather exquisite-looking female on the upper right-hand corner, whom I assumed was meant to be 'Sophia', or Wisdom. The depiction of the figures was in stark contrast to the main codex bearing the face of Jesus. The rendering was Hellenistic in style, with a line of Greek letters bordering the top. My Greek was rusty, but I could just make out the 'AB' of the name Abgar. I was unsure of its authenticity; however, if it did turn out to be authentic, it would be interesting at some point to have a Greek scholar look at the lettering to see if any sense could be made of it – that is, if it was not encrypted, like the lead codices. It was a matter of finding someone we could trust to keep it confidential.

I forwarded these new images to Margaret and Philip, who were as much surprised by the stylistic differences in the artefacts as by the fact that they were made of either copper or bronze (it was difficult to tell which from the images sent). We had been unable to test them metallurgically, as we had the lead codices. The photographs were of poor quality. However, Margaret and Philip thought it was a remote possibility, though unlikely, that they were authentic, owing to the combination of symbols and figures as well as the use of Greek, which we had not encountered before. We all agreed, however, that this codex, if genuine, would have been a reproduction from a much later date – most likely medieval. Philip stated that it was not uncommon to find artefacts from differing dates in the same hoard. In fact, he assured us, this was a point in favour of authenticity. At the site of the Dead Sea hoard in Qumran, parchments from differing dates had been found ranging from the 3rd century BC up to the 3rd century AD. Apparently medieval texts had been mixed in with ancient scrolls. However, we all had our doubts, and decided that it was best to keep the images to ourselves until we had a chance to see them in person and most importantly to have them tested.

## 26 May 2010: Lambeth Palace, London

Thanks to Margaret and Val, Jennifer and I were granted an audience with the Archbishop of Canterbury, Dr Rowan Williams. We showed him the images and briefed him on the scholarly assessment thus far. As one of the world's leading scholars on iconography, we knew that he would be excited about the discovery. He walked across the room and pulled out a book from his heaving library, quoting passages from sources including *Revelation* and the Proto-Evangelium of James. His intellect was razor-sharp. He lacked my preliminary advantage of almost three years of exhaustive research, yet was able to zero in immediately on the context and implications of the discovery.

When I mentioned Margaret's work in his field, the Archbishop's eyes lit up. Like me, he greatly admired her research in *The Great High Priest* and *The Revelation of Jesus Christ*.

'I think Margaret's work is absolutely groundbreaking', I enthused.

'Yes!' he keenly agreed with a twinkle in his eyes. 'That's exactly why I awarded her with her doctorate!'

Jennifer gave the Archbishop a run-down of all of the trials and tribulations we had been through in our efforts to protect the codices, finishing with our concern for their repatriation. His Grace listened attentively and responded with great sympathy. He requested that we keep him up-to-date with developments. He was keen to do what he could to help.

## August to December 2010: The Office of International Treasury Control

At the end of the summer Jennifer and I were introduced by Theo, a close friend, to Danesh, an IT expert Theo had met when they had worked together for a well-known antiquities collector. He knew we had been researching websites for a Foundation we hoped to set up with Charles. He quickly dismissed my attempt to discuss technical matters, and instead handed me a document consisting of numerous pages. Glancing through it I noted hundreds of names and signatures of former and current heads of states from around the world. Beside the names were monetary contributions, totalling many hundreds of billions of pounds sterling. I could not imagine what Danesh was doing with such sensitive information.

He went on to explain that he was in charge of security systems for the Office of International Treasury Control (OITC), an elite and secret branch of the United Nations; and he proceeded to show us his identity card, which indeed bore the recognizable UN logo. He told us that he had been asked, at the highest levels of authority, to approach us in secrecy on behalf of the organization to offer us protection. He went on to inform us that we were not the only people to know about the discovery, that they had heard it from others as well. We were more than disconcerted about this information and felt that it would be remiss not to investigate these claims further, despite being in two minds as to whether we in fact had encountered an ally or an enemy in this powerful organization – if indeed it was *bona fide*. We were instructed that for security reasons we were to refer to each other only by first name and agreed to meet 'Hugo', a contact of Danesh's who was high up in the organization. The only thing we were told about him was that he was well known in the medical profession. He now devoted all of his time to the OITC.

We met at the Bell & Crown pub in Kew, London, a strange choice of venue given the emphasis on secrecy. Hugo's unkempt appearance immediately put Jennifer and me on our guard. Hugo took notes as we told him about Charles and our aims for a Foundation as well as our desire to get the discovery out in the open in order to protect the codices. However, he seemed more interested in discussing our security needs.

'Look, I've got to be up-front with you both,' he said. 'I think your lives are potentially in danger and certainly will be when this comes out.' It was unnerving to hear this from a stranger, and to realize how much he knew about us. He went on to tell us that the Chief of Cabinet had approved funds to set up our Foundation, as well as for our security. Depending on our agreement to disseminate news of the discovery through their organization, the funds would be available by Christmas. Hugo also told us to expect to travel shortly to Russia and the Far East to meet their contacts there.

Despite very much wanting to believe in the legitimacy of the OITC and the sincerity of its concern, we knew neither what to make of it nor what to do next. Jennifer had a hunch that we should speak to her friend Hamish, an academic, and the head of a historic chivalric society. He was well connected; and if our suspicion was correct that the organization might have a Masonic link, Hamish would be the one to speak to.

We told him about Hugo, not expecting any result – it was a shot in the dark.

'Yes, as a matter of fact I have heard of him,' he told us. 'He is a good friend and associate of Allen Ferkel's. I met him briefly about 10 years ago at a conference.' Jennifer and I looked at each other. It was amazing that, after all we had been through, we still had the capacity to be shocked.

### 11 December 2011, Cambridge University: A Breakthrough at Last

Having returned from the Middle East for Christmas, Charles set up a lunch meeting with Dr Neville Morse, a don at Trinity College, Cambridge, with a view to setting up the Foundation. We met up in Cambridge beforehand for a catch-up. Charles was not surprised to find out that the OITC had turned out to be what seemed nothing more than an elaborate hoax. He had smelt a rat long before we had. But he was as surprised as we were that Allen might have been linked to it. He advised us that the only way forward for our security, as well as the security of the artefacts, was to blow open the story in a responsible manner, which is where Neville would be able to help.

Dr Morse was already at our table when we arrived. As Charles had predicted, we got a small lecture on the pitfalls of what we were trying to accomplish, stressing that we should be careful not to raise our hopes too high: there had been countless discoveries that never amounted to much in the end. However, he was intrigued enough to want to hear more, and kindly invited us back to his apartment on campus.

Much to Charles' surprise, Neville appeared to be quite moved by our story and by the significance of the codices: his tack had markedly changed. Following Charles' advice, I initially gave a very cautious account of what I thought the codices were. However, when we got to the image of the Book of the Face, he could not hold back any longer. 'My God!' he exclaimed. 'This really is serious. I totally understand now. This changes everything.'

Encouraged by his interest, I shared with him the more controversial aspects of the discovery. Taking everything on board, he asked our permission to call his senior contact in Jordan. Much to our astonishment, he put in the call then and there.

We could hear a man's voice enthusiastically responding on the other end of the phone. Obviously old friends, they spoke warmly to each other, with much laughter and amusement. The tone became more serious as Neville gave his friend a comprehensive account, expressing concerns for the security both of ourselves and of the artefacts. We had impressed upon Neville that we wanted to hand over not only the tablets but the whole project to Jordan, and that we wanted to help with the repatriation process, which we knew would be a delicate matter.

After putting down the phone, Neville said that his friend in Jordan was extremely interested, wanted to know more, and would like to meet us as soon as possible. 'I am not surprised that all of this has happened,' he had told him, 'we've been waiting for something like this for a long time.' Unfortunately he would not be coming to London until the summer, but hopefully something could be arranged before then. He agreed that a news announcement was absolutely necessary.

Charles suggested that we send him the Due Diligence Report that we had been working on and updating since our first trip to Jordan in 2009, which included analysis from some of the top Biblical scholars around the world. For the sake of confidentiality, we decided to refer to Neville's contact as 'P'. We also offered to put together a further summary document outlining the background story of events, including all the mischief as well as all the supporting evidence.

## December 2010 – January 2011: Surveillance and Hacking

Just before Christmas Hassan rang to tell me that he had just received a call from a 'Mahmoud' in London. He asked me to call him back to see what it was all about. It turned out that Mahmoud, who owned a cargo company, was acting on behalf of someone else who was representing a multi-media company in New York. I was immediately on my guard. However, he sounded genuine, and eager to be as transparent as possible. I asked him the name of the company he was representing. 'SDEMA,' he replied, enunciating each letter carefully as I jotted down the familiar name in my notebook. He went on to say that there are only four academics in the world who can read the codices: all of them British, one a Cambridge scholar. It was remarkable that he knew all this – the precise number stated in our Due Diligence Document. Where did they get their information?

On Boxing Day Hassan called to wish us a Happy Christmas. He told Jennifer that he had received a call from a man named Hugo claiming to be working on media projects with a publisher in New York. I decided to give Mahmoud a call to get to the bottom of this. I asked him directly to confirm that the name of the man who had approached him was Hugo. To my surprise he confirmed it without hesitation, admitting that he was beginning to feel uncomfortable with his involvement in this affair. He explained that he had injured his ankle and needed some easy work so Hugo had offered to pay him to make contact with Hassan. He sounded tired and frustrated, so I softened my tone and asked him if he had been shown the SDEMA report. He admitted to having seen a printed copy of the report as well as other material, including photographs. 'I can tell you, David, he knows an awful lot about you.' I thanked him for his honesty, as he had been most helpful and was innocent in this affair. I warned him that he might get a visit from the police, as the information to which he had been privy had possibly been obtained by illegally hacking into my computer.

Shortly into the New Year we received an email with a Wikipedia web link from Theo. He had been taken aback by Danesh's deception and had since been doing some research on our behalf. The link was to an article exposing the OITC's purported Head, Ray Dam, and his partner in crime. Both men were arrested in Vietnam on Saturday 18 December 2010. The article stated that 'the two were charged with forgery by the Phnom Penh Municipal Court after allegedly fabricating documents claiming ties to the United Nations, the United States government and HSBC Bank'.

The next morning we called Charles to inform him of the events of the past 24 hours. He agreed we now had to work in double-quick time. With our package for 'P' finally ready, Charles sent a draft letter to be sent with our Due Diligence Report to us and to Neville for our approval. It was a brilliant letter. We were thrilled to be getting that much closer to a breakthrough.

* * * *

## Facing God

*God sent His image down to earth in the form of a book.*

7th-century commentary on the Quran

There are not many images of Christ from before the 6th century, and those that do exist show him as a beardless youth, newly ascended into Heaven. He seems very much the new Apollo in these depictions: a Greek-inspired image of perfection. Or is there more to it than this?

In the first few centuries AD, Jesus was symbolized by the image of a fish or by the *labarum*, an anchor-shaped cross. One of the first images of the bearded Christ in Western art is to be found in the catacombs of Commodilla, Italy, dating back to the 4th century. Perhaps the most striking early depiction of Christ is one that managed to survive the destruction of the icons throughout the Byzantine Empire in the years AD 730–87: the Christ Pantocrator (the all-Encompassing) found in the monastery of St Catherine's in Sinai, dating to the 6th century.

Placed alongside the frontal image on the main codex, these faces appear very like each other – so similar, in fact, as to be the same. Both are surrounded by a remarkable halo that serves, aesthetically, to separate the face from its background. The eyes, in each image, are very different from one another: one eye seems to be looking inward, the other outward (in fact, the inward eye is half-covered by shadow, which gives the strange illusion of a face in two halves). The face shows both holiness *and* introspection, but the significant thing about the icon from Sinai is that, although this is difficult to see in reproductions, it has two eight-pointed stars in the top left- and right-hand corners. This is one of the only instances of eight-pointed stars anywhere other than on the codices.

The Syrian icon of Christ Pantocrator, like other icons, portrays Christ carrying a sealed metal book, whereas the codex image is on a metal book – a book that is sealed all around. The front cover of the codex depicts a bearded man, with a halo framing his portrait. The face reveals much. It has suffering written upon it, and yet it is strangely serene. The codex is sealed on all sides with lead binding rings and contains some script. What stands out in the script is the row of Xs – the ancient Hebrew letter form of *Tav*, the letter T; otherwise known in the Palaeo-Hebrew alphabet as the cross. X' is the name of Yahweh – the Lord, the Second God of Israel, Son of God Most High. Quite simply, there is no one other than Christ whom this face could represent. What we are looking at is the first icon. (See figure 1.)

No other theory of identification stands up to close scrutiny. The image is kingly, and it portrays a man who had obviously attained a reasonable level of esteem. The rendering of the image would have been expensive: no one would have gone to this trouble had it not been vitally important to do so. The process of making the face and then setting it in solid lead would have been difficult using the processes of the day. Given the location, it must have been important that the creator was a member of the sect. His silence about what he had created must have been the price of his belief. An early conjecture was that the face was of Simon bar Kokhba, but this is extremely unlikely. The codices are full of Temple symbolism. By the time of bar Kokhba's revolt (AD 132–7) the Temple had already been destroyed. Furthermore, bar Kokhba would not have dared to have himself portrayed in this fashion: he had kingly pretensions but had not been acclaimed as a King. Neither was he a Nazirite, a fact that made his claims weaker. Although his name means 'Son of the Star', a reference to the prophecy in *Numbers* 24.17, that did not impress rabbis of the time. They chose to call him 'Bar Choziba' – Son of the Liar.[2]

It is in the Orthodox Church that the practice of the Holy Image has remained strongest, mostly based upon the traditions of the very early Church.[3] The word *icon* (Greek, *eikon*) means 'image':[4] the 'image' being the heavenly perception of God from beyond the veil of reality – in the form of a divinely appointed representative. This is another reason why Jesus was the only person who could have been represented in such a way.

Before beginning to paint the Holy Image, the icon painter would prepare his ground using a lead-based pigment – lead white. Lead was also symbolic of God, particularly in His Hebrew form, Yahweh. In the portrayal of icons the white ground was seen as giving a clue to the mystical viewer of the vision behind the veil – the veil of the Temple, which divided the Holy of Holies from the inner sanctuary. The iconic portrayal of Jesus is stating, very explicitly, that he was indeed both High Priest and King.

According to the Church, the icons are based upon *the* icon – the Holy Image, in other words the very first ever portrait of Christ. It is a miracle that it has survived at all.

Yet here it is, at once ghostly and haunting, as if offering us an insight into two worlds, beyond the obvious and the ordinary. This world – and the next: two worlds that entered into the mystical realms of God, and both of them conjoined in the figure of one extraordinary man. History and myth had met and merged. For the makers of the original icons, well aware of the theatre of the day, myth was the guiding hand of spiritual thinking; myth sought to surge beyond reality, into an understanding of the place where humanity meets divinity.

The first clue to such divinity is the halo. There are remarkable similarities with Pharaonic Egypt. In dynastic Egypt the elongated circle, called a *cartouche*, was used to delineate the name of the Pharaoh, setting it apart from the physicality of the world. The halo served the same function as a cartouche, being an adaptation of it. Now, the Pharaoh was a living god, and the key to his divine power was his name. The New Testament tells us that Jesus was the Logos: the incarnate Word of God – and here he was, the word inside a cartouche. In the 1st-century context of the codex, the idea was quite possibly to demonstrate that, although he was incarnate as the Word, he was a King in the archaic sense of the word: he was in two worlds at once. In the archaic period he would have been recognized as a kind of shaman, inhabiting two worlds at once, a consensus god of his people, whose job it was to heal the pangs of starvation by conciliating with God or the gods and healing the land upon which the people relied to feed themselves and their families.

By the time of Christ, the theology of the King and his relationship with God had become quite complex, being practised around the holy site of the Temple, believed to mark the navel point of the earth – the point from which a descent of the spirit to the other side was said to be more easily attainable.

The idea of the image of Jesus, or *eikon*, is that this secret image, to be seen by very few, would upon contemplation reveal certain of the mysteries behind the veil – in this case, the veil of flesh. We would be looking into the very nature of God. Such was the immense privilege, but also the tremendous burden, of being the King. What we have here is an example of the old Temple theology meeting the rise of Christianity – in the form of our artefacts.

In this sense the 'image' is the idea of God as seen through God's King/High Priest – his anointed messenger (the Great Angel). This makes Jesus the only person who could have been represented as such without blasphemy.

Great care had been taken to seal the books into their environment and make sure that they were hidden away, beyond prying eyes. Furthermore, from the way in which these books had been bound, in some instances with the binding rings going through some of the symbols, it is very easy and justified to get the impression that this sacred hoard was left *in situ* in a hurry. Moreover, the way in which they had been hidden gives us another clue to their significance. For the 'wall' of icons, or *iconostasis*, is a thing of resplendent holiness in the Orthodox tradition of the Christian Church. There is more than a hint here of a continuation of ancient religious practice: in other words, the traditions of the Temple encased and encrypted within our discovery.

Why, in the icons, is Jesus holding a book? We have to look at this from the Hebrew-Christian perspective: Jesus, the Logos, was holding the Book of the Law, which he came to embody. The book is not his Gospel: it is his New Covenant with God.

On the Book of the Face the facts are assembled in a way that is reminiscent of an identikit picture – a composite. The early Hebrew-Christian idea of the Incarnation, the notion that God became flesh, had been extant from the older Solomonic Temple period and the older theology of all Israel in the 1st millennium BC, in the person of the Messiah, the King or the Priestly Messiah, Son of Aaron. Alongside the depictions of palm trees, *etrogim* and pomegranate flowers indicative of the High Priesthood and alongside, of course, the walls of the Temple, the face of Christ helps us to build a picture that becomes cohesive in the light of its presence. The books, in being the New Covenant, are placing Jesus at the very centre of the Temple – in the Holy of Holies. On another of the codices is a detailed depiction of the Holy Place, showing the food bowls as well as fruits aplenty. On yet others the temple balustrade can be seen, and pillars too. The message could not be more explicit. These are the secrets of the Temple, as known to the Nazoreans; and their Messiah is at the very core of it.

Not everybody was comfortable with truths expressed in imagery: Eusebius in his *Ecclesiastical History* (4th century) is very disapproving of the graven image. This alone is enough to tell us quite how secret these things were. At various times in history sacred imagery has been deemed offensive or impious. The potential power of iconoclasm is enough to tell us quite how secret these things were. Such reverential portrayal of any other figure would have been seen as blasphemy under Jewish Law – particularly if he was a candidate for the Messiahship. Jesus truly was a unifying candidate come to claim the throne of the United Kingdom of Israel, and his claim was seen as good: he was no longer a mere candidate.

All this is the interpretative background, inescapably convincing in our opinion, and that of our collaborators, to the earliest representation of Jesus – in what are therefore some of the earliest Christian documents, if not *the* earliest Christian documents. No wonder we felt so protective toward the codices.

As I have said, this 'true image', or *vera icona*, may well be *the* source of the icons: representations of the Veronica are usually set within a distinct sun disc or halo (as are the faces on the icons) – which has sometimes led to their being mistaken for a representation of John the Baptist's severed head on a dish. This too is redolent of First Temple practice and, of course, speaks of an older and wider usage presaging the foundation of Israel. The face on the cover of the Book of the Face (or Book of Seven Seals) bears all of the messianic hallmarks: the beard, the centre-parted hair, the aquiline nose – all of which are Nazorean/ Nazirite features.

Before the 6th century and the Iconoclastic era in Byzantium, the image of Christ was generally a Romanized version of the image of Apollo – unbearded and shaven. However, long after this period (beginning around the 4th century, there was a startling and dramatic change in the representation of Christ), we see Jesus as a proper Hebrew Messiah with all the familiar attributes mentioned above.

In the years before the Council of Nicaea in AD 325, the Roman image of Jesus has a tendency to look Greco-Roman in character. This portrayal is not the Jewish Jesus, but Christ as the risen sun, splendid and in glory. It is not until shortly after Nicaea that the bearded Jesus begins to emerge, in a more realistic, less idealized look: it is Jesus the man, not the apotheosis of Christ. It is almost as if something in the way of an actual portrait has inspired this sudden change to realism, as opposed to the supernatural.

The codices are in fact Apocalypses, in that they portray the ideal of Christ in the Temple environment – and the Temple to 1st-century Jews, as to the Hebrews before them, was Heaven on earth. The Apocalypse, in terms of the book it describes and the vision detailed within it, reveals the inner secrets of the Temple, what is to be seen there in the secret places and the ultimate vision of God and the Holy Ineffable Name: in this case Jesus. We are in the realms of mystical Hebraism. The Great Angel of Salvation, the King/High Priest, was Yeshu'a, who was *YHWH* incarnate in the form of the King. This would be a definite First Temple survival into the 1st century. As Jesus walked into the Holy of Holies and emerged as High Priest and King, he would have become 'resurrected'; having survived the encounter with the living presence of God, his face would have shone. In the Greek myths Zeus, the King of the Gods on Olympus, is rarely seen by mortals in his true guise: on the few occasions when he is asked to show himself, the poor enquirer is burnt to a cinder instantaneously. The nature of the Hebrew divinity is imbued with a similar flavour.

Such a radical notion of Jesus would have caused great consternation to the Temple authorities, who would have seen it as a challenge to their grip on the politics of Judea. For what James took with him from Jerusalem after the incident on the steps of the Temple is known to have been the archive of his community. The implication is that Jesus passed the secret teachings that he gleaned from his own experience within the Temple to his brother James and to John and Peter. While certain of those teachings would have remained unwritten, this does not mean to say that they were not symbolized, illustrated or enciphered for those who sought access to them. The problem with any assessment of Christianity at its inception has always been that it has been depoliticized, stripped of its circumstantial meaning; and into the lacuna has stepped theology.

It is known that James, after his appalling encounter with Paul, had headed towards Pella, today a run-down city on the road to the cave site – in an arid wonderland that few had ever seen. This gives us a context for the discovery of the codices. The pursuit of James by Paul in the early texts seems illogical and exaggerated. Damascus was way beyond the jurisdiction of the Temple. The Temple authorities were working in cooperation with Rome. It seems more than a little odd, therefore, that they should go to such extremes. Was James really *that* important? Was his person so profoundly holy or so profoundly blasphemous that they were willing to incur the significant costs of pursuit? If so, then the episode is unique and puzzling. However, if he was carrying something the pursuers desperately wanted, not to keep perhaps but to destroy, then perhaps the manhunt becomes more intelligible. The central codex would have contained certain of the secrets of the Temple and its Holy of Holies. If James was thought to be carrying it, that would be enough to justify pursuit and persecution: the Temple authorities had to destroy it at all costs.

\* \* \* \*

### 21 February 2011, Ben Gurion Airport, Israel: The End of the Affair

Jennifer and I looked at each other and burst out with nervous laughter as our plane raced down the runway, heading into take-off. We could not quite believe that we were returning to Israel. Hassan had given us an ultimatum: either do something or he was going to sell. Charles offered to fund the trip and planned to donate the film footage to the Foundation. The footage was to be used for our breaking news story. With us was Karl Weiss, an award-winning documentary film producer who had organized our three-day guerrilla trip to Hassan's to film the codices.

Just before take-off, Hassan called Karl on his cell phone. He had already gathered the codices together ready for filming. The two of them had been speaking regularly for the past week or so, and Hassan had repeatedly expressed his pleasure that we were coming over there.

As the plane started its descent to Tel Aviv, the tension hit me hard, and I knew Jennifer was feeling it too. Despite the past year of a relatively smooth relationship with Hassan, all the bad memories of our last trip to Israel came flooding back. We had no clear idea of what to expect.

Hassan greeted us like old friends and shook hands with Karl, although when he gave me a friendly embrace I could not help noticing the rigidity in his shoulders. He ushered us to the familiar grouping of café tables. As soon as we had all seated ourselves, he wasted no time in asking the one question we were dreading. 'So, I hope you have brought back my tablets?' Any display of camaraderie had gone. The air was fraught with tension.

'Hassan, we discussed this before we came over, and you agreed that we should keep the tablets for analysis.' I tried to reason with him. 'Besides, we all agreed we just couldn't risk it with the current situation in the Middle East. You must have heard that Gaddafi has just fired shots at the protesters, killing over 200 people and injuring thousands. A domino effect is feared – Tunisia and Egypt having already fallen. People are being searched very thoroughly at the airports.'

'We had all of our bags carefully searched, they would have found them,' Karl added.

'You think I'm stupid?' he raged, 'Already you have broken your promise.' He slammed his hand down on the table. 'You have to give me 200,000 dollars for my tablets or you cannot film.' In his fury, he spat out his justification.

'Hassan, listen, we are not trying to cheat you. We were genuinely worried that the tablets would be confiscated. You have to understand, the situation in the Middle East ...' Karl attempted to pacify him, but he was having none of it.

'That's bullshit! I gave you two letters from the IAA. They say I own the artefacts!'

Jennifer corrected him, as tactfully as she could. 'The last letter you sent states that the Antiquities Authority has no interest in your *objects*. Objects could mean anything – it could be this bottle ...' She held up the empty plastic water bottle in front of her. As he started to defend himself, she went on to make a further devastating point: 'OK, well, what about the person who signed the letter? Did you know that his job title is Manager of the Antique Robbery Prevention Unit?'

For a moment he was caught off-guard. He looked at Karl and declared: 'If you put 200,000 dollars in my account I let you film.' It was an obvious tactic to change the subject.

Hassan then started to make aggressive remarks. He turned toward Karl, who was visibly shocked. 'I have friends everywhere. Don't forget what happened in Jordan.' He had not mentioned the Jordan factor once since we had started speaking again a year ago. Obviously Hassaan had been harbouring a silent grudge. Was this what was behind this whole charade? Was he afraid? Was the reality of filming and its consequences at large finally starting to hit him? I could understand that, but why the sudden drastic change? He had been fine just hours ago. We had already picked up our bags and had started to slowly back away from him. Karl was shaken. He could not believe we had endured things for as long as we had. As awful as the situation was, we were glad to have had Karl witness what we had been through. There was no way of negotiating, nor did we wish to. Just over 24 hours later we were back home again.

\* \* \* \*

## Picking up the Pieces

Until St Paul started to expound upon it, the truth of the Resurrection and his vision of the Risen Christ remained the biggest secret of the early Christian movement. It was for this reason, among others, that the Ebionite sect took against Paul in the immediate aftermath of the death of James, brother of Jesus. He was letting Temple secrets out of the bag, but in a way that denied the authenticity of the Law: faith, not good works only, was the view of Paul, in direct contrast to the Ebionites. (In a sense the Ebionites are likely to have viewed this as a case of Paul placing himself at the centre of the revelation, particularly in terms of how he described his vision. Thus, belief in Paul led, by extension, to faith in Christ.) It was at this point that much began to change. In the years after the two Great Revolts against the might of Rome, when Judea was utterly destroyed and the Jerusalem Church too was decimated, the doctrines of Paul won out – whereas before the revolts it seemed as if he was very much on the losing side.

All that we might have known about the Hebrew-Christians was lost at this point: whatever was left over from the First Great Revolt was destroyed in the Second in AD 132–5.

Christianity was the heir to the Temple faith, and the codices are explicit on this point. Some scholars have pointed out how close the codices seem to later Kabbalistic texts, and indeed there are many similarities between the two movements in their use of Temple symbols and script. From the limited analysis thus far, the two seem to have a lot in common. But equally there are differences that point to their separation. Nowhere in Kabbalism is the Face of the Lord to be seen.

Analysis of the surviving texts has revealed a great deal but left many questions unanswered. For example, in the Greek version of the Gospel of Luke, the *Codex Bezae*, reference is made of Jesus going to Oulammaus and breaking bread there after the Resurrection. Oulammaus is the ancient Bethel, the House of God. Why did Jesus go there? (*Genesis 28; LXX; 1 Corinthians*). The suspicion is that it was at Bethel, modern-day Beitin, that the first Hebrew Temple was erected in deep antiquity. Jesus went there because his new Church was a restoration movement, and in order to restore he had to affirm the truths and practices of antiquity: he was making a direct appeal to all of the tribes of Israel not just that of Judah. Bethel is famous as the site of Jacob's dream of the stairway to Heaven. Jesus was making a highly symbolic gesture. He is underscoring the belief that the Jerusalem Temple is illegitimate;

he is harking back to the days of purity, the earliest days of testimony. Bethel is a Samaritan site, and although recent excavations have yet to reveal anything of relevance there, it must surely be only a matter of time before something is found. The Samaritans, the remnant of the 12 tribes of Israel, were the first to recognize Jesus as the Messiah, but this is one of many facts that have become obscured in the power plays of history: much evidence has suffered in the cause of Mother Church.

It comes as a surprise to many people that Kings Solomon and David were Sons of God too. They were Messiahs; they too were semi-divine. But this is another fact that has been obscured, in the race to see Jesus as unique in his status of Messiah. Unique he surely was, in a broader sense. Though a King, he was humble, loyal to the prophetic role expected of the true Messiah. In this he was courageous, in that he tried to restore, against the odds, a movement that had in his eyes – and in those of many others – become illogical and corrupt. Jesus was the Suffering Servant so beloved of Isaiah.

However, there is another point to make here. In his first letter to the Corinthians (*1 Corinthians* 15.4) Paul writes of Jesus that he came to fulfil the prophecies 'in accordance with the Scriptures'. Given that Paul's letters are older than the Gospels and are accorded the status of the oldest documents in the New Testament, what 'Scriptures' can he be talking about? We might naturally assume that they must be the *Isaiah* texts and other texts of the Prophets, but is this really the case? There might well have been Scriptures, which in the coming centuries were altered or rewritten.

The Old Testament with which the modern reader is familiar has come down to us via St Jerome, who used the adjusted Hebrew texts. However, these are not the texts that Jesus and the Christians would have been familiar with, for the Scriptures given to Jerome had been entirely rewritten and edited, to expunge the mention of Jesus, the early Christian movement and certain of the Temple mysteries. A massive loss is that of the original Temple mysteries – until now. The codices offer us more than a glimpse into this highly secretive, controversial world. They give us a deeper understanding of Christian origins. Perhaps a long-lost chance has fallen into our laps?

The Jewish canon (Masoretic Text or *MT*) was formulated at Jabneh in AD 70–132. However, the earliest surviving scripts that are at present known to exist date back no further than AD 1000. The Greek translation of the Hebrew Bible, the Septuagint (*LXX*), by contrast, dates back to the 3rd century BC. Many versions of this translation contain longer passages than those to be seen in the later Masoretic texts and a comparative analysis of the telling differences between the two reveals that much was indeed removed. The discovery of the Dead Sea Scrolls in the late 1940s has only served to provide more evidence for this view. The connections and links between the Old and New Testaments have yet to be fully explained by scholars, and this is partly because of the early Church Fathers who tried to either alter or eliminate the Old Testament. The influence that they have cast over Biblical studies is dark and substantial. A direct result of this influence is the vogue in the last 30 years or so to see Christianity as a Hellenistic-inspired cult that had little or nothing to do with the fundamental tenets of Hebraism. Classicists like to see Christianity as a Helios/Sun-god-inspired, Greco-centric sect which emerged as a result of Hellenistic influence upon Palestine. This could not be further from the truth. Churches in the early period chose to retain the Old Testament for a specific reason, and that reason was that they wished to retain the traditions that went back way beyond the Babylonian exile, to the days of Solomon's Temple and its theology, all of it based around the ancient royal cult of the semi-divine King.

Strangely enough, confirmation of this account comes from the fact that, as the Jews made new translations of their Scriptures in the 2nd century, the Christians continued to use Greek translations of the Old Testament. Both sides accused each other of alterations. This demonstrates that the Old Testament was indeed important to early Christianity – particularly in way that Jesus, according to Christians, was the fulfilment of the prophecies contained within the old Scriptures. The Jews altered their texts for many reasons: the destruction wrought on Judea by the Romans was one reason, since they needed to protect themselves. The death of James was said to have provoked the Fall of Jerusalem. To many early Hebrew-Christians the Temple authorities were to blame for his death; however, for their part the Jewish authorities blamed James and the early Church for the messianic fervour that led to the Fall of the Temple. It was a painful memory. Within the early Church, as we have seen, James had a significant support base and these early persecutions of his movement, by the Temple authorities, left their mark: the Christians became sundered from the Jews.

The priesthood at Qumran saw itself as a Royal priesthood, concerned with the 'Preparation of The Way', a phrase that appears often in the New Testament. The emphasis was on restoring purity through ritual in the worship of God. The point here is that the community at Qumran and Essene communities elsewhere were very much aware of one special event that was related to the theology of the end-times. This event was the Great Jubilee of Jubilees.

The Jubilee came every 49–50 years – and the Great Jubilee only after 10 times that number: 490–500 years. Such a Jubilee would bring the Day of Judgement, and it is described vividly in the Dead Sea text *11QMelch*. This states how Melchizedek would take his place in the heavenly assembly. Dr Margaret Barker has discovered that 'This was to be the year of Melchizedek's favour, a very significant alteration to *Isaiah* 61.2, which proclaims the Jubilee as the year of the *Lord*'s favour [...] *The only possible conclusion is that Melchizedek, the heavenly high priest, was the Lord, the God of Israel* [my italics].' Jesus's ministry begins at precisely the hour the Great Jubilee begins. Jesus is Melchizedek, who brings divine judgement – but he also brings renewal, the renewal of God's Covenant with humanity, which must be renewed on the Day of Atonement in the year of the Great Jubilee. *Hebrews* 10.12 tells us: 'When Christ offered for all time a single sacrifice for all sins, he sat down at the right hand of God.'

The six seals described in the *Revelation* were 'prophecies of events during the Jubilee and, as each event happened, so a seal was believed to have been opened'. Each of the events described in *Revelation* actually occurred. The Fifth Seal was the martyrdom of James the Just and the Sixth was Nero's persecution. The opening of the Seventh Seal was to be the return of the heavenly High Priest to complete the great Atonement at the end of the tenth Jubilee – which was, at that time, imminent.

The prophecy of the Seven Seals contained in *Revelation 5–8* must have had a sizeable impact on the mood and attitude of the people. Times were hard and Palestine, during the years of the Tenth Jubilee (AD c16–66), was in turmoil owing to famine, war and Roman mismanagement. As each of these events happened, a prophecy was held to have been fulfilled; and so the prospect of the opening of the Seventh Seal created a high pitch of expectation – a state of affairs that must have horrified the Temple authorities.

Jesus called for a new self-understanding in the face of the Kingdom of God. He was earnest in his desire for the population to share in his thinking of the last days and the coming of the will of God. In order for the people to be ready for the ultimate sacrifice and the appearance of the Holy One, their thoughts had to be drawn towards the Temple, so that the focus of the ultimate rite was complete. As Otto Betz and Rainer Reisner put it, 'The royal priesthood of the Qumran community was to achieve what the sacrificial cult in Jerusalem was meant to achieve but could not because of its impure priesthood; it was to expiate for the polluted land and in this way protect it from the divine judgment.'[5]

The renewal of the Covenant was all about the cleansing of the Temple, and the purifying of the land – and ultimately of the people. During the Sermon on the Mount, Jesus went up the mountain in an echo of Moses on Mount Sinai. But he went further than Moses, the first redeemer. Here, Jesus spoke to the people camped before him on the mountain and proclaimed the God who rescues from slavery (*Matthew* 5.3–12). This is another element of the lost secret teaching: it appears that Jesus is actually making a statement not about Moses but about the Deuteronomist and his rewriting of Scripture long before the 1st century. Here Jesus is seen to be releasing the people from the 'Thou

Shalt Not' mentality, the state-centred priesthood of the Temple that was now being exposed as corrupt and collaborative. Jesus, by contrast, exhibits a great concern for the individual sinner, which would only have added to the allure of this man of 'amazing learning'.

The Seventh Seal would bring the return of the Great High Priest, the Melchizedek figure, to complete the greatest of all Atonements. Fervour was high on all sides but particularly among those who were followers of Christ.

Now, when a good man dies, seemingly for the wrong reasons, those who admire or even revere him, are likely to get angry. Thus, some of the first Christians may well have become Zealots. It is possible that certain of the disciples may well have been connected with the nationalist movement that eventually led the outbreak of the Revolt.

Josephus deplored the actions of these 'pretended messengers of the deity who led the wretched people astray' with their belief that the Lord would return to His city.[6] It was hardly the fault of the first Christians if these prophecies were misunderstood in later times – hard times that many wanted to come to an end. It was during this period that the term 'apocalypse' became synonymous with doom rather than revelation. Jesus spoke of what he had seen in Heaven. The vision was now spilling into the wider world as a reflection of something more insidious: the use of prophecy to provoke the masses.

In the aftermath of these troubles the Christians and the Jews went their separate ways for good – and so too did their texts. The Gospels became more Roman in their message: anything to do with the Temple was expunged, since the memory was still too fresh. The religion of Judaism now underwent a period of fundamental reform, by which aspects of earlier Temple culture and the monarchy were removed or reinterpreted. It was during this period that the concept of the Suffering Servant became re-cast in the mould of not one specific individual but of an entire people – the long-suffering Jews. The Nazarenes were fiercely opposed to the new rabbinic movement.

It is interesting to observe that with the appearance of Jesus, the Essene movement seems to disappear. It is Church Father Epiphanius (AD 315–403) who remarked that the first Christians were in fact Essenes.

Looking back on this fascinating and complex period of history, we have to re-evaluate much that previously has been seen as 'gospel truth'. The irony of this is that the Gospels themselves have undergone so much rewriting and so much editing and translation that it is sometimes difficult to get a sense of what they are really saying. Scholars are now questioning the original role of those who were, early on, labelled 'heretics' – that is, various of the Gnostic groups. These sects claimed to be the inheritors of a secret inner knowledge. It seems that for too long now this inner knowing has been misconstrued as knowledge of the self and beyond: but what if they did 'know' (Greek, *gnosis*) in a more outward, objective sense? What if they were inheritors of the ancient traditions too, whether directly from the Temple or from Jesus himself? A significant part of their many writings displays a remarkable knowledge of the inner workings of the Temple and its surrounding theology. We must not forget that more than one movement sprang out of the destruction of the Temple; for without a central authority to guide these believers and to rein in some of their later theological excesses, it was inevitable that they should at some point diverge from their original inspiration.

\* \* \* \*

### 3 March 2011: A Chronicle of Errors

Things had been quiet for two weeks since our speedy return from Israel. Jennifer and I were busy working on a press release and planning a media strategy with the cooperation and backing of Jordan, with input from Margaret, Philip and Charles. Through Margaret we were put in touch with Robert Pigott, the Religious Affairs Correspondent for BBC. He was bowled over by what we had to show and tell him, and very eager to help us put our story together and announce it on the *Today* show on BBC Radio 4 – the ultimate slot.

Our new-found tranquillity was soon interrupted. The phone rang, disturbing an otherwise delightful early spring afternoon. It was Hassan in one of his manic phases. I was not in a mood to speak to him, but as always, thought that perhaps I should listen to what he had to say, as he tended to reveal useful information.

'We've got a surprise for you!' He taunted me gleefully, then rambled on incoherently. I put him on speakerphone and we listened for about 20 seconds before hanging up. We could not make out most of what he was saying, except for the clearly discernible words, '*Jewish Chronicle*'. Over the weekend Jennifer looked up the *Jewish Chronicle* online and came across the feature: *Heavy metal secrets from a Mid-East cave; Israel's archaeological establishment believes they are a fake. But could a collection of metal books be an early example of Kabbalah?* A photograph showed Allen, posing in front of the mouth of a cave – in Jordan.

### April 2011: Announcement to the World's Press

'Hello?' I responded eagerly, putting the caller on speakerphone. It was the call we had been waiting for. 'P's' office had responded with urgency to our latest report. They had fully agreed with our strategy to make a news announcement and informed us that we were to expect a call from Dr Ziad al-Saad, the Director-General of the Department of Antiquities of the Hashemite Kingdom of Jordan in Amman. Although the line was not the best, we were just about able to hear him.

'Hello, this is Ziad al-Saad from the Department of Antiquities. I would like to offer my congratulations. I have read your report and I must tell you, it is excellent! We also want to give you our thanks for all of the things you are doing for Jordan and to say that we are completely amazed at the wonderful thing you have given us.'

Jennifer and I were speechless at first but were able, after a few seconds, to thank our caller for his kind words.

'We are very much looking forward to working together with you for a happy conclusion,' he continued. 'We must get started working on the repatriation as soon as possible. However, we will need to do some investigations first and, of course, further testing – and of course you must come to Jordan. Let us be in close touch via email. Oh, and I've read your press release – it is very good and I am happy to authorize it for release. I wish you luck.'

A few days later, Jennifer went online and sent the announcement to everyone on our already-prepared media list. By 6am the BBC's *Today* programme had already posted their announcement on their website and by 8.30am our interview with Robert Pigott had been aired. Our banner was flying freely across the world. The fate of the codices was now in the realm of the Jordanians, where it belonged.

Although we had fulfilled our mission, our work was not over yet. Robert Pigott called us later that day requesting that we show up at the BBC the next day for interviews on BBC *News 24*, the 10 o'clock news, and various radio programmes.

Meanwhile, Allen was having a meltdown. Jennifer and I, as well as Philip, Margaret and our agent, received a copy of an email he sent out to the Press Association, all the major international broadsheets and Rex Features, our photographic agency, stating that we had no right to associate ourselves with the discovery. He signed his own name as Hassan's press agent. The main points were that a) all information on the discovery of the lead codices is the subject of confidentiality agreements covering publication and exploitation in any media; b) the material is owned by Mr Hassan Saeda, who has exclusive rights in all publicity and display or exploitation through his agent Allen Ferkel. Legal action was threatened for anyone in unauthorized breach of these entitlements. Unsurprisingly, he had chosen to ignore the overruling issue: that the discovery was the legal property of the Hashemite Kingdom of Jordan.

### 25 April 2011: A Call from the Department of Antiquities – On Our Way at Last

We were on our way to the BBC headquarters at White City, West London, when Jennifer answered the phone. It was Robert Pigott. He sounded strained and tense.

'Jennifer, we have a problem. A certain young man has just left reception where he commanded that I come down and see him. He demanded that we remove the web article on the *Today* show site.' Fortunately, the matter was resolved in our favour. The opposition had beleaguered us until the very end. But it was now out – no one could stop it.

Jennifer and I were then whisked away for BBC *News 24* and the 1 o'clock news. Robert pulled back a dark heavy curtain and introduced us to the producer. Much to our surprise we found ourselves in a dark studio facing a familiar lit-up red and white counter and backdrop. The newsreaders were off-air for a 10-minute break. We recognized them immediately: Louise Minchin and Chris Rogers. Jennifer unwrapped the little package containing the tablets and handed them over. Before we knew it, the red light flashed. We were on air.

We were exhausted when we finally left BBC White City and headed toward the tube station to meet Charles for dinner. He was eager to hear how our day went. We told him about our various broadcasts and ended with the visitation of Horace.

'He obviously still has an axe to grind,' Charles said. 'You don't think he could have been behind the reluctance of the JMI to pursue further involvement with the codices?'

'That's exactly what we've thought for a long time,' Jennifer replied. 'We're pretty sure he's been in touch with Jordanian officials, declaring the codices to be forgeries and not to take David seriously.'

We had done what we had set out to do. Now we could only sit back and hope that our strategy would have the desired effect, that the Jordanians would be pleased and that we could now begin the process of repatriation.

On 5 April 2011, Dr al-Saad delivered the strength of his conviction in an article in *The Jordan Times* stating that the codices may represent 'the greatest discovery on the eastern banks of the River Jordan' and 'have been billed by Jordanian experts as more historic than the Dead Sea Scrolls'. Dr al-Saad affirmed that 'we have every indication that these texts were excavated from Jordan illegally in recent years and smuggled across the border'. He confirmed that 'authorities are working at every diplomatic and legal level in order to return the books from across the river and into Jordan. These manuscripts are a part of Jordan's heritage and global heritage, and we hope to share it soon with the rest of the world.' The article ended with a promise that Jordanian authorities would work to house the codices in a museum on the eastern bank of the River Jordan near the site where its authors sought refuge some two millennia ago. We were absolutely thrilled by Jordan's support and could not have hoped for a better outcome.

Over the course of the next week we were amazed by the response. Although we always believed the discovery to be of huge importance, it was hard to gauge how the rest of the world would perceive it. We were inundated by calls from journalists from around the world. Thanks to Robert Pigott's superb journalism, the standard of worldwide press was impressive and, to our surprise, wholly supportive. Although a huge burden had been lifted from our shoulders, the journey was not over yet. We had been quietly invited to Jordan by the Department of Antiquities to debrief them on all that had happened to us surrounding the codices as well as to escort their team of archaeologists to the site to survey it. It was the beginning of yet another chapter.

# Conclusion

## The Origins of Yesterday

*All matter originates and exists only by virtue of a force ... We must assume behind this force the existence of a conscious and intelligent Mind. This Mind is the matrix of all matter.*

Max Planck (1858–1947)

## The Second Coming

What is myth? The etymology of the term gives us a revealing insight. *Myth* is 'ritual', *mythein* in Greek: 'that which is spoken' – that is, spoken in ritual *by the King or Priest* whose word was law. These simple words, 'that which is spoken', express the essence of the greatest survival in human history: for myth is the earliest intellectual achievement to have come down to us from a deeply archaic past. Religion and spirituality cannot be lightly dismissed, for the same reason that myth cannot lightly be dismissed: they are survivals of our earliest memories, complex memories whose substance became the foundation of civilization. Myth, though it might lose its superficial currency, shows an uncanny ability to retain information and understanding on a complex level.

On the BBC *News 24* channel in late September 2013 a 20-minute report told of how Muslims in Damascus were expecting the appearance of one of their greatest prophets above a mosque in the city. The prophet concerned is Jesus, whose name appears more than 100 times in the Quran, and his appearance was to take place in the form of a *baraki* – a small sealed book. Possibly this is the seventh sealed book of *Revelation*.

The main codex of the hoard is closed with seven seals – and it has a portrait of Jesus on the cover. As we look at the cover of the book we can see that on the left-hand side there are three binding rings; there are four rings at the top and four rings at the bottom; and on the right-hand side, *where the book is finally to be opened and the revelation uncovered*, there are the seven seals. Seven is a significant number, associated symbolically with perfection. Eight is symbolic of completion and of Jesus Christ. Jesus therefore has emerged from the book to complete the next Great Jubilee cycle, at which point a great Atonement, a period of prophecies and visions, would take place. The Great Jubilee took place every 490 years and lasted for 50 years. The height of the vision was that The Lord would return to His place in the Temple. The Old Testament prophet Daniel mentioned 70 'weeks' of years (490 years) that would end when sin and iniquity were removed and Jerusalem destroyed (*Daniel* 9.25). There were Great Jubilees in the time of the reformist King Josiah, c622 BC, and in 424 BC: 'Jewish tradition,' Dr Margaret Barker writes, 'remembered that the 490 years ended in AD 68; calculation from the Second Temple Jubilee sequence beginning in 424 BC gives AD 66. A two-year discrepancy is hardly significant in the light of what this implies, namely that the tenth Jubilee began in AD 17/19.'[1] As Dr Barker goes on to point out, this describes the context for Jesus's ministry.

What is even more extraordinary is that if we then calculate the next expected Jubilee forward to the present, we can see that it is expected about now – within the next two or three years. Myth once again has become reality.

It is startling to realize that Jesus Christ is much nearer to the period of King Tutankhamun than to our own time. Tutankhamun lived around 1300 BC – 1,300 years before Jesus. Yet we live 2,000 years after Christ. Even more startling is that we are still profoundly influenced by a man who, it is rapidly becoming apparent, sought to preserve even more archaic traditions familiar to the likes of Tutankhamun. And yet we still like to think of ourselves as modern and progressive, even in the face of the fact that we are still drawn to ancient ideas of the divine and the profound.

The persecutions by the Roman Emperor Nero around AD 68 are among those described in *Revelation* as the Sixth Seal. However, the question we have to ask is why did the Romans at this stage abominate the 'new' religion, so shortly after the death of James? Tacitus is sympathetic to the plight of the persecuted but says, all the same, that they warranted it. Was this the confused idea of the Resurrection? That only the Roman emperor could be a god – not a mystical King of Israel, and a poor one into the bargain? The great tragedy is that at such an early stage Christianity was already so at odds with its history: though in the end it seemed to conquer all, this came at the price of identity.

The idea of a spiritual Resurrection is in many ways more powerful than the idea of the physical resurrection. Jesus's followers thought in these terms. Grieving disciples saw him 'beyond' death, and this to them was a sign of hope. The idea was consistent with the entrance of Jesus into the Holy of Holies. This is not a matter of a mere mortal raised from a state of actual death. Whether he survived or not is immaterial: what the Apostles were seeing was the Risen Lord as the spiritual vision of the Second God, the Son of the Most High. As John Dominic Crossan has pointed out, although Paul remarks that Jesus 'appeared' to him, a more accurate translation of the Greek would be 'revealed to [him]'. This complements the idea of the spiritual vision of the Lord enthroned as the King of Israel, the Great High Priest, the arbiter between humanity and God.

The problem for Jesus was that he had found himself, by virtue of who he was, caught between the Rock of Sion and a hard place. Very soon after his acclamation as King, he was arraigned before the Sanhedrin, to be followed by trial by the Romans and then crucifixion.

In the apocryphal book *1 Esdras*, written by a Hebrew-Christian community in the 1st century, we find the following:

> And Esdras said to the people, 'This Passover is our Saviour and refuge. And if you have understood and it has entered into your hearts that we are about to humiliate him on a cross and afterwards hope in him, then this place will never be forgotten saith the LORD of Hosts. But if you will not believe him nor listen to his teaching, you shall be the laughing stock of the Gentiles.'[2]

Evidence that this text was deleted from the original text of *1 Esdras* is borne out by Justin Martyr in his *Dialogue with Trypho.* Thus was the tragedy of Jesus summed up: everything, no matter how gruesome, was a fulfilment of the prophecy of the Suffering Servant – even unto death. For Jesus as the last King, his was the attempt to make his people self-aware by an act of supreme self-sacrifice. He had been on this path all his life and now the time was come for completion – and for renewal.

The question is often asked, was Jesus a rebel? The answer to this must be a firm *yes*. But he was a rebel with good cause: he was in rebellion against what the Temple had become and what it was in danger of doing to the people, the very 'children of Israel', now scattered so widely that it would only be the itinerant Paul who would attempt the improbable task of bringing them together. It is commonly said that Jesus was not trying to found a new religion: this is true in as much he was trying to re-found an old religion.

The Church was born at Pentecost, when the Holy Spirit (Wisdom) descended on the 12 disciples and allowed them to speak in a language that they had not known before: it was the language of the ancient royal liturgical cult, the language of the codices. It was Palaeo-Hebrew. In this context, Paul becomes not so much the 'inventor' of a new religion, but the inheritor of the Jesus family secret in the aftermath of the Great Revolt – predicted with such clarity by the Messiah himself when he stated that he could destroy and rebuild the temple in three days (*Mark* 13). This secret was also the Ebionite secret of Jesus's divinity. Thus, the irony of the situation is that the Temple Jews were outraged by James' knowledge of the secret teaching, only for the 1st-century Ebionites themselves to be annoyed by Paul's teaching of the secret and thus by his possession of it too.

However, a mere two and a half centuries later the Nazarenes had accepted Paul, according to the writings of St Jerome, and this indicates that they were not following Jewish Law and customs to the letter. How interesting it is that this particular group should be seen by scholars as Syrian Christians: our books were found in a cave not far from the Syrian border. In ancient times this area was probably the most influential in the rise of the Way and the spread of the Word.[3]

Paul's Christ is Risen: he is the Risen Lord, the one who will come again: this time to deliver us from evil. From Paul's travels, we quickly appreciate that he is in a hurry. He expects Christ to return soon: the end-days are upon him; he and his followers have no time for those with a long-term agenda – which is why he seems at times rather blasé about the advice he gives to those who have the nerve to enquire.

However, although Jesus's prophecies about the Temple came true, he returned only in spirit, and we get the feeling that Paul eventually came to the same conclusion. Paul intimates in his letter to the Corinthians (*1 Corinthians* 15) that Jesus's return would be not so much as a phantasm, but as an inspiration to those who would live by the example that he sought to give, both in his preaching and his living.

It is these rites that have survived, even from deep antiquity, in the Church today, particularly the Orthodox Church; these same rites that celebrate the crowning of a divine King, a crowning that has been preserved in the form of the basest metal of all – the lead of the codices. For what else could be used to transfer the teaching symbolically to those who would know? – what else but a very poor metal

The centralized Temple had been formed as a focus for a cult of sacrifice, in honour of a fearful God and a strict code of law that was criticized by Jesus Christ. In becoming the sacrifice, Christ freed the people and decentralized the Temple, by allowing them to go hither and thither. He gave them a precious gift: freedom of movement. The old law was, in Gnostic eyes, the Devil. Christ as King ended the Devil's sway.

This is apparent from the icons, in which Jesus is to be seen as 'resurrect' and carrying a codex. Jesus was the Messiah, he was Israel: '*The Man Who Saw God*'. It is through him that we see the divine: this is the experience of the icon – the image of The Lord on the cover of the Book of Seven Seals. The codices are the New Covenant: the object of Paul's vision – the Face of The Lord.

In icons Jesus gives the sign of the Father and his head is backed by a cross, encapsulated in a halo. His look is the look of the divine – the look of ultimate attainment, the enlightened sense that radiates from Him who speaks of the living presence of God, incarnated in the Son, so that humanity might reach out to this presence. Jesus must have been a truly remarkable man to have attained such a level of enlightenment – and then to share it with his flock. With one eye looking out and the other looking in, it is the impression of a spirit and a body half in this world, half in the next; the bridge from here into the timeless zone of eternity.

And yet God knows that until all humanity is brought to the same level, perfection will always be a step too far – the act of stepping into the unknown and unknowable. This is because perfection and the perfect state are not about needing to know on the outside – the phenomenal view of the world – but about the *inner* sense of knowing, which is possibly why the first book of the Bible has this comment:

*Terribilis est locus iste ('This place is terrible')*

*Genesis* 28.17 *Isaiah* 53.3–6

# Endnotes

**Prelude** (pp xvii–vxiii)

1 John Dominic Crossan, *Who Is Jesus?*, p79.

**Part I: Signs and Wonders** (pp 1–64)

2 Robin Lane Fox, *The Unauthorized Version*, p90.

3 Richard Heller, review of Robin Lane Fox, *The Unauthorized Version*, in *The Mail on Sunday*, 15 December 1991.

4 Flavius Josephus, *Antiquities of the Jews*, xviii, 63–6, trans. William Whiston.

5 Justin Martyr, *Dialogue with Trypho*, 71, in Alexander Roberts and James Donaldson (ed.), *The Ante-Nicene Fathers*.

6 Justin Martyr quoting deleted words from *1 Esdras*, in Alexander Roberts and James Donaldson (ed.), *The Ante-Nicene Fathers*.

7 Preface to *The Wisdom of Sirach*, also called *Ecclesiasticus*, a part of the Old Testament Apocrypha (*Orthodox Study Bible, Jerusalem Bible* et al). Ben Sira is translating a part of the Jewish Scripture into the Greek Septuagint, the Greek translation of the Old Testament from the late 2nd century BC.

8 These people would have been known in the pre-Christian years as messianic Jews or Messianists, as opposed to the Pharisees or Sadducees who comprised the Sanhedrin, the Council of Elders, which presided over matters spiritual and legal.

9 Seleucus was one of Alexander the Great's Generals who shared the division of the empire at Alexander's death with Ptolemy of Egypt. The Seleucids considered Judea to be a part of their empire.

10 Robert Graves and Joshua Podro, *The Nazarene Gospel Restored*, Cassell, 1953; review by Hyam Maccoby, in *Gravesiana: the Journal of the Robert Graves Society*, p46, issue 1.

11 The author of St Matthew's Gospel exhibits a number of characteristics common among Jewish-Christians in the area of Antioch, AD c90. He has a theological outlook, a good command of Greek and a rabbinic training. He is very likely a second- generation Judaeo-Christian.

12 Oracular re-telling of various traditions was common throughout Asia Minor and Palestine at the time of Jesus.

13 J R Porter, *Jesus Christ*, p74.

14 Papias in Eusebius, *The History of the Church*, Book iii, p36.

15 Papias in Eusebius, *The History of the Church*, Book iii, p39.

16 Hyam Maccoby, *The Mythmaker*, p173.

17 The 1st-century *Ascensions of Isaiah* mentions 'the remnant'. The gist of the text is that a group of 'prophets' withdrew from Bethlehem and went to live in the desert, on a mountain, where they subsisted frugally on herbs (*Ascensions of Isaiah* 2.7–11).

18 St Jerome, *De Viris Illustribus* (On Illustrious Men), ch. 2.

19 According to Eusebius (Hugh J Schonfield, *The Essene Odyssey*, p53ff), the Hebrew-Christians practised the Essene arts of healing.

20 For further information and a different point of view, see Robert Eisenman, *The New Testament Code*, p413.

21 Clement of Alexandria, *Hypotyposes*, in Eusebius, *The History of the Church*, 1.12.2 and 2.1, trans. G A Williamson.

22 Clement of Alexandria, *Hypotyposes*, in Eusebius, *The History of the Church*, 1.12.2 and 2.1, trans. G A Williamson.

23 Eusebius, *The History of Church*, 3.20, trans. G A Williamson.

24 From the long-standing excavations at Qumran we know that the movement inhabiting the area lived along monastic lines.

25 On the one side we have Peter, and on the other John, brother of James, both sons of Zebedee. In the Gospels of *Matthew* and *Mark* there is a considerable amount of negative comment about James and John.

26 The idea that the two factions were opposed and 'at war' with each other runs counter to the idea of what Christianity was supposed to represent in the light of Jesus's words. What such an interpretation does is to highlight the often, until now, overlooked importance of the role of politics both in the early movements of the time and in the wider influence of such issues abroad. Given his divisiveness it is perhaps a little too ironic that in *Acts* 24.5 Paul is called a 'ringleader of the Nazarene sect'. However, it is still an accurate representation of the state of the early Church at that time. Soon Paul would separate completely from the Jerusalem Church, but a Nazarene he remained in the eyes of all around him.

27 Margaret Barker, *The Great High Priest*, p299.

28 Eusebius, *The History of the Church*, 3.5.3. Professor Gerd Lüdemann argues against this on the grounds that Eusebius does not indicate Hegesippus as the source, as he does in other areas of his work. A likely candidate is Aristo of Pella, AD c150, whom Eusebius does mention as a source for his story on the bar Kokhba revolt.

29 Epiphanius, *The Panarion*, 29.7.7–8, trans. Frank Williams. Epiphanius makes a distinction in his *Panarion* between the Nazoreans and the

Ebionites. By the time he came to write his text, these two groups had become separate and distinct, having emerged from out of one original grouping – the Jerusalem Church.

30 Werner Jaeger *et al* (ed.), *Gregorii Nysseni Opera*.

31 St Jerome, 'Prologue to his Translation of Isaiah', in J F A Sawyer, *The Gospel According to Isaiah*, Expository Times, vol. 113, no. 2, 2001, pp39–43.

32 Philo, *The Life of Moses*, 2.34, 37–41. The translators were 'prophets and priests of the mysteries whose sincerity and singleness of thought has enabled them to go hand in hand with the purest of spirits…'.

33 This translation was much praised by the rabbis. For example: 'Aquila the proselyte translated the Torah for R Eliezer and R Joshua and they congratulated him saying: "You are fairer than the children of men."' *m. Megillah* 1.9, J Neusner, *The Talmud of the Land of Israel*, vol. 19, Chicago and London, 1987.

34 A 5th-century text, the *Dialogue of Timothy and Aquila*, thought to be a reworking of much earlier material. Timothy, a Christian, writes of the corruption not only of the Greek text of Scripture but also of the Hebrew: 'If you find that a testimony to Christ has disappeared from the Hebrew or has been concealed in the Greek, it is Aquila's plot.' (F C Conybeare, *The Dialogues of Athanasius and Zaccheus and Timothy and Aquila*, Oxford, 1898, fol. 119ro.)

35 Marcion, a 2nd-century Church Father, AD c160, suggested abandoning the entire corpus of Hebrew tradition but this idea was rejected and condemned by the Church, which kept the older Scriptures. The question was, what were these Scriptures? As early as the 2nd century the Christian and Jewish versions were different.

36 *Clementine Homilies*, 18.20, with a similar account in 3.50. Alexander Roberts and James Donaldson (ed.), *The Ante-Nicene Fathers*, vol. 8.

37 See Margaret Barker, *The Great High Priest*, p298ff.

38 Josephus, *The Jewish War*, 6.311–13.

39 A possible reference to the image on the main codex, the Book of the Face (or the Book of Seven Seals).

40 Letter of Clement of Alexandria in Morton Smith, *Clement of Alexandria and a Secret Gospel of Mark*, p254ff.

41 Letter of Clement of Alexandria in Morton Smith, *Clement of Alexandria and a Secret Gospel of Mark*, p254ff.

42 Morton Smith, 'The Secret Gospel', p14ff, and J K Elliot (ed.), *The Apocryphal New Testament*, OUP, Oxford, 1993, p148ff.

43 Bart D Ehrman, *Lost Christianities*, introduction.

44 Church Father Tertullian (AD c160–225) had stated only one 100 years
   before the accession of Constantine: 'The world may need its Caesars,
   but the Emperor can never be a Christian, nor a Christian ever be the
   Emperor.' (Quoted in Peter Rosa, V*icars of Christ*, London, Bantam Press,
   1988, p155.)

## Part II: From Afar (pp 67–139)

1 In November 1990 the late Professor John Strugnell, former head of the
   international team on the Dead Sea Scrolls, gave an interview to the Israeli
   newspaper *Ha'Aretz* in which he denounced Judaic belief with surprising
   ferocity: 'Judaism is a horrible religion, based on folklore. It is a Christian
   heresy.'

2 Margaret Barker, *The Great High Priest*, p1.

3 Margaret Barker, *The Risen Lord*, introduction, p xi.

4 Margaret Barker, *The Great Angel*, p3.

5 Amir Ganor: at the time, Detective, Rockefeller Museum, Jerusalem.
   Currently Head of the Robbery Prevention Unit of the Israel Antiquities
   Authority.

6 The term 'Judaism', as used in the Book of Nehemiah, would seem by
   implication to refer solely to the returnees from the Babylonian exile who
   opposed the idea of the Samaritans helping with the reconstruction of the
   Temple. It was at this stage that a distinct 'Judaism' began to emerge: see
   Geoffrey Troughton, *Journal of Biblical Studies*, issue 7, 2003, p4.

7 Margaret Barker, *The Revelation of Jesus Christ*, p xii. The pre-Christian
   Essenite document *The Assumption of Moses* speaks of the time of
   chastisement and the cleansing of the Second Temple. 'For they will
   not follow the truth of God, but some will pollute the altar [...] they will
   forsake the Lord.' *The Assumption of Moses*, trans. R H Charles, ch. viii, in
   Hugh J Schonfield, *The Essene Odyssey*, p22, note 7.

8 Posidonius, Strabo and Marcus Vipsanius Agrippa are the classical source
   material on the Essenes. See Stephen Goranson in *The Journal of Jewish
   Studies* (*JJS* 1994, p295–8). These sources date from the time of Herod
   the Great (d.4 BC). See Wise, Abegg and Cook, *The Dead Sea Scrolls, A
   New Translation*, p49, on the Scrolls/Essenes question. As Professor
   Norman Golb has pointed out, the differences of handwriting, spellings
   and contents do not point to any consistent chronology or single source

(Norman Golb, *Who Wrote the Dead Sea Scrolls?*, p367).

9   See Otto Betz and Rainer Riesner, *Jesus, Qumran and the Vatican*, p90. The Qumran community was anti-Zealot: see note 23 regarding an important Qumran text that 'was originally headed "On the Resurrection" but is now called the Messianic Apocalypse'. In the commentary, reference is made to 'the gentle and the faithful' – a common theme in Christianity.

10  See Otto Betz and Rainer Riesner, *Jesus, Qumran and the Vatican*.

11  Josephus, *Antiquities of the Jews*, 18.1–5, trans. William Whiston.

12  Robert Eisenman, *James, Brother of Jesus*, p34.

13  Matthew Black, *The Dead Sea Scrolls and Christian Origins*, pp 20, 24.

14  Josephus, *The Jewish War*, book 2, ch. 8, 5–11. In this vein Josephus calls the Essenes 'good men', by which he means 'men of God'. He also calls them 'poor men', which is exactly the name given to the Ebionites.

15  See Joan E Taylor, *The Essenes, The Scrolls and the Dead Sea*, OUP, Oxford, 2012, p188ff for Geza Vermes' etymology of the Essenes and other arguments; and see Otto Betz and Rainer Riesner, *Jesus, Qumran and the Vatican*, p152 for the etymology of the word 'Essene'.

16  Allen H Godbey, *The Lost Tribes: A Myth*, p512.

17  Robert Graves, *The White Goddess*, 1st edn, Faber, London, 1948, pp138–9.

18  In the Book of Job, Evil, *the Destroyer*, is identified with the dark side of the Lord. (See Philo, *On the Contemplative Life*, 1 *Exodus* 12.12, 23; *Job*; 1QSVIII; *m.Yoma* 6.1).

19  See note in Josephus, *The Jewish War*, trans. H St J Thackeray, Loeb edition, book 2, pp372–3, note (a).

20  Matthew Black, *The Dead Sea Scrolls and Christian Origins*, p99.

21  SDEMA report: p3, Section IV, Background on Hassan Saida [Saeda], D.D. Criminal Background & Connections.

## Part III: Opening the Seventh Seal (pp 141–207)

1   Dionysus the Areopagite, *On the Divine Names*, ed. Colm Luibheid, Classics of Western Spirituality, Paulist Press, 1987, 5992B.

2   In this sense it is telling that St Paul in his letters refers to Jesus as 'Christ' but never as 'Son of Man', the Hebrew-Christian appellation.

3   The story of Paul's vision parallels an account of Julius Proculus, direct ancestor of Julius Caesar, who had a vision of the founder of Rome, Romulus, which is remarkably similar to that of Paul.

4   Paul, in his writings, contrasts the physical and the spiritual bodies: *soma*

*psuchikon* and *soma pneumatikon*. In his view, the resurrection body is the body of the first creation. It is incorporeal, *not* physical; it is incorruptible and made after the image of God (*1 Corinthians* 15.42–50; see also Philo, *Creation*, 134); it is neither male nor female.

5 Paul had his vision on the road to Damascus. Pella is south of Damascus, around 60 miles (95 km) away. It took its name from the Greek god Apollo, whose image was the rising sun.

6 The story as told in *Acts* 9.7 and 22.9 is contradictory. In 9.7 they hear but do not see. In 22.9 they see but do not hear.

7 John Dominic Crossan, *Who Killed Jesus?*, p204, comments on *Corinthians* that Paul's list of people to whom Jesus 'appeared' (including himself) would be more accurately translated as 'revealed to' – this gives a more striking sense of an inner experience, rather than the supernatural.

8 Freemasonry, in its history, imagery and hierarchy, provides a very telling description of the imparting of a temple-based doctrine of secret teachings, such as those Clement mentions in his *Hypotyposes*.

9 Hugh J Schonfield, in *The Essene Odyssey*, p82, speculates that Paul was on the road to Damascus in pursuit not of the new movement of Christians, as we would recognize them, but an older movement linked to the Essenes which had, in the light of Jesus and of John the Baptist, converted to the new way – they were soon to be known as Christians.

10 In his letters Paul states that grace was all not good deeds, just simple faith, but James refutes this in *James* 2.17: 'In the same way, faith by itself, if it is not accompanied by action, is dead. Show me your faith without deeds and I will show you my faith by what I do ...'

11 Margaret Barker, *The Revelation of Jesus Christ*, pp 2–3.

12 The *Kerygma Petrou* or *Preaching of Peter* is a polemic against this view, written by Ebionites in the latter half of the 1st century. In it, Paul's view is condemned: 'This God you must worship, not after the manner of the Greeks [...] carried away by ignorance and not knowing God as we do [...] they show ingratitude to God since by these practices they deny that he exists.' Clement, *Stromata*, vol. v, 39.

13 The Church Fathers Epiphanius and Jerome state in their writings that James was indeed a High Priest and that he did indeed walk into the Holy of Holies.

14 *Acts* tells us that Saul followed his father into the profession of tent-making. His father must have prospered in the work, for to have purchased citizenship he would have needed the princely sum of 500 drachma.

15 In the *Infancy Gospel of James* (19.15, in J K Elliot [ed.], *The Apocryphal New Testament*, OUP, Oxford, 1993) there is the following description: 'A great light appeared in the cave so that eyes could not bear it, and then when the light withdrew a baby appeared.'

16 Josephus, *The Jewish War*, ii, 124; Philo, *Apology*, 1.

17 The Dead Sea Scroll found in cave 4 at Qumran, *The Damascus Document* (CD 6.5ff; 7.15ff; 8.21; 19.34; 20.12). See M Wise, M Abegg and E Cook, *The Dead Sea Scrolls, A New Translation*, pp51–2.

18 B Pixner in Otto Betz and Rainer Riesner, *Jesus, Qumran and the Vatican*, p145, note 13.

19 Hugh J Schonfield, *The Pentecost Revolution*, p280.

20 Karaites are members of a strict sect of Jews who adhere to the literal interpretation of Scripture, as opposed to rabbinical traditions and laws.

21 Leon Nemoy, 'Al-Qirqisani's Account of the Jewish Sects and Christianity', *Jewish Quarterly Review*, li, 1960–61.

22 CD B19–20. Geza Vermes (trans.), *The Complete Dead Sea Scrolls in English*.

23 'But David had not read the sealed book of the Law which was in the Ark of the Covenant.' CD V in M Wise, M Abegg and E Cook, *The Dead Sea Scrolls, A New Translation*, p55; Geza Vermes, *The Complete Dead Sea Scrolls in English*, p102.

24 CD VII. Geza Vermes (trans.), *The Complete Dead Sea Scrolls in English*. Professor Vermes translates '*images*' as '*statues*'. Statuettes of Christ as the Great High Priest were found within the hoard, alongside the sealed books. See Vermes, p105.

25 *Matthew* 19.1, 4.25; *Mark* 10.1, 3.7–8; R Riesner, *Bethany Beyond the Jordan: Topography, Theology and History in the Fourth Gospel*, Tyndale Bulletin 38, 1987, 29ff.

26 The Thanksgiving Hymn is also found in Handel's *Messiah*, as a Christmas hymn. (The words are from *Isaiah* 9. 6–7: 'Unto us a child is born.')

27 See Otto Betz and Rainer Riesner, *Jesus, Qumran and the Vatican*, p147.

28 Marvin Vining, Jesus, *The Wicked Priest*, p118. A good point is raised here: with the rise of James, brother of Jesus, Essene practice lingered within the early Christian circles.

29 Cf Mark 15.43; *Luke* 23.51. Joseph of Arimathea is described as 'waiting for the Kingdom of God'. This implies an Essene/Nazorean connection, as he is waiting literally for the Messiah to come and institute the proper codification of the Law: this is not a Second Temple way of thinking.

30 Epiphanius (AD c315–403), the early Church Father, wrote that 'They who

believed in Christ were called Essenes before they were called Christians.'
*The Panarion*, 29.5.6.

31 *Acts* 6.7 has the words: '...and a great many of the priests became obedient
to the faith'. This is a possible reference to the conversion of Essenes.

32 Private email from Dr Margaret Barker, 1 August 2013.

33 'Oh God, send thy curse upon the Nazirites,' from *Birkat haMinim*, 2nd
century; see also Justin Martyr, *Dialogue with Trypho.*

34 Geza Vermes, *The Dead Sea Scrolls in English; The Community Scroll* and *The
War Scroll;* cf *Thessalonians* 5.5.

35 Martin Hengel quoted in Gordon Strachan, *Jesus the Master Builder*, p163.

36 The Dead Sea Scrolls Fragment 7 contains the fragments of a Christian
Gospel of St Mark (Carsten Peter Thiede in Otto Betz and Rainer Riesner,
*Jesus, Qumran and the Vatican*, p117). It is significant that it is written on
both sides.

37 It has been suggested that the reference in Acts 6.27 to 'a great many of the
priests [who] became obedient to the faith' actually refers to the Essenes
(G. Strachan, *Jesus, the Master Builder*, p172; and Otto Betz and Rainer
Riesner, *Jesus, Qumran and the Vatican.*

38 Petri Luomanen, in Matt Jackson-McCabe, *Jewish Christianity Reconsidered*,
p89ff.

39 Otto Betz and Rainer Riesner, *Jesus, Qumran and the Vatican*, p141ff.

40 Otto Betz and Rainer Riesner, *Jesus, Qumran and the Vatican*, p144.

41 Irenaeus is the first writer to mention the Ebionites, in *Against Heresies*,
1.26.2 (introduction, note 1).

42 Comm. Isa. 31.6–9; in A F J Klijn and G J Reinink (trans.), *Patristic Evidence
for Jewish-Christian Sects*, 1973. Petri Luomanen comments on this: 'This
passage reveals a viewpoint that is nothing short of the formative Catholic
view: the Jews are expected to convert and accept the apostolic faith.' Matt
Jackson-McCabe, ed., *Jewish Christianity Reconsidered*, p113.

43 R P C Hanson, *The Acts in the Revised Version*, introduction.

44 According to Epiphanius, the Ebionites only accepted a truncated version
of the Gospel of Matthew, with the first two chapters excised. This is called
The *Gospel of the Ebionites*, though its original title remains unknown. It is
indeed very similar to Matthew, with the infancy narratives omitted. We are
solely dependent on Epiphanius for details of this text.

45 *The Apocryphon of James* (CG I.2.1) in James Robinson (ed.), *The Nag
Hammadi Library in English*, p29ff.

46 Epiphanius, *The Panarion*, 3.8–9, trans. Frank Williams, 3.8–9.

47 Epiphanius, *The Panarion*, 2.11.7ff, trans. Frank Williams.

48 Timotheus, the Bishop of Seleucia, who lived AD 726–819 tells how a group of Jews from Jerusalem sought, in the light of the discovery, admission to the Church. (Letter in Syriac, dated AD c800, quoted in G R Driver, *The Judaean Scrolls*, Basil Blackwell, Oxford,1965, p8.)

49 See M Barker, P Davies, D Elkington and K Hearne, *The Case for the Jordan Codices*.

50 Mark has said that the impurities analyses point strongly to the metal being of volcanic origin – from directly *inside* the earth. To undertake further analysis along these lines it is now necessary to find a control: a sample of volcanic metal from the same region at around the same period.

51 Higher isotope ratios may yet prove the limitations of present testing by showing an active radio presence indicating that the material is sub-terra and not initially worked from ore.

52 Volcanic metal is 'of the gods'. This is both a reference to the mountain of the gods, in this case Mounts Sinai and Olympus, and to the Temple. See P Kingsley, *Ancient Philosophy, Mystery and Magic: Empedocles and the Pythagorean Tradition*, p172ff.

53 See *Acts of Paul*.

54 See M Barker, P Davies, D Elkington and K Hearne, *The Case for the Jordan Codices*.

55 See C W King, *The Gnostics and Their Remains*, p362ff.

56 *El* appears in the Old Testament a number of times, for this is the name given to God, as in *El Shaddai* (*Exodus* 6.3), *El-Jireh* (*Genesis* 22.14), *El Olam* (*Genesis* 21.33), *El Bethel* (*Genesis* 35.7), *El Roi* (*Genesis* 16.7–14), *El Berith* (*Judges* 9.46) and, most significantly, *El Elyon* – 'God Most High' (*Genesis* 14.18–20). King David was reputedly a devout worshipper of God in the highest form, of whom, according to recent research, the God of Judah, Yahweh, was a son. See Margaret Barker, *The Great Angel*.

57 The Hasmonean (or Maccabean) rulers were also the High Priests, and in order to hold the title legitimately took it after the Order of Melchizedek (that is, they were not Levites), calling themselves Priests of the Most High God.

58 Hugh J Schonfield, *The Pentecost Revolution*, p97.

59 *Damascus Document*, ix 4–9: 'the Books of the Law are "the Tabernacle of the king".' The King is the congregation, in that he represents their presence before God, whose spirit enters into the King. The King's word thus becomes the Law.

60 Dr Margaret Barker, private communication, May 2012.

61 *Daniel* 5–12, the 'Son of Man' text, was possibly written by Maccabean rebels, who may have been Essenes.

62 *Daniel* 12.2 is a *Resurrection* text: 'Then many of those who sleep in the dust of the earth shall awake, some to everlasting life ...'

63 Dr Margaret Barker, private communication, 25 February 2013.

64 Robert Hayward, academic paper, 'Melkizedek as Priest of the Jerusalem Temple in Talmud, Midrash and Targum', November 2008, p15, bottom.

65 *2 Esdras* 14.42 is a damaged text and thus the Latin translation is corrupt. The translation here is from the Syriac, supported by the Ethiopic and Armenian translations.

66 Margaret Barker, *The Great High Priest*, p105ff.

67 *Acts* 2.3–4 appears to be an intimation of the possible understanding of Palaeo-Hebrew.

68 *The Shepherd of Hermas*, vision 2.1, in *The Apostolic Fathers*, trans. K Lake, vol. 2, Loeb Classical Library, 1913, 1948.

69 The explanation of Gnosis is that it is a kind of 'knowing through experience' rather than knowledge that has been taught. As Elaine Pagels puts it, 'Contrary to Orthodox sources, which interpret Christ's death as a sacrifice redeeming humanity from guilt and sin, this Gnostic gospel [*The Gospel of Truth*] sees the Crucifixion as the occasion for discovering the divine self within' (Pagels, *The Gnostic Gospels*, p95). Recent surveys of the age of *The Gospel of Truth*, dating as it does from the early 2nd century, have thrown doubt on its identification as truly Gnostic, although its author was later to become associated with Gnostic ideas and was outlawed by the Church as a heretic. The formulation of Gnostic ideas or Gnosticism as a separate movement was still only in its embryonic stages at this time.

70 For example, some scholars have stated that the Gnostic text *The Apocryphon of John* is a forgery: this is an outmoded concept. *The Gospel of Truth* is describing the main codex, the Book of the Face (or Book of Seven Seals) – and the point here is that you do not imitate something that comes itself from a fake, thus lending support to the authenticity of at least this particular codex.

71 *The Gospel of Mani* has 22 parts, each labelled by a different letter of the Aramaic alphabet, in the same random fashion as *The Gospel of Truth*.

72 *The Gospel of Truth*, i.23f, in James Robinson, *The Nag Hammadi Library in English*, p43.

73 The Book is a symbol for knowledge (*gnosis*). *Aeon* in Greek is 'age' or 'lifetime' – this is the meaning given in *The Gospel of Truth*. Each letter represents a divine idea: each letter is perfect truth.

74 See James Robinson, *The Nag Hammadi Library in English*, pp245–6. *The Dialogue of the Saviour*, an early 2nd-century text, shares some parallels with *The Gospel of Truth*: it mentions the 'Place of Truth' defined as a physical place, a place of Exile; it also mentions that 'The Lord' is the earthly Jesus, *not* the exalted risen Lord (cf *The Gospel of Truth*).

75 *See Romans* 4.16, 2.29; *Galatians* 3.27–9; *John* 4.22; 2 *Corinthians* 11.13–15 and *Matthew* 7.15–20.

76 SDEMA report: p2, Section III, Transporting the Codices from Jordan to Israel.

77 Letter from Eversheds of London, July 2009.

78 *Initial Report on the Codices in Due Diligence Document for the Jordanian Government*, June/July 2011.

79 In an email to the BBC Radio 4 *Today* programme, Kevin Connelly, 23 July 2011.

80 Professor Philip Davies' contribution in M Barker, P Davies, D Elkington and K Hearne, *The Case for the Jordan Codices*.

81 See Professor Philip Davies' contribution in M Barker, P Davies, D Elkington and K Hearne, *The Case for the Jordan Codices*.

82 Amer al Fayez, the Jordanian Royal Court, private communication.

83 *The Gospel of Truth*, verse 23, in James Robinson, *The Nag Hammadi Library in English*, p43.

84 The Department of Antiquities has applied to the United Nations for World Heritage status for the site.

85 Extreme enlargements of the images taken at Hassan's house have confirmed his story. See M Barker, P Davies, D Elkington and K Hearne, *The Case for the Jordan Codices*.

86 Including Richard Barker, private communication, 21 August, 2013.

87 *Independent Assessment and Analysis of the Metal. Summary of Technical Analysis of the Jordan Codices*, [private Chartered Civil Engineer], BEng, MSc, CEng, FRINA, MAPM, CDipAF, MIET, RCNC. The following five quotations are also from this source. See M Barker, P Davies, D Elkington and K Hearne, *The Case for the Jordan Codices*.

88 In French the word for 'lead' is *plombe*, indicating its historical application – plumbing.

## Part IV: Dénouement (pp 209–241)

1 Michael Baigent and Richard Leigh, *The Dead Sea Scrolls Deception*, p80, referring to an interview with Professor Philip Davies, 10 October 1989. Philip wrote in 1988: 'Any archaeologist or scholar who digs or finds a text but does not pass on what has been found deserves to be locked up as an enemy of science. After forty years we have neither a full and definitive report on the dig nor a full publication of the scrolls.'

2 'Bar Kokhba' was a pun on Simon's hometown, Choseba.

3 The Council of Trullo in AD 692 laid down the rules for the painting of icons, as well as other aspects of worship.

4 The first gift of Pentecost is to see and think differently: the gift of vision. This is very much the tradition in the East, where one confesses not to a priest but to the icon.

5 Otto Betz and Rainer Reisner, *Jesus, Qumran and the Vatican*, p131.

6 Josephus, *The Jewish War*, 6.286, trans. H St J Thackeray.

## Conclusion: The Origins of Yesterday (pp 243–250)

1 Margaret Barker, *The Great High Priest*, p37.

2 Alex Roberts and James Donaldson (ed.), *The Ante-Nicene Fathers*, vol. 1, ch. LXXII; see Margaret Barker, *The Great High Priest*, p294, note 9; see also note 11.

3 John Dominic Crossan, *Who Killed Jesus?*, p204.

# Appendix: The Press Release, March 2011

*For Immediate Release*

**On Behalf of David and Jennifer Elkington**

**SECRET HOARD OF ANCIENT SEALED BOOKS FOUND IN JORDAN**

One of the biggest and best-preserved hoards of ancient sealed books, which had been secretly hidden for centuries, has been discovered in Jordan. Early indications are that some of the books could date from the first century CE/AD and may be among the earliest Christian documents, predating the writings of St Paul. Leading academics consider that the find might be as pivotal as the discovery of the Dead Sea Scrolls in 1947.

The hoard consists of up to 70 ring-bound books (codices) made of lead and copper. Many of them are sealed on all sides. Scrolls, tablets and other artefacts, including an incense bowl, were also found at the same site. Some of the lead pages are written in a form of archaic Hebrew script with ancient messianic symbols. Some of the writing appears to be in a form of code.

There is likely to be considerable academic and political debate about the collection's authenticity, meaning and interpretation. But now there is also a race against time to safeguard the collection's future. Having been originally discovered some five years ago in a remote cave within a militarised zone by a Jordanian Bedouin, the hoard was subsequently acquired by an Israeli Bedouin, who illegally smuggled them across the Border into Israel, where they remain hidden under his protection.

However, legal advice has confirmed that the find qualifies as treasure trove under Jordanian law, and is rightly the property of the Kingdom of Jordan. The Jordanian Government is now working at the highest levels to repatriate and safeguard the collection. The British team leading the work on the discovery fears that the present Israeli 'keeper' may be looking to sell some of the books on to the black market – or, worse, destroy them.

The collection appears to be of mixed provenance. But initial metallurgical tests indicate that some of the books made of lead could date from the 1st century CE/AD, based on the form of corrosion which has taken place, which experts believe would be impossible to achieve artificially.

Sealed books were used by early Christian writers as a code for secret teaching; they were heavily persecuted and needed to protect their knowledge. Until now, no such book has ever been found. The codices were discovered in an area to which Christian refugees are known to have fled after the fall of Jerusalem in 70 CE/AD, and where important documents from the same period have previously been found. The existence of a significant, hidden collection of sealed codices is mentioned in the Christian Bible's Book of Revelation and in other biblical books.

The team involved in bringing the find to the world's attention has been led by David Elkington, a British scholar of ancient religious history and archaeology. David has been supported by his wife Jennifer and a small team of leading international academic experts, including Dr Margaret Barker, co-founder of the Temple Studies Group and former President of the Society for Old Testament Study, and Professor Philip Davies, Emeritus Professor of Biblical Studies at Sheffield University and an authority on the Dead Sea Scrolls.

David and Jennifer Elkington informed the Kingdom of Jordan about the find at an early stage and, following more recent briefings, are now working with the Department of Antiquities in Amman in order to safeguard its future.

Much further investigation will be needed to confirm the authenticity, meaning and full significance of the find. It is intended that an educational foundation will be created to promote long-term research into this find and related discoveries, to enable greater understanding of the fragmented – often conflicting – origins of Christianity, for the benefit of the whole world.

Preparations are being made for a documentary film about the discovery, in conjunction with a leading television network, and the publication of a book.

In announcing the find, David Elkington said: 'It is an enormous privilege to be able to reveal this discovery to the world. But, as ever, the find begs more questions than it answers. The academic and spiritual debate must now commence, and this needs a calm and rational environment to be most productive. So it is vital that the collection can be recovered intact and secured in the best possible circumstances, both for the benefit of its owners and for a potentially fascinated international audience.'

Dr Ziad al-Saad, Director-General of the Department of Antiquities of the Hashemite Kingdom of Jordan, said, 'The Department believes that this important collection was discovered within the Kingdom of Jordan. We are delighted to be working with David and Jennifer Elkington in order to repatriate and safeguard it, to enable detailed research, authentication and understanding. We much appreciate David and Jennifer's work to date.'

Commenting on the discovery, Dr Margaret Barker said: 'The Book of Revelation tells of a sealed book that was opened only by the Messiah. Other texts from the period tell of sealed books of wisdom and of a secret tradition passed on by Jesus to his closest disciples. That is the context for this discovery. So if they are forgeries, what are they forgeries of?'

Professor Philip Davies said: 'My own scrutiny suggests to me and to several of my colleagues that the form of the archaic Semitic script corresponds well to what was used in the era 200 BCE/BC–100 CE/AD. The codex format of the documents is also known to have been adopted by Christians from about the 1st century CE/AD. However, much of the writing appears to be in code and many of the images are unfamiliar. The possibility of a Hebrew-Christian origin is certainly suggested by the imagery and, if so, these codices are likely to bring dramatic new light to our understanding of a very significant but so far little understood period of history.'

London 28 March 2011

**Notes to Editors**

David Elkington has been shown many of the artefacts by the current possessor of them, who wished to understand their significance, and was allowed to photograph some of them in their present location for research purposes. But he makes no claim of ownership, which, based on the legal advice he has received, rightly rests with the Kingdom of Jordan.

Given the controversy and competition which the discovery of ancient artefacts always promotes – both academic and commercial – David is keen to ensure that the find can now be properly and professionally investigated, in a safe and secure place, with the full support of the Kingdom of Jordan and with the benefit of access to the world's leading experts.

David has worked to date entirely on a voluntary basis, with the support of many friends, alongside the generous help of many leading experts in this field.

bce and ce are increasingly used by classical scholars in place of the more colloquially used terminology of BC and AD respectively.

Particular observations from the codices include:

The codices show many symbols of the Feast of Tabernacles, Sukkot, which was associated with the enthronement of the ancient Davidic kings in Jerusalem, and later with the coming of the Messiah.

There are clear images of the menorah (the seven-branched lamp), leafy branches and etrogim, the large citrus fruits used at Tabernacles.

There are also fruiting palm trees, well known from coins of the late Second Temple period and the time of the bar Kokhba war.

There are blocks of Palaeo-Hebrew script, which could be from the Hasmonean period, 2nd–1st century BCE/BC, but the experts consulted to date believe these to be in code.

Further information will be released in due course once the security of the artefacts has been assured.

# Select Bibliography

See the authors' website, www.sevensealedbook.com, for more information on the lead codices and for a full set of endnotes, with additional scholarly background and citations.

## Biblical and ancient texts consulted

*The Jerusalem Bible*

*The King James Bible – Pure Cambridge Authorized Version*

*NIV, RSV, NKJV Bibles*

*The Orthodox Study Bible*

*The Quran*

*Septuagint (LXX)*

*Epistle of the Apostles*

*Hypostasis of the Archons*

*The Letter of Aristeas*

*The Letter of Barnabas*

*Didache*

*Diodorus Siculus*

*The Gospel of the Egyptians*

*1 Enoch*

*2 Enoch*

*3 Enoch*

*4 Enoch*

*2 Esdras*

*Questions on Genesis*

*The Gospel of the Hebrews*

*Hypotyposes*

*The Apocryphon of James*

*The Ascents of James* (in Epiphanius, *The Panarion*)

*The Gospel of James*

The Wisdom of Jesus Christ

The Apocryphon of John

Jubilees

1 Maccabees

2 Maccabees

The Gospel According to Mary Magdalene

Babli Megillah

Melchizedek

Mishnah

The Apocalypse of Moses

The Assumption of Moses

The Secrets of Moses

On the Origin of the World

The Acts of Paul and Thecla

The Gospel of Peter

The Gospel of Philip

The Martyrdom of Polycarp

Babli Sanhedrin

The Dialogue of the Saviour

The Three Stelae of Seth

The Shepherd of Hermas

The Teaching of Silvanus

Pistis Sophia

excerpts from *Theodotus*

*The Gospel of Thomas*

*Dialogue of Timothy and Aquila*

*The Gospel of Truth*

*The Testimony of Truth*

*Wisdom*

*Babli Yoma*

*The Talmud and Toldoth*

Apuleius, *On Plato and His Doctrine*

Basil of Caesarea, *On the Holy Spirit*

Cerinthus (in Irenaeus, *Adversus Haereses*)

Clement of Alexandria, *Stromata (Miscellanies)*

    *Hypotyposes* (only extant in quotation in Eusebius, *The History of the Church*)

Clement of Rome, *1 Clement*

    attributed to Clement, *Clementine Recognitions* (in Roberts, A, and

Donaldson, J, *Ante-Nicene Fathers*, vol. 8)

Cosmas, *A Christian Topography*

Dionysus the Areopagite, *On the Celestial Hierarchy*

    On the Divine Names

Epiphanius, *The Panarion*

Eusebius, *Preparation of the Gospel*
    *Proof of the Gospel*
Hegesippus, *Commentaries*
Hippolytus, *Refutation of All Heresies*
Iamblichus, *Theology of Arithmetic*
    *Life of Pythagoras*
Ignatius, *Ephesians*
    *Magnesians*
    *Philadelphians*
    *Trallians*
Irenaeus, *Against Heresies*
    The Demonstration of the Apostolic Preaching
Jerome, *On Ezekiel*
    On Isaiah
    Letters
    On Matthew
    On Illustrious Men
    On Psalms
Josephus, *Antiquities of the Jews*
    Contra Apionem
    The Jewish War
Justin Martyr, *Apology*
    Dialogue with Trypho
Lucian, *De Morte Peregrini*
Martial, *Epigrams*
*Martyrdom of Polycarp*
Origen, *Against Celsus*
    On Exodus
    On Ezekiel
    Jeremiah
    Letter to Julius Africanus
    Commentary on John
    Commentary on Luke
    Commentary on Matthew
    On Numbers
    On Psalms
Papias (in Eusebius, *The History of the Church*)
Philo, *The Contemplative Life*

*On the Creation*

*The Life of Moses*

Plato, *Critias, Timaeus*

Porphyry, *Life of Pythagoras*

*Against the Christians*

Strabo, *Geographica*

Tacitus, *Histories*

Annals

Tertullian, *Against the Jews*

## Source texts

Allegro, John Marco, *The Shapira Affair*, W H Allen, London, 1965

Anderson, William, *The Rise of the Gothic*, Hutchinson, London, 1988

Assman, Jan, *Moses the Egyptian*, Harvard University Press, Cambridge, Mass., 1997

Aubrey, John, *A Natural History of Wiltshire*, 1656

Baigent, Michael, and Leigh, Richard, *The Dead Sea Scrolls Deception*, Jonathan Cape, London, 1991

Barker, Margaret, *The Great High Priest: The Temple Roots of Christian Liturgy*, T & T Clark, Edinburgh, 2003

*The Revelation of Jesus Christ*, T & T Clark, Edinburgh, 2000

*On Earth As It Is in Heaven*, T & T Clark, Edinburgh, 1995

*The Great Angel*, SPCK, London, 1992

'Temple Mysticism, Seeking the Face of The Lord', academic paper, June 2006

*The Risen Lord*, T & T Clark, Edinburgh, 1996

Barker, Margaret, Davies, Philip, Elkington, David, Elkington, Jennifer,

Hearne, Keith, *The Case for the Jordan Codices*, Watkins, London, 2014

Barnstone, Willis, *The Restored New Testament*, Norton, London, 2002, 2009

(ed.) *The Other Bible, Ancient Alternative Scriptures*, HarperCollins, San Francisco, 1984

Beckhough, Harry, *In the Beginning*, Book Guild, London, 2002

Bernheim, Pierre-Antoine, *James, Brother of Jesus*, SCM Press, London, 1997

Bettenson, Henry (ed.), *Documents of the Christian Church*, OUP, Oxford, 1999

Betz, Otto, and Riesner, Rainer, *Jesus, Qumran and the Vatican*, SCM Press, London 1994

Black, Matthew, *The Dead Sea Scrolls and Christian Origins*, SPCK, 1969

Bloom, Harold, *The Book of J,* trans. David Rosenberg, Grove, New York 1990

Bond, Helen, *Pontius Pilate in History and Interpretation,* Cambridge University Press, 1998

Borg, Marcus J. (ed.), *The Lost Gospel Q,* Ulysses Press, Berkeley, California,1996

Bowden, John, *Christianity: The Complete Guide,* Continuum, London, 2005

Burleigh, Nina, *Unholy Business: A True Tale of Faith, Greed and Forgery in the Holy Land,* Smithsonian and HarperCollins, London, 2008

Butler, A J, *The Ancient Coptic Churches of Egypt,* 2 vols, OUP, 1884

Chadwick, Henry, *The Early Church,* Penguin, Harmondsworth, 1967

Charles, R H, *The Book of Enoch,* SPCK, London, 1994

   *The Apocrypha and Pseudepigrapha of the Old Testament,* 2 vols, Oxford, 1913

Charlesworth, James H, *The Bible and the Dead Sea Scrolls,* Bibal Press, D & F Scott, Texas, 2000

Child, Heather, and Colles, Dorothy, *Christian Symbols: Ancient and Modern,* G Bell & Son, London, 1971

Churton, Tobias, *The Gnostic Philosophy,* Signal, Lichfield, 2003

   *The Gnostics,* Weidenfeld & Nicholson, London, 1987

   *The Missing Family of Jesus,* Watkins, London, 2010

Chyutin, Michael, *The New Jerusalem Scroll from Qumran: A Comprehensive* 'Reconstruction (Journal for the Study of the Pseudepigrapha)', Supplement 25, Sheffield Academic Press, 1997

*Complete Anglican Hymns, Old and New,* Kevin Mayhew Ltd, Stowmarket, 2000

Crossan, John Dominic, *Who Is Jesus?,* Westminster John Knox Press, Louisville, 1996

   *Who Killed Jesus? Exposing the Roots of Anti-Semitism in the Gospel Story of the Death of Jesus,* Harper, San Francisco and NY, 1995

Danielou, J, *The Theology of Jewish Christianity,* ed. J A Barker, London, 1964

Davies, Philip, *Memories of Ancient Israel,* Westminster John Knox Press, Louisville, 2008

Dodd, C H, *Historical Tradition in the Fourth Gospel,* Cambridge University Press, 1963

Doresse, Jean, *The Secret Books of the Egyptian Gnostics,* Viking, New York, 1960

Edmonds, Michael, *The Hidden Mysteries, Revelations of Early Christianity,* private publication, 2010

Ehrman, Bart D, *Lost Christianities: The Battle for Scripture and the Faiths We Never Knew,* OUP, Oxford, 2005

   *Lost Scriptures: Books That Did Not Make It into the New Testament,* OUP, Oxford, 2003

*The Orthodox Corruption of Scripture,* OUP, Oxford, 1993

Eisenman, Robert, *The Dead Sea Scrolls and the First Christians,* Element,
Shaftesbury, UK,1996

*James, the Brother of Jesus,* Faber, London,1997

*The New Testament Code,* Watkins, London, 2006

Eisenman, Robert, and Wise, Michael, *The Dead Sea Scrolls Uncovered,* Element,
Shaftesbury, 1992

Eisler, Robert, *The Messiah Jesus and John the Baptist,* Methuen, London,1931

Elkington, David, *In the Name of the Gods,* Green Man Press, Sherborne, 2001

Elliott, J K (ed.), *The Letter of James, The Apocryphal New Testament,* OUP,
Oxford,1993

Ellegard, Alvar, *Jesus, One Hundred Years Before Christ: A Study in Creative
Mythology,* Century, London 1999

Epiphanius of Salamis, *The Panarion,* trans. Frank Williams, 2 vols, E J Brill,
Leiden, 1987

*Ancoratus,* trans. Karl Holl, Walter de Gruyter, Berlin, 2002–04

Eusebius, *The History of the Church,* trans. G A Williamson, Penguin,
Harmondsworth, 1965, 1989

Fallon, F T, *The Enthronement of Sabaoth: Jewish Elements in Gnostic Creation Myths,*
E J Brill, Leiden, 1978

Farbridge, M H, *Studies in Biblical and Semitic Symbolism,* Dutton, New York, 1923

Farmer, David, *The Oxford Dictionary of Saints,* OUP, Oxford, 1982

Ferguson, E (ed.), *Encyclopedia of Early Christianity,* Garland, NY, 1999

Finaldi, Gabriele, *The Image of Christ,* National Gallery, London, 2000

Frend, William, *The Rise of Christianity,* Darton, Longman & Todd, London,
1986

Furneaux, R, *The Empty Tomb,* Panther, London, 1963

Gabriel, I M, *The Holy Valley and the Holy Mountain,* Hurst Village, 1994

Gaffney, M, *Gnostic Secrets of the Naasenes, The Initiatory Teachings of the Last
Supper,* Inner Traditions, Rochester, Vermont, 2004

Gesenius, H F W, Brown, Francis, Robinson, Edward, Driver, S R, and Briggs,
Charles A, *A Hebrew and English Lexicon of the Old Testament,* OUP, Oxford,
1906

Getty Museum, J Paul, *Alpha and Omega: Visions of the Millennium,* Los
Angeles,1999

Ginzberg, Louis, *Legends of the Jews,* original German edn 1909; trans. Henrietta
Szold, Jewish Publication Society of America, 1968; reprinted, Johns
Hopkins University Press, Maryland, 1998

Godbey, Allen H, *The Lost Tribes: A Myth*, Duke University Press, Durham, NC, 1930

Golb, Norman, *Who Wrote the Dead Sea Scrolls?*, Michael O'Mara, London, 1995

Goranson, Stephen, 'Posidonius, Strabo and Marcus Vipsanius Agrippa as Sources on Essenes', *Journal of Jewish Studies*, 1994, 295–8

Gordon, C, and Rendsburg, G, *The Bible and the Ancient Near East*, Norton, London, 1997

Graves, Robert, *King Jesus*, Cassell, London, 1946

Graves, Robert, and Podro, Joshua, *The Nazarene Gospel Restored*, Cassell, London, 1953

*Jesus in Rome*, Cassell, London, 1957

Groothuis, Douglas, *Christian Apologetics*, I V P Academic (Inter Varsity Press), Illinois, 2011

Hanson, R P C, *The Acts in the Revised Version*, Clarendon Press, Oxford, 1967

Harpur, Tom, *The Pagan Christ: Is Blind Faith Killing Christianity?*, Walker, New York, 2004

Hasking, S, *Mary Magdalene: Myth and Metaphor*, HarperCollins, London, 1993

Hastings, James, *Encylopaedia of Religion and Ethics*, T & T Clark, Edinburgh, 1908–26

Hayward, Robert, *Melkizedek as Priest of the Jerusalem Temple in Talmud, Midrash and Targum*, Durham University, 2008

Hodge, Stephen, *The Dead Sea Scrolls: The Essential Guide to their Origin and Significance*, Piatkus, London, 2001

Hoeller, Stephan A, *Gnosticism: New Light on the Ancient Tradition of Inner Knowing*, Quest, Illinois, 2002

Holl, Adolf, *Jesus in Schlecter Gesellschaft*, Deutsche Verlags-Anstalt GmbH, Stuttgart, 1971

Horbury, Will'm, *Jewish Messianism and the Cult of Christ*, SCM Press, London, 1998

Hume, Basil, *The Mystery of the Cross*, Darton, Longman & Todd, London, 1998

Isserlin, B S J, *The Israelites*, Thames & Hudson, London, 1998

Jackson-McCabe, Matt (ed.), *Jewish Christianity Reconsidered*, Fortress Press, Minneapolis 2007

Jaeger, Werner, *et al* (ed.), *Gregorii Nysseni Opera*, E J Brill, Leiden, 1960–98

James, M R (trans.), *The Apocryphal New Testament*, OUP, Oxford, 1924

Jonas, H, *The Gnostic Religion*, Beacon Press, Boston, 1958

Jones, A H M, *The Herods of Judea*, OUP, Oxford, 1967

Jones, F Stanley, *An Ancient Jewish Christian Source on the History of Christianity:*

*Pseudo-Clementine Recognitions* 1.27–71, Society of Biblical Literature, 1995

Johnson, A, *The Cultic Prophet in Ancient Israel*, University of Wales, Cardiff, 1944

*The One and the Many in the Israelite Conception of God,* University of Wales, Cardiff, 1961

*Sacral Kingship in Ancient Israel,* University of Wales, Cardiff, 1967

Josephus, Flavius, *Antiquities of the Jews,* trans. William Whiston, W P Nimmo, Edinburgh,1865

*Jewish Antiquities,* trans. H St J Thackeray, Loeb Classical Library, Harvard University Press, 1930

*The Jewish War,* trans. William Whiston, W P Nimmo, Edinburgh,1865

*The Jewish War,* trans. H St J Thackeray, Loeb Classical Library, Harvard University Press, 1989

*Contra Apionem,* trans. H St J Thackeray, Loeb Classical Library, Harvard University Press, 1976

*Jewish Antiquities,* trans. H St J Thackeray, Loeb Classical Library, Harvard University Press, 1930

Kamm, A, *The Israelites,* Routledge, London, 1999

King, C W, *The Gnostics and their Remains, Ancient and Mediaeval,* Bell & Daldy, Cambridge, 1864

King, L W, *Legends of Babylon and Egypt in Relation to Hebrew Tradition,* Schweich Lectures, British Academy, OUP, Oxford, 1916

Kingsley, P, *Ancient Philosophy, Mystery and Magic: Empedocles and the Pythagorean Tradition,* OUP, Oxford, 1995

Kirsch, Jonathan, *The Harlot by the Side of the Road, Forbidden Tales of the Bible,* Rider, London 1997

Klijn, A F J, and Reinink, G J (trans.), 'Patristic Evidence for Jewish-Christian Sects', Novum Testamentum Supplements, 36, E J Brill, Leiden, 1973

Knappert, J, *Middle Eastern Mythology and Religion,* Element, Shaftesbury, 1993

Knight, J, *Christian Origins,* T & T Clark, Edinburgh, 2008

Knight, Richard, 'A Discourse on the Worship of Priapus', academic paper, London, 1786

Kokkinos, Nikos, *The Herodian Dynasty,* Sheffield Academic Press, 1998

Kostova, Elizabeth, *The Historian,* Time Warner, New York, 2005

Lane Fox, Robin, *The Unauthorized Version,* Viking, 1991

Lang, Bernhard, *The Hebrew God: Portrait of an Ancient Deity,* Yale University Press, New Haven, Connecticut, 2002

Leeming, H, and Leeming, K, *Josephus Jewish War and Its Slavonic Version,* E J

Brill, Leiden, 2003

Leick, Gwendolyn, *A Dictionary of Ancient Near Eastern Mythology*, Routledge, London, 1991

Letham, Robert, *The Holy Trinity*, P & R Publishing, Phillipsburg, New Jersey, 2004

Luckert, Karl, *Egyptian Light, Hebrew Fire*, SUNY, New York, 1991

Lüdemann, Gerd, *What Really Happened to Jesus?*, Westminster John Knox Press, Louisville, Kentucky, 1995

Lundquist, John A, *The Temple: Meeting Place of Heaven and Earth*, Thames & Hudson, London, 1993

Maccoby, Hyam, *The Mythmaker: Paul and the Invention of Christianity*, Weidenfeld & Nicholson, London, 1986

MacDermot, Violet, *The Fall of Sophia*, Lindisfarne Books, Great Barrington, Massachusetts, 2001

Magee, Michael D, *The Hidden Jesus*, AskWhy Publications, Frome, 1997

Marcus, Amy Dockser, *Rewriting the Bible*, Little Brown, London, 2000

Martin, Ernest L, *The Temples That Jerusalem Forgot*, ASK Publications, Portland, Oregon, 1999

McCrum, Michael, *The Man Jesus*, Janus, London, 1991

Mead, G R S, *The Virgin of the World*, G Redway, London, 1885

Meyer, M, and Smith, R (ed.), *Ancient Christian Magic: Coptic Texts of Ritual Power*, Harper San Francisco, 1994

Milik, J T, *The Aramaic Books of Enoch of Qumran Cave 4*, OUP, Oxford, 1976

Murray, Peter, and Murray, Linda, *The Oxford Companion to Christian Art and Architecture*, OUP, Oxford, 1996

Nemoy, Leon, *Al-Qirqisani's Account of the Jewish Sects and Christianity*, Hebrew Union College Annual, vol. vii, Cincinnati, 1930

Neusner, Jacob, *Foundations of Judaism*, Fortress Press, Philadelphia, 1989

Newton, Isaac, *Observations upon the Prophecies of Daniel and the Apocalypse of John. In Two Parts*, London, 1733

Noth, Martin, *The History of Israel*, SCM Press, London, 1960

Ouspensky, Leonid, *Theology of the Icon*, SVS Press, New York, 1992

Pagels, Elaine, *The Gnostic Gospels*, Weidenfeld & Nicholson, London, 1980

Panati, Charles, *Sacred Origins of Profound Things*, Penguin Arkana, London, 1996

Parfitt, Tudor, *The Lost Tribes of Israel*, Weidenfeld & Nicholson, London, 2002

Parrinder, Geoffrey, *Jesus in the Quran*, Faber, London, 1965

Patai, Raphael, *The Hebrew Goddess*, New York, Wayne State University

Press, 1967

Pines, Shlomo, 'The Jewish Christians of the Early Centuries of Christianity according to a New Source', *Proceedings of the Israel Academy of Sciences and Humanities* 2, no.13, Jerusalem, 1966

Pope Benedict XVI, *Jesus of Nazareth,* Bloomsbury, London, 2008

Porter, J R, *Jesus Christ,* Duncan Baird, London, 1999

Powell, Enoch, *The Evolution of the Gospel,* Yale University Press, New Haven, Connecticut, 2011

Procopius of Caesarea, *The Secret History,* trans. R Atwater, University of Michigan Press, 1961

Quispel, Gilles, *The Origins of the Gnostic Demiurge,* Gnostic Studies, Istanbul, 1974

Riley, Gregory J, *One Jesus, Many Christs: How Jesus Inspired Not One Christianity But Many,* Harper San Francisco, 1997

Ringgren, Helmer, *Israelite Religion,* SPCK, London, 1966

Roberts, Alexander, and Donaldson, James (ed.), *The Ante-Nicene Fathers,* in 10 vols, T & T Clark, Edinburgh, 1867–73, reprinted Eerdmans, Grand Rapids (ANF), 1950–52

Robinson, James M (ed.), *The Nag Hammadi Library in English,* E J Brill, Leiden, 1977

Rowley, H., H., *From Joseph to Joshua,* British Academy, OUP, Oxford, 1948

Sanders, E P, *The Historical Figure of Jesus,* Allen Lane, London, 1993

Schonfield, Hugh J, *The Pentecost Revolution,* Hutchinson, London, 1974
  *The Essene Odyssey,* Element Books, Shaftesbury, 1994

Shorto, Russell, *Gospel Truth,* Hodder & Stoughton, London, 1997

Smith, Morton, *Clement of Alexandria and a Secret Gospel of Mark,* Harvard, Cambridge, MA, 1973
  *Jesus the Magician,* Harper & Row, New York, 1978

Stanton, Graham, *Gospel Truth,* HarperCollins, London, 1995

Stone, Merlin, *When God Was a Woman,* Harcourt Brace, 1976

Stoyanov, Yuri, *The Other God,* Yale University Press, New Haven, Connecticut, 2000

Strachan, Gordon, *Jesus the Master Builder,* Floris, Edinburgh,1998

Suetonius, *Lives of the Caesars,* trans. Robert Graves, Penguin Classics, Harmondsworth, 1957, 2007

Temple, Richard, *Icons and the Mystical Origins of Christianity,* Element, Shaftesbury, 1990

Thiede, Carsten P, *The Emmaus Mystery: Discovering the Evidence for the Risen*

*Christ,* Continuum, London, 2005

*The Quest for the True Cross,* Weidenfeld & Nicolson, London, 2000

Thompson, Thomas, *Early History of the Israelite People,* E J Brill, Leiden, 1992

*The Messiah Myth,* Jonathan Cape, London, 2006

Trocme, Etienne, *The Passion as Liturgy,* SCM Press, London, 1983

Tubb, Jonathan N, *Canaanites,* British Museum Press, London, 1998

Vermes, Geza, *The Complete Dead Sea Scrolls in English,* Allen Lane, Penguin, London, 1997; and Folio Society, London, 2000

*The Changing Faces of Jesus,* Allen Lane, Penguin, London, 2000

Vining, Marvin, *Jesus the Wicked Priest: How Christianity Was Born of an Essene Schism,* Bear & Co., Rochester, Vermont, 2008

Watts, Alan W, *Myth and Ritual in Christianity,* Thames & Hudson, London, 1954

Werblowsky, R J, and Zwi, Wigoder, Geoffrey, *Oxford Dictionary of the Jewish Religion,* OUP, Oxford, 1997

Wheatcroft, Andrew, *Infidels,* Viking, London, 2003

Whitelam, Keith, *The Invention of Ancient Israel: The Silencing of Palestinian History,* Routledge & Kegan Paul, London, 1996

Wilson, AN, *Paul, The Mind of the Apostle,* Sinclair-Stevenson, London, 1997

Wilson, Ian, *Jesus: The Evidence,* Weidenfeld & Nicholson, London, 1996

Wise, Michael, Abegg, Martin, and Cook, Edward, *The Dead Sea Scrolls, A New Translation,* HarperCollins, London, 1996

Wolfson, H A, 'The Pre-Existent Angel of the Magharians and al-Nahawandi', *Jewish Quarterly Review,* 1960

Wiseman, T P, *Remus: A Roman Myth,* Cambridge University Press, 2001

Yahuda, Joseph, *Hebrew is Greek,* Becket Publications, Oxford, 1982

## Websites

*www.theleadcodices.com*

*www.sevensealedbook.com*

*www.margaretbarker.com*

*www.templestudiesgroup.com*

*www.ebionim.org* (gives a good assessement of the Ebionites and their milieu)

*www.earlychristianwritings.com* (a good starting-point for those interested in the writings of the early Church Fathers)

*www.dailygrail.com* (a good general newsfeed site which often has links to articles that do not appear in the mainstream press; an attractive mix of the orthodox and unorthodox)

# Acknowledgements

Hassan Saeda, to your initial trust and good will, we owe our gratitude. We are sorry that you have been ill used by those who should have known better.

Margaret, we cannot thank you enough for being there for us, in every respect, every step of the way.

We are grateful to many people for their time and support in answering many questions and providing much important information: Dr Margaret Barker, Richard Barker, Tim Blades, Dr JCB, Prof. George Brooke, Prof. Philip Davies, HKF, Prof. Robert Haywood, MH, Charles Merchant, John Stuart Reid, Prof. John F A Sawyer, Dr Rowan Williams and Prof. Roger Webb. Any errors theological or academic are our own.

Much gratitude goes also to our Jordanian friends: Dr Ziad al-Saad, Prof. Khasawneh, Dr. Amer al-Fayez, Colonel al-Hewayan, General Manaseer, Captain Hussein, General Manaseer and Ra'ad Tawalbeh, with all of whom we look forward to celebrating a happy conclusion for the codices.

Our especial thanks goes to Jonathan Lloyd and Lucia Rae at Curtis Brown for their enduring belief in the project and for their very extraordinary support. Our thanks goes as well to John Tintera at The Osprey Group and Jeff Scott of Platypus PR for their much appreciated moral support and professionalism. And for those whose very valued friendship has enabled us to succeed in our endeavours: Hilary Baker, JCB, Linda Browne, John Gibson-Forty, Phyllis Gray, Brian Matthew, Ted Suhaka, Count Peter Schoenborn. And *most especially*: Susan Leather, Dorothy Perks, Julian and Hege Usborne and Maisie Usborne, Chris and Caroline Woodard and Ralph Whittaker and Clare Lawrence.

And for much appreciated friendship, kindness and support, our thanks goes to: Jacob Arback, Martin Asser, Neil and Lesley Beverley, Tim and Clair Beardson, Honor Blair, Nigel Blair, Paul Bridger, Paul Broadhurst and Gabrielle, Gillian Brooke, Andrew Brown at Intertek, Marion Campbell, Anna Cox, Stephen and Miranda Crouch, Andre

Durand, Christopher Eddy, Michael W Edmonds, Alon Farago, Anne and Lucy Fisher, Sarah Gray, John and Dinah Griffey, Stephan Hoeller, Lee Hoffman, Gillian Humphreys, Mike Ives, Martin Kipp, Simon and Caroline Knowles, Charles Law, Mike and Freddie Lawrence, Liam and Lily from Digiprint, Alex Lesseps, Anne Lindsay, Charles Maxwell, Dr. Hugh and Hermione Montgomery, John and Elizabeth Moody, Julian Mounter, George Parnell, Robert Pigott, Claire Palmer, Philip Playfer, Reverend Valerie Plumb, Alison Powell, Prue from Marshfield, St. Edward's School Oxford (and in particular, Philip Jolley, Lewis Faulkner, Mark Taylor and Pasha Francisco 'Miss P'), Azim and Zeenat Suleiman, Joe and Helen Taylor, Robert Watts and Gary White; and to all of our many followers on the Jordan Codices Facebook page for their support and enthusiasm.

We are grateful to all those who have kindly allowed us to quote published and unpublished writings in this book. Every effort has been made to secure permissions to reproduce material protected by copyright. The authors and publishers will be pleased to make good, in future editions, any omissions brought to their attention.

# End Statement

We have risked all for a cause, a moral cause: to stop the codices from being sold off on the black market by unscrupulous figures, many based in Europe and the USA who really should know better.

Some of these figures have academic positions; some of them are merely self-interested; none of them has a good excuse for partaking in illegal activities; all of them will be aware of the potential for the codices to transform our knowledge of the origins and connections of three great religions. Our experience has taken us through periods of police protection, coming in the light of serious threat and considerable expenditure on our part in order to demonstrate the worthiness of further analysis into the hoard.

We have been accused by certain parties of 'being in it for the money': nothing could be further from the truth. That others have sought to take advantage of our position is sadly indicative of the present state of civilization – one that is far from the words of the man represented on the codices. It is extraordinary that 2,000 years after these events they should still exert such influence on a modern, transformed and technological society.

Bureaucracy has no conscience: the empty space of its soul is banality, behind which individuals hide the truth of both other people and themselves. The hoard has been suppressed in Jordan and certain individuals demoted and removed from their posts – no explanation has been given, no reasons for such a turn of events. Unfortunately, the worst mistakes of history are made when we try to gloss over them and to rewrite them rather that confronting them and learning.

In the West there have also been concerted attempts to suppress all knowledge of the discovery: opinion-based blogs representing hidden and secret causes have offered only opinion – but on the basis of no scientific analysis, no proper investigation of the hoard, only *ad hominem* attacks on both of us and on the eminent experts who have advised us. We have even been inhibited from telling some of our story owing to the fear of legal reprisals; despite the fact that most of the defendants are not in a position to morally defend themselves. No doubt, now the text is published and accompanied by an academic companion, the bloggers and detractors will redouble their efforts in writing to the press and broadcasters.

Given that the codices are supposed, in large part, to be 'fakes', the interested parties have been surprisingly passionate in their denunciations. If the codices are fakes, surely they would be disinterested?

Academic presses, when approached, expressed initial interest only for such interest to mysteriously evaporate when the time came to prepare for publication: the same too with publishers. In the USA, broadcasters were warned off, even though they were impressed by the extent of the evidence offered by us.

Senior political figures whom we consulted confirmed the suppression. Despite the many obstacles put in our path, almost seven years later, the book telling our story has finally been published. We are also glad to finally release the historical and scientific analysis that the public has long been waiting for.

For further and detailed scientific and scholarly analysis please see *The Case for the Jordan Codices,* by Dr Margaret Barker, Professor Philip Davies, David Elkington, Jennifer Elkington, Dr Keith Hearne and others.